Migrant Women's Voices

Migrant Women's Voices

Talking About Life and Work in the UK Since 1945

Linda McDowell

Bloomsbury Academic
An imprint of Bloomsbury Publishing Plc

B L O O M S B U R Y
LONDON · OXFORD · NEW YORK · NEW DELHI · SYDNEY

Bloomsbury Academic

An imprint of Bloomsbury Publishing Plc

50 Bedford Square	1385 Broadway
London	New York
WC1B 3DP	NY 10018
UK	USA

www.bloomsbury.com

BLOOMSBURY and the Diana logo are trademarks of Bloomsbury Publishing Plc

First published 2016

© Linda McDowell, 2016

British Library Cataloguing-in-Publication Data

A catalogue record for this book is available from the British Library.

ISBN:	HB:	978-1-4742-2447-5
	PB:	978-1-4742-2448-2
	ePDF:	978-1-4742-2451-2
	ePub:	978-1-4742-2450-5

Library of Congress Cataloging-in-Publication Data

A catalog record for this book is available from the Library of Congress.

Typeset by RefineCatch Limited, Bungay, Suffolk
Printed and bound in India

*For the Daisy side of the family: Sarah and Cecil
and their son, CJ, born in October 2014*

CONTENTS

Figures   ix
Preface and acknowledgements   x

1   The Working Lives of Migrant Women   1

2   Moving Stories: Journeys to the UK   21

3   Making Things: Textiles, Toys, Shirts, Seat Covers and Engines   55

4   Waged Domestic Work: Cleaning, Catering and Childcare   85

5   Body Work: Nursing, Occupational Therapy and Caring for the British   109

6   Brain Work: Banking, Medicine, Scientific Research and Teaching   139

7   Serving the Public: Offices, Hotels, Shops, Salons and Buses   171

8   Home Life: Housework, Family, Community and Retirement   195

9   Afterword: British Identity and 'the Other'   217

Appendix 1   Half a Century of Change: UK 1951–2001   229

Appendix 2   Interviewees in Alphabetical Order   237

Appendix 3   Post-War Immigration Legislation   241

Appendix 4   Questions Raised by the Narratives   245

Notes   247
Select Bibliography   251
Index   259

FIGURES

1. A young Irish migrant arrives alone in London, October 1955   32
2. Seven hundred Caribbean immigrants in the Customs Hall, Southampton, May 1956   34
3. South Asian migrants from East Africa at London Airport, February 1968   39
4. Working at the BMW Mini plant, Cowley, Oxford, November 2013   82
5. A nurse from Jamaica working at a hospital in Eastbourne, January 1952   116
6. Women employees leaving Lehman Brothers after the crash, Canary Wharf, London, September 2008   147

PREFACE AND ACKNOWLEDGEMENTS

Migration, both to and from the UK, has always been a central part of the history of the country. Without population movements, there would have been no Hadrian's Wall or Roman baths, no Hanoverian monarchy, no Albert Hall, no Empire, no reggae or post-imperial novels. And many (perhaps most) of the people who currently define themselves as British, or as Scottish, Welsh or English do not have to search far in their family histories to discover an ancestor from elsewhere. My paternal grandfather was born in Germany, my husband's father in Ireland and my daughter's father- in-law in Dominica. Yet as I write in Spring 2015, the contribution of the population born elsewhere to the British economy, to politics and culture is under attack as a xenophobic rhetoric about strangers, foreigners and migrants dominates the political debate in the run up to the 2015 election. This book addresses the persistence of attitudes to strangers through the stories of 74 women, born outside the UK, but who came here to work.

The details of waged work have always fascinated me. My own working life has been spent entirely in universities, but sometimes I longed to know what other jobs might have been like. The solution was to go and talk to other people, both women and men, about their working lives and so the stories here were collected as part of various academic projects that I have carried out, sometimes single-handedly, at other times with research assistants. Studs Terkel's book *Working* (1977 [1974]) was the book I have long wanted to write: a book with an immediacy, that allows what are often termed 'respondents' or 'subjects' by oral historians and social scientists to speak for themselves, without filtering their voices through the net of conventional forms of history. I wanted to capture, in their own words, women talking about their jobs, their hopes and fears and their agency in their everyday life, as they struggled against disadvantage and discrimination, as well as their energy and their joy in doing a job well. Unlike Terkel, though, I am an academic rather than a broadcaster and journalist, and so there is somewhat more 'interpretation' and explanation here than in his text. I am also a feminist and so this book is about women's lives, placing them at the heart of the history of post-war change in the UK.

As I hope the voices of the 74 migrant women in this book make absolutely clear, the contribution to the UK of people born beyond its borders has been hugely significant. Throughout their long working lives, as they cared for, looked after, served and made goods for the British public over six decades since the end of the Second World War, as well as raised their own families, these women have contributed labour, taxes, good humour and energy to Britain. My gratitude to and admiration of the women who told me their stories are immense. I cannot thank them enough and hope that, should they read this book, they will find it an acceptable reflection of their lives. I hope too that other readers find the book makes them think again about the significance of migrant women in the labour market, as well as providing a useful source of information about women's lives since 1945. I hope that readers might be inspired to collect similar narratives themselves, whether about strangers or members of their own family. The aim of the book is not only to record individual stories that may be forgotten but to provide a set of sources for fellow academics, for students at different stages of their career and for the general reader. The narratives might be used for methods teaching, for writing classes and for filling in or challenging conventional histories and geographies of post-war change in British society, as well as, with careful contextual work, a source for a global history, connecting women's lives across space and time over seventy years of migrations and socio-economic change.

All the stories were collected between 1992 and 2012, during which time I worked at four different universities. They are based on interviews with investment bankers as the excessive expansion of jobs in the City stuttered in the early 1990s; with early post-war refugees from Latvia still living in the UK in 2002 and 2003, anxious to capture their astonishing journey and work in the UK before the end of their lives; with agency workers in a London hospital and hotel in the mid-2000s and with women migrants living in Oxford toward the end of that decade. Short extracts from some of these women's stories have been included in two of my earlier books (McDowell 2005, 2013), but this is the first time that these women's voices have been presented in full or at greater length, permitting them to speak for themselves, without a carapace of academic argument, multiple references to other texts, or lengthy interpretation. More recent interviews were undertaken especially for this book, in an effort to capture both the diversity of labour market change as casual, precarious and zero hours contracts became more common and as the origins of migrants became increasingly diverse. I should like to thank all these interviewees for the great privilege of hearing their life stories.

I also want to thank my co-researchers and my students in all four institutions for their advice, support and assistance over the years, and my immediate family for their patience as I spent far too long telling them stories about migrants' lives. Thanks to Chris, Hugh and Jessica McDowell and Cecil and Sarah Daisy for listening. The School of Geography, COMPAS, St John's College Oxford and the colleagues working on the Oxford Diaspora Programme have made Oxford University, where I have worked since 2004, a stimulating place to be thinking about migration: so thank you too. At different times over the last three decades, the interviews at the heart of this book have been funded by grants from the Economic and Social Research Council, the Arts and Humanities Research Council, and St John's College Research Centre. I am grateful for their financial support.

1

The Working Lives of Migrant Women

This is a book about migration and work – two of the most important issues in the lives of people living in the UK today. Public opinion polls in recent years have been consistent in showing that immigration and making a living are at the top of many people's concerns about their own lives and those of their children. Most people nowadays expect to have a job for almost all of their life before reaching the age of retirement, barring periods of unemployment. This includes women as well as men, and mothers as well as women without children, albeit often on a part-time basis when children are still at school. Many more women now work for wages than they did as this book opens in 1945. Then, their first responsibility was as wives and mothers. Women's participation in waged work, however, has been under-recorded in official figures, especially in earlier years. It was often on a casual basis, 'off the books', for cash in hand or based on reciprocity, as well as unwaged work in the home. Over the second half of the twentieth century, however, women were drawn into the labour market in rising numbers as the nature of waged work changed significantly. Male-dominated manufacturing employment was replaced by service sector work, employing many more women than in previous decades. Attitudes also changed and by the end of the twentieth century, all women under retirement age were expected to join the labour market, unless they were unfit or their children were very young.

Just as women's large-scale entry to the labour market over the post-war decades altered the gender composition of the workforce, in-migration added to its diversity as workers born outside the UK sought employment in growing numbers. Britain's population began to change after the end of the war and grew steadily until the mid-1990s, when net in-migration accelerated. The annual number of people born abroad who moved to live in the UK increased significantly from the end of the last century, rising from about 48,000 in 1997 to 298,000 in 2014. By 2015, in some parts of the UK – in Greater London, for example, but also in smaller towns such as Luton – about one third of all workers are now first generation migrants, or the sons and daughters or grandchildren of people who came to live here after 1945. Elsewhere, the proportion is much smaller, although growing, as from 2004 migrants from new European Union member states have joined the workforce in towns and cities all over the UK, as well as in rural areas. Many people, however, have little accurate idea of the percentage of the UK population that was born abroad (about 13 per cent in 2015) and often over-estimate it when asked. Britain remains a predominantly 'white' society in which people of colour and in-migrants, including people from the new European Union member countries, are constructed as the Other, different from the norm, still strangers and sometimes, although not always, visibly different and subjected to unequal treatment.

These changes – in the composition of the population and in waged work – are two of the most significant social and economic trends that have transformed the UK since the end of the Second World War. This book is about the history of these changes and the connections between them. It is not a conventional history, however, but is instead one seen through the eyes and reported through the voices of migrant women, talking about their lives and the types of jobs they have undertaken since their arrival. The reactions of the British public, and of politicians and officials regulating migration flows, are not a central aspect of the book, although they are addressed in the final chapter. Through migration controls, the state influences who might work in the UK, and the general public, as co-workers, neighbours and friends, as well as through the media and other cultural institutions, constructs the UK as a place that sees migrants as different from, and too often regarded as inferior to, the host population.

At the heart of the book – Chapters 2 to 8 – are oral narratives: stories told by more than 70 women migrants. Migrant women have often been ignored both in discussions of the changing nature of post-war migration and in the structure of the labour force. My aim is to provide a rich and vivid source through which to counter conventional narratives of post-war change, as well as to record for posterity individual stories that are in danger of being forgotten. Readers anxious to hear the voices should turn to Chapter 2 immediately, perhaps returning to this context-setting chapter later. My hope is that these stories will not only be of intrinsic interest to readers but will also be a useful resource for fellow academics in history and labour studies, in geography or cultural studies and for students at different stages of their career. The narratives might be used in a variety of ways to stimulate further work to fill in some of the gaps in this text. I hope the book will be useful for methods teaching in all those disciplines that draw on interview techniques of different kinds, for life history or for autobiography writing classes. I hope too that it will help to fill in and challenge conventional histories and geographies of post-war change in British society that ignore women's lives, as well as, with careful contextual work, prove to be a useful source for a global history, connecting women's lives across space and time over seventy years of huge migrations and socio-economic change.

I also hope that there is an audience among the wider public, among readers who want to know more about the circumstances in which they, their mothers or their grandmothers grew up. The individual stories illustrate not only the continuities and changes in women's opportunities for employment since 1945, but other significant changes in British society and, indeed, across the wider world over the second half of the twentieth century. The narratives include, for example, information about the ways British-born co-workers treated women from elsewhere, about some of the major struggles by workers including participation in strikes, but also details about housing, about childcare and meals, about illnesses, including TB and the polio epidemic in the 1950s, and many other aspects of everyday life, including unwaged work undertaken by women in their own homes. Work is what dominated these women's lives as they forged a new identity in post-war Britain but the term 'work', when women are the focus of attention, captures not only employment for wages but all those jobs and tasks undertaken 'for love' in the home. The stories also touch on significant events in the wider world, events that precipitated migration, including the effects of wars, independence in India and Pakistan, the decolonization of East Africa, and ethnic strife in many parts of the world. These world events had national and local effects as British towns and cities became more diverse across the second half of the last century.

From the vantage point of 2015, now seventy years since the end of the Second World War, it is salutary to recall that, before 1945, official and public fears were about *losing* population, about emigration rather than immigration. Between the two world wars, governments had encouraged people to leave the UK, in part to relieve poverty at home but also to strengthen the position of the white population in what were then called the Dominions, among them Australia, New Zealand and Canada. From the mid-1940s, however, everything changed: in the UK labour was needed for the post-war reconstruction effort as well as to replace women who left the workforce after the war and so new sources of labour had to be found. Independence movements in Britain's imperial possessions destabilized populations in India and Africa and resulted not only in white returnees but also new movements of people of colour to join the migrants from the Caribbean who had rallied to the call for labour from the 'mother land' in the late 1940s and the 1950s. From this moment the idea of migrants as people of colour became firmly set in the British imagination, not to be challenged in any significant way until the expansion of the European Union in the first decade of the twenty-first century, despite not inconsiderable numbers of white migrants to the UK from different parts of the world across the entire second half of the twentieth century. By the start of the new millennium, the origins of the most recent migrants were far more diverse than when this book opens in 1945.

Preceding the post-colonial movers as potential workers, however, were migrants who are often forgotten in the story of Britain's transformation into a multicultural society. They came from continental Europe, displaced during the war: from the Baltic States, Ukraine and Poland, joining migrants from Ireland as well as from Mediterranean countries, including Italy. Later they were followed by women and men from Cyprus, by Hungarian refugees in 1956 and Czechs in 1968. However, from about 1947 the numbers of women and men moving from 'New Commonwealth' countries became more significant than these European migrations, altering older patterns of in-migration and changing the composition of the UK population, especially in Greater London and other large cities. It was from this date that the conflation of the terms immigrant and people of colour became established, so that, as Brian Harrison (2009: 82) notes, 'by the 1970s the terms . . . were being used almost synonymously, even though by then only one in three immigrants entering Britain came from these regions, that is from India, Pakistan, Africa and the Caribbean'. Further, growing numbers of people of colour were not migrants at all, but British citizens born in the UK.

However, right across the decades, even in the few years in the late 1940s when labour was needed and migration was relatively unregulated, new entrants to the UK found that their welcome was a qualified one. Suspicion, rather than acceptance and assistance to settle, was the habitual response, both to the women and men who came from continental Europe as post-war refugees, but were transformed into workers by a government decree, and to people from the Caribbean, heeding the call from Britain for workers, As the years went by and as regulation increased, restricting the right to enter the UK (see Appendix 3 for a summary of the changes), the atmosphere hardened, especially during recessionary years, when the native population was wont to argue that migrants were 'stealing our jobs'. The grip of a vision of the UK, or perhaps an imaginary England, white, middle class, united by customs and beliefs, as a 'homeland with its own people, known and loyal to itself and distinct from strangers from another land, remains vice-like' (Amin 2012: 1). The construction of a sense of national identity and belonging to Britain that excludes the Other is the subject of the final chapter.

Finding employment in a changing labour market

Many of the new entrants to the UK from 1945 onwards either came to work, or soon found that they had to seek employment to survive. Some had been promised a job before they left home, others looked for work when they arrived. Some women had been employed before leaving their homeland, others had not. If, in the immediate post-war years, many British women were leaving the labour market, women migrants were joining it, some as employees in the newly expanding public sector, including the National Health Service. However, over the course of the second half of the twentieth century, waged work became part of the lives of more and more women as women from all backgrounds moved into the labour market. Rising standards of living, home ownership and the prospect of purchasing new consumer goods necessitated a second income in many households, pushing women to seek employment. Women's lives changed too as they stayed at school longer, went to university in growing numbers, began to restrict the numbers of children born, and, especially, worked for wages for longer and longer periods over their lifetime. By the end of the century almost as many women as men worked outside the home, facilitated by the radical transformation in the types of jobs and occupations available.

In 1955, the majority of the workforce, albeit mainly men, worked in the manufacturing sector, but its significance began to decline from that date. The sorts of hard manual labour in mines, steel mills, shipyards and factories that dominated men's working lives in the early post-war years have now largely disappeared. The violence and bodily dangers involved in these forms of work are also in the past, at least in the UK if not elsewhere, as manufacturing has become more technologically advanced and aided by new robotic methods, or has moved elsewhere in the world as new global connections separate ownership of multinational companies from the location of the workforce. The decline of manufacturing was, however, uneven over time and space and women working on the line, manufacturing car components or parts for the growing white good industries, sewing car seats for Ford or shirts for Marks and Spencer all tell their stories here. By the start of the new century, however, working in services, rather than manufacturing, was the norm. In the UK by 2001, almost three in every four workers were employed in the service sector, rising to more than eight in every ten women workers.

The growth of service employment is the second great transformation in the post-war era. Termed deindustrialization in a male-centred view of the world of work, it is better captured in more positive terms as the feminization of the labour market, opening up the world of work to millions of women, providing wages and some degree of economic independence. However, the growing service economy proved not to be one of unalloyed opportunity for women. Many women undertook secretarial and clerical work in both the public and private sectors, where women's 'pink collar' employment typically was lower paid compared with the 'white collar' jobs done by men. Women's clerical work, though often tedious, was at least reasonably secure, despite the rise of new computer-aided methods in the office, until contracting out and off-shoring routine tasks, by insurance companies and the NHS, for example, reduced female employment. More recently, the post-crisis austerity programme and cuts in public sector budgets since 2008 have further reduced women's options. Even so, clerical work was, and remains, better paid than the jobs many women found looking after the children and elderly relatives of other women, in private homes and care homes, in schools and hospitals, as well as in other parts of the consumer service industries.

Over the post-war era, but especially since the 1970s, many 'traditional' feminized jobs of serving and caring for others, previously undertaken for love in the home, moved into the market, in part in response to women's rising employment participation rates. The tasks involved – mopping up, cleaning, loving, empathizing with others, socializing children – continued to be seen as appropriate for women. Based, it was assumed, on the 'natural' attributes of femininity, rather than on long apprenticeships and the acquisition of specialized skills, these jobs typically are defined as unskilled and so poorly paid. Despite their significance in the reproduction of the population, they are regarded as low status. Domestic service, which employed millions of women before the First World War, is now being reconstituted: sometimes in the homes of individual workers, although probably in a middle class household, in a crèche or a care home, rather than in the kitchens and nurseries of the local aristocracy as in the past. Servicing the upper class, however, still remains significant as a glance at the situations vacant in publications such as *The Lady* makes clear. These are the jobs that are hard to mechanize or to transfer to the consumer, to the patient or child. Looking after people is close-up personal work, hands, often literally, on the bodies of others, demanding and unrelenting, and not amenable to a nine to five routine. It remains quintessentially 'women's work' and the sort of work undertaken by thousands of women migrants over time, as the chapters that follow show.

Other service sector occupations, at the top end of the labour market, typically based on cerebral attributes such as calculation and opinion (the law, higher education, banking perhaps) are constructed as part of the new 'knowledge economy' rather than the 'body work' done by women for low wages. Knowledge work is seen as highly skilled, demanding academic and vocational credentials, and it became, and has remained, a largely masculine domain, although open to middle class women with the appropriate educational backgrounds. But even for these women, who tell the stories of their working lives in Chapter 6, their femininity tends to disqualify them from some of the most senior positions, and they are not immune from various forms of discriminatory treatment, despite significant changes in workplace cultures and acceptable behaviours in the office, the trading floor or the operating theatre in more recent decades.

This increasingly polarized world of service work, as well as women's work in the now-residual manufacturing sector, is the focus here. Migrant women, moving to the UK in growing numbers after 1945, found that although opportunities in the labour market were expanding, they were often restricted to less well-paid jobs. These were jobs that typically white women preferred not to do, some of them dubbed the 'dirty work' of caring for others. As the narratives show, looking after other people, sometimes people who are ill or ageing, demands huge resources of energy and resilience.

Women from other countries, other cultures, with different voices, bodies, beliefs and habits, found, right across the post-war decades and into the new millennium, that they were seen as less suitable or less eligible employees for many occupations, in part because of stereotypical assumptions about their attributes by employers, co-workers and even the people whom they served. Through these mechanisms, 'the production of difference' (Roediger and Esch 2012) remained a central mechanism of discrimination in the British labour market. As the women who tell their stories here reveal, in often painful detail, waged work often involves daily humiliations, and insufficient recognition of the value of the tasks performed. These women, often key workers in caring services, were sometimes regarded as too slow or too uneducated, too un-ambitious or too placid to be appointed to positions of trust or responsibility, or even eligible for certain jobs at all.

Some women came to the UK already trained – as teachers, doctors or lawyers – but found that their qualifications acquired abroad were not necessarily transferable or recognized in the UK and so they too were restricted to low waged work, at least in their initial years in the UK. Elvira, for example, who came to the UK in 1947, had qualified as a primary school teacher in Latvia but worked as a factory hand in the textile industry in Yorkshire and in the hosiery industry in Leicestershire, before she eventually found employment as a teacher, the job she had trained for as a young woman. Women from the Caribbean who became nurses found in the 1950s and 1960s that a combination of institutional discrimination and individual racism restricted their promotion prospects across their working lives. Women lawyers, bankers and doctors, from both Old and New Commonwealth countries, also found that discrimination, typically on the basis of gender rather than nationality, limited their opportunities. Yet as the narratives reveal too, work was also a source of pride, as women migrants built a life in the UK and forged new relationships, within and beyond the workplace. Their hope, pride in their work and their resilience shines through their stories.

Women talking about employment, work and life

For most women, 'work' includes not only working for wages but all the daily tasks of what feminist authors sometimes term 'daily reproduction' or more simply 'domestic labour'. This includes getting everyone up and ready, making meals, keeping the washing done and the house clean(ish), helping with homework, talking to children and partners, helping elderly relatives or friends, shopping: that mix of repetitive work involving keeping things clean and a household ticking over and the emotional or affective labour of loving and caring for family members. When undertaken by individual women in their own homes and for their own family it is work that is unpaid, and so unmeasured and invisible in national economic accounts. If women ever stopped doing this work, however, it seems likely that households would not function smoothly, children might not be delivered to school and workers would find that their clean clothes or packed lunches were no longer delivered on a regular basis.

Over the seventy years here, however, life has changed for many women and the work they used to do in the household, the services they provided (love, care and affection, mending, washing, basic health care) and the goods they made for love (jam, clothes, meals) became more widely available for cash in the market. As these jobs have moved (back) into the cash economy in recent decades they remain types of work undertaken predominantly by women, as idealized notions of femininity, including deference and caring for others, define many of these jobs as suitable for women. In the narratives, as women talk about what they do all day and how they feel about it, the focus is not only on waged work but on the connections between it and unwaged domestic labour.

The term work–life balance is often used to capture this connection between employment and domestic work, and the growing awareness by policymakers that if even more women are to be persuaded and encouraged to enter the labour market then domestic labour, and especially childcare, has to become a focus of public policy. This notion of balance, however, suggests a too easy accommodation between what used to be termed 'women's dual roles'. Negotiation and struggle are more accurate terms. As the stories reveal, women use all sorts of strategies to combine the tasks involved in their waged work and home lives. I have not used any of these terms – balance, struggle or negotiation – in the book's sub-title, instead referring to life and work, not intending to see these as separate spheres, but instead insisting on their inevitable intersection in the lives of all 'working' women.

The key emphasis of the chapters that follow, however, is on the tasks of waged labour. Most women took it for granted that I, as a woman, a mother and an employee, someone who had been in the labour market all her life, apart from brief periods of maternity leave, as most of these women had, would understand what was involved in running a home and in negotiating the demands of waged and domestic work. 'You know how it is', many would say, when I asked about their daily lives in the home, but were much more forthcoming when I asked them to explain exactly what was involved in, for example, working in a woollen mill in 1948, for a London hospital in 1960, in an investment bank in the City of London in 1980 or as a nanny in 2010. If doing housework and managing childcare through cobbling together a range of strategies such as help from relatives, working shifts and paying babysitters unites women, their position in the workforce, the jobs they do and the rates of pay often divides them, especially women in higher paid and higher status jobs, who tell their stories in Chapter 6, from women in the other chapters working in lower paid and lower status jobs.

Migrant origins

The migrant women whose voices are heard here were born in many different places between 1917 (the oldest) and 1982 (the youngest), both of whom, by chance rather than design, were born and lived until they were young women in Latvia. Grieta, the older of the two, left in 1944 fleeing the advancing Russian front. Karina, the younger of the two, left by choice, just before Latvia joined the EU in 2004, attracted by the hope of earning better money in the UK. Between them are women born in different years over eight decades of the twentieth century and from different countries of origin: Jamaica and Barbados, the US, Canada, Australia and New Zealand, Malaysia and the Philippines, India, Pakistan and Sri Lanka, Kenya, Uganda and Tanzania, Estonia, Ukraine, Poland, Latvia, Kosovo and Russia. Some of them grew up in middle class or professional households, with fathers who were doctors or soldiers, small business men and government officials. Among the older women from these households their mothers often did not work, in the sense of for wages, but other mothers did. Dagnija's mother from Latvia, for example, whose husband was a high ranking soldier, was an opera singer between the wars and Dagnija's most precious possession, destroyed during her forced labour sorting coal in Germany, was a pair of her mother's opera gloves.

Other mothers were teachers or nurses, setting their daughters an example of women's dual roles as workers and housewives. Yet other women came from working class backgrounds, from families who were part of the industrial working class, with fathers who were miners or steel workers and whose mothers found the demands of domestic labour with a husband in a heavy and dirty job precluded formal waged work but who nevertheless took casual jobs when necessary. Many women came from rural backgrounds in Ireland, India, the Caribbean and the Philippines, where women's work on the land was often, although not always, part of a family enterprise and so typically unwaged. These women spoke of the sacrifices their parents, especially their mothers, had made to support them in their dreams of migration and their passage to a new life. What is also noticeable is how many of these women came from large families, with numerous siblings, some of whom came to the UK with them but many remained in their country of origin, or moved elsewhere in the world, stretching their family across the globe as the years went by.

Most of the women came to the UK as young women, some already married, some with children and others who left their children behind, but most of them came as single women or, for the small number of older women, as widows. Some intended to return 'home', once independence arrived, once money for a new life had been accumulated; others planned to stay permanently, or to return in later life, after retirement perhaps. For most of the women here, however, new ties, new relationships, raising children in the UK, looking forward to grandchildren meant that, whatever they had planned initially, eventually they decided to stay in the UK. Some returned, for a visit or planning a permanent return, but they often found themselves out of place in their country of birth, disoriented by the changes that had occurred in their absence. Post-war refugees, for example, found their old compatriots resented them, perhaps incorrectly assuming a life of luxury in the UK. Vieda, on a visit to Latvia, found she 'no longer spoke in a way that could be understood'; others found that the property that they had hoped to reclaim was no longer the idyllic cottage of childhood but had been swallowed up in industrial suburbs or post-war state housing developments, if indeed it could still be identified. As Diana, who left Latvia in 1944, explained when I talked to her in 2003:

> It is completely different though, Latvia now. It is not the Latvia I remember. Everything has changed. In 1991 or 1992 both my sisters went but I haven't been. I am too scared. . . . I sometimes think I am too old. The house we had, my father liked to garden and there was flowers and fruit trees but when they went there, it was different. There was nothing and the house looked dilapidated. They could hardly recognize the place. Just before we left my father planted a new garden with apples and pears and cherries and there was nothing. I want to remember as it was. Maybe it is cowardly, maybe for you it looks sentimental or childish but for us . . .

Reading the text: stories of change and continuity

Although the narratives in the following chapters are told in women's own words, only lightly edited for sense or repetition, they are not innocent of the interviewer's presence. Being there affects what migrant women decide to reveal, as well as what they think an interviewer might find interesting. They sometimes challenge or change the intended focus of the researcher. Women displaced during the Second World War, for example, told me that my questions about Britain in the 1950s had to be preceded by the stories of their wartime journeys in order to understand the decisions they made later. But there is also another key way in which texts are not innocent of both the author and the readers. Clearly, my choice of what to ask and what to include here has influenced the text. Furthermore, how these interviews are read, depending on readers' own prejudices, life experiences, backgrounds and politics, will also affect their interpretation. Younger readers may know relatively little about the early post-war migrations or about the struggles by women of colour to achieve recognition and respect and higher pay in the labour market, nor indeed the different reasons why women from different

parts of the world came to the UK. Some of this may be familiar to older readers, especially if they too are migrants, but overall, this long story of seventy years of hard work by women born in increasingly diverse places outside the UK is one that has been left untold.

The early years of this history women's migration reflect the aftermath of war and empire, as displaced people from Eastern Europe came to the UK. This story of women from the Baltic States and elsewhere, who came to the UK via Germany, is one that is little known by the British public. Imperial and post-imperial migrations – from the Caribbean, the Indian subcontinent and East Africa, countries connected to Britain by a long and contested history – are more familiar. Women who came to Britain in the later 1940s and through the 1950s were often recruited for specific jobs. East European women in the late 1940s came to work as domestics in hospitals and unskilled hands in the textile industry. Many women from Eire and the Caribbean worked as nurses and so these jobs are central in their narratives. As the decades passed, however, migrant women found employment in a more varied range of jobs and careers, many of which are included here. But there are omissions from the text. The most notable absence is of sex workers; there are also no clergy, no journalists, no police, no airline stewards, although Maria, whose tells her story in Chapter 3, originally from East Timor, and working at a car plant in the UK, had been an air steward in her own country, as well as a hotel receptionist in Brunei. Machinists, packers, traders, writers, care workers, nurses, doctors, shop assistants, cooks, cleaners, child carers, occupational therapists, teachers, translators, and numerous other jobs undertaken by women over their life course are represented, revealing an extraordinary story of the huge commitment made to Britain, to its economy and to its population by 'ordinary' women, women who were not born in the UK, but who, through choice or force of circumstance, made the decision to move across national borders and make a life elsewhere.

The conventional story of labour market change in Western economies is too often one of loss and nostalgia, of the lost world of manufacturing, or of nine to five jobs, of working for a single employer across the lifetime. This was always a masculine story, a world of heroic masculinity, of male effort, whether by brawn or by brain, in which women's work was an afterword at best. Arguments about new patterns of casual attachment to the labour market, about the growing precariousness discerned in contemporary theoretical discussions of employment, ignore the ways in which women have combined waged work and domestic labour for decades, as well as the less spectacular sort of jobs undertaken by millions of women, sometimes in their own or other women's homes, but also in factories, hospitals, universities and banks. Caring for children and for the elderly is just as meaningful employment as building aircraft or cars, although nowadays women are almost as likely as men to do the latter jobs, and as Harbhanan's story in Chapter 3 shows, some exceptional women were assembling car engines in Dagenham almost forty years ago. But placing women, especially women migrants, at the centre of the story of labour market change produces a different narrative: one marked by continuity as much as a radical transformation of the nature of employment. It has long been an important aim of feminist historians and social scientists to challenge narratives of temporal transformation that take for granted men's experiences as the unchallenged norm.

Although migrant women's contribution to the British economy has been substantial and important since 1945, in the early post-war years, they were excluded by the very fact of their employment from the dominant image of acceptable femininity, which was based on an ideal of domesticity and maternity. Migrant women, however, have had high participation rates across the second half of the twentieth century as their reason for migration, or their condition of entry to the UK, from 1945 onwards, was, in the main, to take waged work. Immediately after the Second World War, however, many British-born women left the labour market for a domestic life, dominated by childbirth and child rearing. In the Beveridge Report (1942), laying out plans for new forms of social provision and welfare support after the war, it was suggested that full employment was the policy goal for men only. 'Women had a different role', one that was 'vital to British ideals in the world' (Beveridge Report 1942: 53). For women, at least white British women, their life's work was to produce children and rebuild family life in the privacy of the home. Their work was unremunerated and largely unregulated, although health visitors began to investigate the conditions in British homes and to offer advice to mothers. Beveridge reflected the dominant assumptions of that time: that men's responsibility was to seek lifelong full-time employment in order to support a home-based wife and children. To reflect and reward this responsibility, men should be paid 'a breadwinner wage' which became the basis for claims by the union movement for higher pay for men than for women. If, after the war, British-born women were to be persuaded to return to their 'traditional' role as wives and mothers, then an alternative labour force was needed for those jobs constructed as appropriate for women workers.

The British state turned to women born abroad to fill vacancies on a full-time basis, while British women worked on a part-time basis in female-dominated jobs, permitting them to combine what was then termed 'women's dual role', that is domestic tasks and waged work. In the 1950s it was commonly suggested that women worked for 'pin money': a derogatory term that ignored the key contribution of women's wages to many family budgets. In 1951, 6.3 million women were in employment, including 40 per cent of all married women, although almost all of them were in part-time work. By the end of the century, however, over 13 million women worked for wages; just over 70 per cent of all women of working age (16–60). Indeed, the number of men in the UK labour market remained static between 1970 and 2001, and so 'women have made up the entire net expansion of the UK workforce over the period' (Connolly and Gregory 2007: 144). In this sense, British-born women's lives are now more similar to those of women migrants, as in recent years most women tend to remain in the workforce over their lifetimes, albeit with differences in patterns of employment before and after having children. There are also important class-based differences in participation: larger numbers of highly educated women than women with fewer credentials work on a full-time basis. In the early twenty-first century, however, women, as well as men, are expected to work for wages, although currently an unpleasantly xenophobic debate about the labour market rights of migrants, including but not only asylum seekers, has developed.

Individual stories and world events: talk, memories and recollections

The stories migrant women tell about their working lives in the UK illustrate changes and the continuities in women's employment since 1945. They also reveal enormous changes in the wider world. Patterns of migration into the UK have become significantly more diverse over the last seven decades, as have reasons for migration, the origins and backgrounds of migrants and their status, as well as the rights and obligations of in-migrants, once in the UK. New technologies have made it both easier to migrate and more difficult to enter the UK, as electronic connections and surveillance techniques have become more sophisticated. Distances have been reduced by changes in transport technologies, as well as by new ways of keeping in touch with 'home'. Migration patterns themselves have changed, not only as more women now move across national borders, but also as more people, women included, become transnational migrants: people who move to a second or third country, rather than make a single move from home to a host country where they remain for the rest of their lives. The initial reasons for moving to the UK and the freedom to move elsewhere, of course, are dependent on social and political conditions in different parts of the world, on political changes, on 'natural' disasters as well as smaller-scale changes in families' and households' intimate lives. Individual stories touch on many of the major political and social changes of the second half of the twentieth century, from the consequences of the Second World War to the effects of 9/11, 7/7 and the events in Paris in January 2015.[1] World wars and civil wars, internecine strife, persecution in Uganda and other African countries, the fall of the USSR, changing governments, shifts in public opinion and changes in immigration regimes and legislation are all reflected in these women's stories.

How to place stories in context, how to add sufficient information about global events and large-scale changes so that readers are able to interpret individual accounts raises an important question for all authors of life stories. It is the one that the noted biographer, Hermione Lee, drawing on an image of Virginia Woolf's, has termed the problem of 'the fish in the stream'. How much detail about the events (the stream) that influence individuals' (the fish) lives is it necessary to include for readers to make sense of narratives? To place each story told here in its historical context is impossible within the pages of a single book. Instead I have chosen to let the women speak for themselves. I hope, however, that this immediacy will be met by a desire to know more, to set the events in their wider context. Where it seemed necessary for understanding the stories, notes are added and to help in capturing the radical changes in the UK since 1945, some of the key changes between 1951 and 2001 are outlined in Appendix 2. Appendix 3 lists the main changes in immigration legislation. I have also included in the Bibliography a small number of other books that describe some of the main social and economic changes in the UK since 1945.

I strongly believe, however, that as well as providing broad-brush analyses that aid in an understanding of the key features of post-war change, it is important to listen to the individual stories of migrants, both refugees and those who moved by choice to the UK. All migrants who move across national borders are affected by loss and grieving, even those for whom the journey marked the start of a successful new life, but they are not an undifferentiated mass. Their stories vary and it is only though exploring the details of individual lives that a sense of the agency of migrants, the choices and decisions they made and failed to make, both before, during and after displacement and movement might be adequately captured. But stories are exactly this, a version of a life constructed for others to hear, and so the question of how to assess such stories must be addressed.

Two issues are important to think about when using narratives as source material. The first is a question about the status of talk, of telling stories, and the second is about the reliability of past stories and narratives that are retold in the present. It is talk or discourse, both speech and text that allows certain things to be said and prevents or inhibits others and so both shapes and permits experiences to be shared. Speech is, as Purvis and Hunt (1993: 485) suggested, 'a vehicle for thought'. The way migrant women talk about their circumstances reveals not only patterns and processes of economic and social exclusion and how they have changed over time but also the extent to which migrant women make sense of a new and unequal world with which they are unfamiliar and may not always fully understand. All the women told a chronological story, prompted, of course, by initial questions about their early lives. For most women, the tale of leaving home had been told before, often to family, sometimes to friends, although seldom to an unknown researcher. Some women, however, had not so far told the 'whole story', as it were, putting together their migration and their later working lives. All the narratives are presented virtually as they were spoken. In most cases, I have not altered the order in which events were recalled, nor how they were expressed, other than when it helped to make sense of the narrative. For readers familiar with the voices and accents of women from different parts of the world, it may be possible to hear the tone and inflections of their spoken words, even when re-presented as text.

Telling life stories typically follows literary conventions or tropes. Migration stories often take the form of a heroic struggle, of overcoming the odds, or of a journey to personal fulfilment. But these are conventions that more easily capture men's, rather than women's, sense of themselves. When women are at the heart of a narrative, the traditional trope is that of a romance but the stories here are ones of loss and displacement and of struggles to make a new life rather than romance, although love, marriage, partners and children do feature. In the initial telling, narratives are not always straightforward. Instead, life stories, or less ambitiously, recollections of searching for work sometimes take an unwieldy or non-chronological form in the storyteller's mind that might nevertheless typically become a more coherent story as it is retold. The very act of telling – the language used in recollection not only reflects but also constructs experiences of labour market changes. Stories are part of the ways in which participants, representing their life working life, make sense of their world. As Gabriel (2000: 4) has pointed out, 'the truth of a story lies not in the facts, but in the meaning'. The function of stories is multiple: they may undermine or support versions of particular events; they may support the dominant structures of power or subvert them; they may unite or divide the workforce, building solidarity or division. They may help a narrator make sense of her world, perhaps, in the moment of retelling, resolving past tensions, frustrations or disappointments, as well as celebrating successes or hardships overcome. Many of these traits are evident in the stories that follow.

For young migrant women, often facing uncertainty and insecurity, and sometimes discriminatory attitudes from the British population, unfamiliar with the customs and experiences of the incomers, a story that exaggerates certain aspects or deflects blame elsewhere may be part of trying to make sense of their new lives. The young Latvian women, for example, felt betrayed by the British government as Latvia became part of the USSR at the end of the war. Some of them suggested that the new Labour government was part of a Communist-led plot, finding the term socialist, used to describe it, had unpleasant associations for them. Each of the stories told by migrant women from different backgrounds about their initial struggle to find work and their experiences in the years that followed is constructed in the context of an overarching social and political narrative about citizenship, employment and the place of migrants within the UK. This context is constructed through the interactions of migrants with the 'settled' population, as well as by changes in governments, new legislation and new customs and practices in the UK – matters discussed in Chapter 9.

Migrant stories are also about the past; they are recollections of previous experiences and so are based on memories. There is now a large scholarly and methodological literature (some of it listed in the Bibliography) about memory, about its construction and shaping, about issues of recall, about the extent to which stories that are retold became solidified over time or forgotten as storytellers age. Narratives also change as stories once not able to be told may emerge as times and customs change. For many women, stories about sex, about harassment, about trading sexual favours or about rape in times of unrest or in the aftermath of war, once deemed unrepeatable, or not believed at all, are now able to be told. In this sense, as Connerton (1989) and others have argued, a simple or uncontested notion of 'the past' is not tenable. The past is continuously reconstructed in the present and so all memory is a continuous process of what might be termed retranslation. Yet, the assumption that memories are a way of providing direct access to the past remains strong in popular notions of the role of historical reconstructions based on recollections. Paradoxically, it is also widely accepted that memories dim or alter with age and that stories may be changed as unpleasant incidents are forgotten or nostalgia outweighs more accurate recall of particular events.

One way of thinking about the problems inherent in recollections is to compare the stories told by different women in similar jobs, by women from similar and different backgrounds and to compare the combination of all the narratives as a source with larger-scale histories of the times, based on different, typically official, sources. However, both the authors and the audience for these larger stories affect their form and content. Stories told by the victors, by the powerful, who are often men, or stories deemed acceptable by the establishment tend not to reflect the experiences of the less powerful or events that challenge conventional notions. As E. P. Thompson (1963) suggested so powerfully in the preface to his influential book, *The Making of the English Working Class*, stories of the lives of ordinary women and men have been erased by 'the enormous condescension of posterity'. The collection of statistics, the preservation of records, the inclusions in official histories and physical representations in galleries, as statues in urban squares, are all influenced by the decisions made by those who pull the different levers of power, whether in government, in the universities or in other arenas. Representations of women, especially working class women, have often been absent.

Since E. P. Thompson's claim, however, both academic and popular histories have changed significantly, as exciting work by feminist historians and by historians anxious to place working class men and women at the centre of their work constructs counter-narratives to what Henrietta Marshall (1905) in her children's history of Britain termed 'our island story'. These counter-narratives, including Raphael Samuel's *Island Stories* (1999), in a reference to Marshall but suggesting more complex and multiple stories, spell out the crucial contributions to the British economy made by people not born in the UK, as well as to the First and Second World War efforts and to the changing culture of their adopted country. New histories, reflecting the voices of the 'Other' – the working class, women, people of colour, recent migrants – have been published, drawing on sources as varied as diaries, notebooks, cartoons and novels, as well as reconstructed from statistical series initially collected for different purposes. Health records, for example, of the heights and weights of soldiers or the weights of children taken to clinics, applications for hardship grants from charities, details of loans made by pawnbrokers, or women's shopping lists are all useful sources in constructing more complex and immediate histories.

The collection of oral histories is but one method among many that has begun the task of putting women at the heart of the story about change in post-war Britain. Migrant women, especially the working lives of those in poorly paid and low status jobs, however, are not always reflected, even in the turn to history from below. In most of the stream of books recently published that draw on oral narratives and diaries (see for example, Arthur 2004; Garfield 2004; Holmes 2007) working class women in general, and working class women migrants in particular, largely are absent. Jean McCrindle and Sheila Rowbotham's (1977) innovative book about working class women *Dutiful Daughters: women talk about their lives* provided an early corrective to this neglect but the interviewees are mainly white British-born women. Selina Todd's (2014) more recent book *The People* tells the story of twentieth century change through the eyes of the working class, but there is relatively little mention of the role migrants played in the UK economy. In both the texts, however, women's lives are central to the story, altering the lens through which history is normally seen, as well as challenging the condescension towards the working class still evident in some histories of the twentieth century. The long struggles of working class women for equal treatment and higher pay – some of them reflected here – provide a clear example of how important they are in Britain's labour history.

The class position of migrant women is often difficult to pin down. Some of the women in this book were born into middle class families, but in the UK ended up in working class jobs and living in less affluent parts of British towns and cities. Some women from middle class backgrounds with higher educational qualifications retained their class position after their migration and others, from poor or rural backgrounds, were upwardly mobile as they moved into semi-professional occupations such as nursing or primary school teaching. The class position of women is also complicated by marriage, as they move into households in which they and their husbands may have different positions, incomes and values. Further, as is common among many migrant groups, ambition for their children, and the desire to recapture social status among the downwardly mobile groups, often influences ambitions and lifestyle and makes it more difficult to categorize their status. For all the women who tell their stories here, however, their gender and their nationality have had a huge impact on their lives, as they sought work in the UK where the intersection of gender, nationality and class significantly influenced the types of jobs open to them and the extent to which opportunities for promotion were available or not.

The organization of the book

The chapters that follow are organized to reflect the decline of manufacturing and the rise of the service sector. Some of the women worked in several jobs over their lifetime, moving not only between jobs but between sectors, from manufacturing perhaps earlier in their working life, into service employment later on and so their stories straddle easy distinctions between different types of work. As service sector employment increased its dominance as the years passed, more space is devoted to this type of work than manufacturing jobs. Chapter 3 is about making things, and Chapters 4 and 5 are about different types of caring. The jobs that women talk about in these chapters include low waged body work – cleaning and caring – as well as nursing and elder care. Chapter 6 is about higher paid employment, 'mind' work rather than body work, a dichotomy that Brush (1999) captured as 'hi tech' and 'high touch' tasks. Here university teaching and banking exemplify types of work based on cerebral rather than bodily attributes, although paradoxically medicine is also often defined, not least by practitioners, as cerebral and high status, despite its evident attention to the bodies of patients and sometimes demanding physical work.

A great deal of service sector employment, however, is both body and mind work, termed interactive work as providers of services are in direct contact with customers, clients, patients or students. Here bodily presentation – size, shape, clothes, expressions and gestures – matters in the interaction. For many migrant women, new to the UK, often struggling with language or with habitual forms of interaction that may be strange to them, establishing acceptable social relations with the people that they serve is not always easy. Although these interactions are addressed in several earlier chapters, in Chapter 7 they are explored directly, looking at the UK public through the eyes of women workers employed variously as shop assistants, as a bus driver, a receptionist and in hotels. An unflattering picture of the attitudes of the UK public to the women that serve them emerges here.

The larger narrative of the book is a chronological one as service work replaced manufacturing over the post-war decades, as precarious forms of contract, especially for women, replaced more secure forms of employment and as the numbers of migrant women looking for waged work increased across the second half of the twentieth century and into the twenty-first. However, within each chapter, there is also a sense of time, as women workers of different origins replace one another in the same types of work. Women from the Baltic States, for example, worked in the textile industry as mill hands in the 1940s, South Asian women sewed car seats at Fords or garments in their homes in the 1970s, and women from countries from East Timor to Poland worked on the line assembling cars and packing goods as varied as toys, biscuits and pharmaceuticals in the 1990s and 2000s. Presenting all these forms of manufacturing employment together allows comparisons over time and between women of different origins to be drawn, revealing the similarities in the ways in which gender, ethnicity and nationality in combination construct migrant women as cheap labour. But these women were regarded as hard and reliable workers by employers, and, significantly, in their own eyes, providing them with a sense of self-worth as they labour over the decades in the service of the British state and the British public.

In each chapter common themes are evident. These include stories about disruption and dislocation, about rebuilding a life both in the workplace and at home and in the community. And as the chapters progress, the women whose stories construct them begin to age, to think of retirement and perhaps return to a homeland that they left in some cases more than half a century earlier. Behind all the decisions, however, whether about employment, children or retirement, the initial story of migration and the journey to Britain continues to loom large. For all the women in this book, leaving home, often as a very young woman, had an unparalleled effect on their life, even for the young women who made a short-term decision based on an assessment of the advantages of migration for their future career or who moved in order to travel. For this reason, the next chapter is about leaving home where it is clear, perhaps especially for the women who were unwilling migrants, torn from their families and futures by war or ethnic conflict that memories of migration remain vivid, not fading with age.

There are evident continuities in migrant women's narratives, as they left home and re-established lives in Britain. All of the women in the pages that follow found employment, often immediately they arrived, and many of them worked continuously across their lifetime. Typically they found employment in what are regarded as appropriate jobs for women, in feminized sectors, serving or caring for others, making or assembling fiddly components in the manufacturing sector or doing that quintessentially feminine job of sewing. They often faced discrimination, trapped in the lower ends of job hierarchies and even those women who established themselves on a career path often found that their gender or their nationality was the basis for less equal treatment. The voices of these women are vivid and engrossing. Their courage and agency shines through and each narrative provides a counter to commonly held views, particularly widespread in the second decade of the twenty-first century, of migrants as a burden on the British state.

The white British population is largely absent from the heart of the book, other than as an amorphous group of 'co-workers', neighbours and less often friends. In the short concluding chapter, I turn more directly to the majority population in a brief history of changing attitudes and policies towards 'strangers' living in the UK. In Appendix 4 there is a list of questions that might be helpful to keep in mind when reading the rest of the book, aiding comparisons and in seeing common themes across the chapters. This guidance may not be necessary though as the extraordinary voices of these women who consider themselves 'ordinary' reveal both the centrality of 'work', both waged and domestic, in their lives across seven post-war decades. Their stories illustrate the complexity and contradictions that migrant women faced in the labour market, at home and in their everyday lives as they built communities and interacted with the British population. As the narratives show, waged work entails pleasure and pain, as well as providing an income. Labour market participation was essential for all these women to maintain individual and family life in a new country. The different workplaces described here are arenas where social relations between newcomers to Britain and the longer established population have had to be negotiated over time, where individual women found meaning, developed a sense of self-worth and built new identities, as well as being one of the key sites in the negotiation of and struggle between all those responsibilities that fall on women's shoulders. What is clear is that for all women, waged work has come to play a much more significant role in their lives than the post-war planners who emphasized women's domestic duties ever envisioned. Beveridge's post-war vision of a domestic home-based life for most women has vanished.

2

Moving Stories:

Journeys to the UK

This chapter is about leaving home and the journey to Britain. Although the term 'odyssey' is often used in connection with migrants' journeys, it seemed inappropriate here as typically it embodies male experiences. Like Odysseus, the idealized migrant in many stories of journeys is a heroic masculine character. There are numerous accounts of long walks to freedom (Eksteins 1999; Mandela 1994; Rawicz 1999 [1956]) in which the protagonist is a man, often alone, sometimes with his dependents, but typically in charge of the journey and able to overcome the difficulties encountered during it. As feminist critics of this genre have noted, while not doubting or diminishing the horrors and difficulties of displacements of different kinds, women less typically place themselves at the heart of such narratives and often feel uncomfortable in recounting their heroism. Instead, many women tend to pass over their own bravery and may tell their story with a focus instead on the mundane or the everyday and its shocking contrast with the reality of flight.

*Twenty-four-year-old **Elvira**, telling of her narrow escape from discovery by Russian soldiers as she fled westwards across Latvia in late 1944, focused on the bad luck of deciding that day to wear her favourite yellow blouse, one of the few garments she still possessed that reminded her of home.*

One morning the sun was shining and although we were all anxious, it seemed quite bright in a way and I thought 'I'll put a summery blouse on' and it was bright yellow. And I needed to go into the bushes. There I was, squatting there, the sun shining on my bright yellow blouse and I heard some Russians talking. They had found us. I slid down and crawled further into the bushes and thought 'why did I put this blouse on? It is so bright'. And one of the girls was just standing there and they took her into the bushes and raped her. If I had been there, it would have been my turn.

All 74 women who tell their stories here left to start their new lives in a country that they often knew little about. Although the rise of mass media and more recently the internet has to a large degree countered this lack of knowledge, nevertheless myths about the UK often loom larger than realities, even for many of the most recent migrants. The early post-war migrants, women displaced by the war in Europe, like Elvira, were perhaps the most ignorant of the country in which they landed between 1946 and 1949. They had no attachment to the UK and sometimes they had to borrow an atlas to find the towns and cities where they were sent to work. In 1947, Eva was placed in a hospital outside Warwick, a town in the Midlands. As she reported, 'I thought "oh well, in the middle that would be best, not far away from anything"'. Most of these young women could not speak English and if they could, they often found the accents of the local people and of their co-workers difficult to understand. Eva and her sister were allocated work in a mental hospital and 'we had to look up the word "mental" in a dictionary'. Valda, on her arrival at a small hospital in rural Scotland, was asked if she wanted 'fash' to eat for her supper, something she had never heard of but which, when it arrived, she discovered was fish.

These women, the first to arrive in Britain at the end of the war, had been displaced by the hostilities, leaving home as the Soviet army advanced westwards and housed temporarily in displaced persons camps in Germany. Although they considered themselves refugees, the British government transformed them into economic migrants by a single decree. Women recruited in displaced persons camps in the British sector were to be termed 'European Volunteer Workers' (EVWs), allocated to a job and not permitted to change it for a fixed period, usually three years. The first entrants to the UK were recruited in a scheme in which they were termed 'Baltic Cygnets'. For these women the loss of their homes and their country and their subsequent displacement – months and years in camps and then a journey to the UK – runs through their memories of migration.

The label 'economic migrant' is a better description for women from the Caribbean, who like women from the Baltic before them, were regarded as valuable workers by the British state. Unlike the EVWs, however, women from the Caribbean imagined they belonged to Britain through a joint history and citizenship in the Empire. They arrived in increasing numbers from the end of the 1940s, rising to a peak in the late 1960s, when about 100,000 women born in the Caribbean then lived in the UK. The 1962 Immigration Act, however, had begun to impose restrictions on their entry that were tightened in later years. These women answered the call from the British government for workers to fill 'female' jobs. They responded to recruitment drives in the Caribbean by hospital matrons and administrators looking for nurses, or young women prepared to train as nurses, to staff the new NHS, and by London Transport officials seeking public transport workers in ticket offices, in canteens and sometimes on buses and trains. They came largely by choice, although some were propelled by poverty and settled mainly in larger British towns and cities, particularly in London and Birmingham. Their journeys and recruitment paralleled longer-established moves across the Irish Sea by young women from Eire, many of whom came as nurses in the post-war years, and also tell their stories here.

If women from the Baltic States were refugees (at least in their own eyes) and women from the Caribbean and Ireland actual volunteers, rather than migrants with little choice, then women from South Asia and of South Asian origins who left East Africa from the mid-1960s onwards, as independence and Africanization programmes precipitated their emigration, were a hybrid category. These women were not looking for work initially, nor were they allocated employment by the state but were instead more representative of a commonly held view of women migrants. In this view, women were 'trailing wives', accompanying or following their husbands, or if younger, their fathers and mothers or other family members. Bina, whose story is included in this chapter, came to London, for example, with her sisters. As the stories told by these women of South Asian origin reveal, most of them came as part of a family, unlike the European and Caribbean young women who were more likely to be single and to travel alone. Many of the women from South Asia and East Africa had not been employed before, but economic necessity ensured that they had to find work soon after arriving in the UK.

All these women's stories are full of a sense of loss and displacement, as well as, for some, shock to find that what they thought of as the motherland was not welcoming. Disbelief about the weather, the food and the difficult accents run through their narratives. For women from the Caribbean and South Asia being unable to decipher what people said, and worse, not being understood themselves although they spoke English, was galling, and they were quickly disabused about their knowledge of the country based on their school curriculum. Shivering in light clothing, Brie, for example, found it hard on her arrival in 1957 to reconcile inner London with England's 'green and pleasant land' familiar to her from hymns sung in church in Trinidad. Jaba, born in India, but moving from Tanzania in 1968, found the climate and the locals inhospitable and the houses cold.

The oldest of the 74 women, women like Elvira and Diana whose stories of leaving Latvia follow, grew up in the 1930s. Most of the Cygnets came from middle class families and expected to lead a conventional middle class life, employed perhaps before marriage – Diana and Elvira both trained as teachers – and leaving the labour market when they had children. In 1940, however, 'everything changed'.

Leaving Latvia

Elvira was born in 1920, the daughter of a soldier. Her family lived in a rural area and after compulsory schooling she held a series of clerical jobs before she trained as a teacher in the early 1940s. During the Russian occupation between 1939 and 1941 she was also involved with a guerrilla partisan group. She fled with friends in late 1944, and after a period in a displaced persons camp, came to the UK as a Baltic Cygnet in 1947.

I was born in the country, on my grandfather's farm. My father was in the army and later on we went to a smallish town where my father's unit was. We lived there while I was going to primary and grammar school and I finished grammar school when I was 19. My dream was to be a teacher but I was a very thin girl, healthy I think, so my mother just packed me off to my grandmother's farm, like we did in the summer. She packed me off there til the autumn and so it was too late to put in any applications anywhere. So I found a job in a factory, in the office, typewriting and that sort of thing. That was 1939–40 and everything changed. All the dreams had to be scrapped because the Russians came in. They came [to the small town where she lived] in June 1940. It was a very frightening time. We didn't know what was happening; we didn't know what to expect.

I was a year in the office and then I changed. I got a job at the police station, again as a typist and tea maker. That was just before the Russians came in. And that was really the worst place to be when the Russians came in and to see the people taken out and never seen again. All the staff had to go. We all had to leave.

And then I found work in the forestry office and that was where my grandparents were. I was in the village and they were on a farm and I lived in the forestry office and it was really a very nice time in a way because there were quite a lot of young people, and we arranged a choir and we were putting on plays. And although it was Communist time and we had Russian lessons as well but of course we just listened to what was happening, who had been taken away for questioning and so on. It was a frightening time, but we were twenty or twenty one and we didn't think the worst.

And then the deportations happened in June 1941.[1] The phone rang and my boss answered it and he went absolutely white and he said 'you know what has happened tonight? Some people have been taken away. The lorry had taken people from the telephone exchange and they are headed your way.' And so he said 'Elvira, go and get some things together because it may be for us.' What do you get together? It was the middle of summer but if it was for a long time you need winter clothes and so I just got some things together. We put some things together and just waited but they didn't come for us. Later we heard who had been taken away.

The war didn't really affect us til 1941 when the Germans came in. All the deportations happened just before. Whether they [Russian occupiers] knew before, I don't know. The Russians just fled and took some Latvian people with them and some went by their own free will who had been involved. Then the Germans started sorting out who had been helping the Russians and so that was an awful time as well. For us as individuals, although it was very frightening, at least we knew the Germans were more intelligent, better people than the Russians, or that is what we thought. We did not know that they would kill us too and take people away. We had no real say in our lives when the Germans came. They made the rules and we had to obey. We were occupied and we had to obey.

When the Germans came in and things quietened down in a way, I thought 'well, I could go to the teachers' training college now'. There were some entrance exams but I passed and that was marvellous. . . . I made it just in time. I went in 1942. And then in 1944 it all happened again.

The Germans were losing the war and the Russian front was advancing west.

We could hear the bombing and see the lights. We knew we had to go. We all decided we would go to Germany but later on my parents changed their mind. They didn't want to leave my sister. She was pregnant and her husband was in the army. I didn't want to leave my parents but I decided to go with friends. My mother said 'go with them and then perhaps later on you can get us out if the worse happens'. So I went with those farmer friends. If my mother had said 'don't go', I wouldn't have gone. I never saw them again.

Elvira sailed from Leipaj, Latvia's main port, to Danzig.

From Danzig we were sent to Colberg [in Germany], to work in a paper mill.[2] It wasn't all that hard really but we had to walk a long way from the camp which was in a factory. We had to walk and sometimes I did night shifts. We were Latvians together. The front was coming closer and closer, so one day we decided we must go, go somewhere away. So we started going on the train, not really a train, just a goods train with only two wagons. It was all open flat trucks and two closed: one for mothers and children. There were bales of straw to sit on and it was March. We just went and went and stopped somewhere and people had to jump off to do their business and there were some soup kitchens but we never stopped at any towns. I was about three days on the train and in the end I was so cold, feeling awful. I decided at the next stop I'll get off and I don't know what I'll do, but it happened to be Rostock on the north coast and we were shunted out, not in town but out of town to an estate and we stayed there.

As the front approached again, Elvira and her companions attempted to leave, taking a horse and cart.

For three or four days and nights we just kept going and then, near the coast, in northern Germany, there was a big field and we decided to catch a few hours sleep and my cousin said she heard people shouting 'don't sleep; you don't know the danger coming up'. I never heard them. We did stop and about six the next morning with a nice sun coming up, we boiled some water for tea and all of a sudden, just like mushrooms out of the ground, there were Russians with the red star. And they said 'uri, uri', watches. I had this ring, my godmother gave it me on confirmation day and I put it in my boot and I said I had nothing. . . . And we were all turned back.

We knew there were those zones – English and American – and we thought we must see if we can find any way to get to the English zone or at least out of the Russian zone. We told the Russians we were going back to Latvia, not just to Berlin. So we got things together, just what we could carry and we went on the train to Berlin. The train was absolutely packed; it was awful. We just sat there for nearly three days. We finally got to Berlin about one o'clock on Saturday [after getting on the train on Thursday] and the offices were closed where we were supposed to register. So we had to wait all through Saturday and Sunday. On Monday morning the station was bombed, just ruins. Only where the tickets were collected was left. And so we all huddled together. And one night it rained, it was really awful. This friend, he was very good. He organized a van, a baker's van, for the children and the luggage. And working on the farm I had had my legs scratched and they were infected. I couldn't really walk so I was in the van with the luggage. And he took us to a British camp and we were taken in as refugees.

I was there a year and a half and then the chance came to come to England. Someone came from England to recruit. It was just for single people. I came in 1947. Before I came people were taken only to work in hospitals. I was still hesitating then, when those people came. I was offered work, weaving in Bradford and so I said yes. I arrived in August and started work in September [1947].

Vieda grew up in a small village with her mother. Her father died when she was young and her mother did casual work to get by. When Vieda was 15, her mother died and six months later, in early 1945, she left Latvia with friends. Like Elvira her memory of leaving and the journey to Germany is constructed around objects – the loss of her photographs and the pleasurable shock of white bread and oranges given to her by officials in the American zone.

At the last minute we got on a ship with all civilians and army and so and we got out of there into Germany. I had a bundle of clothes and photographs and I carried them with me. At first we arrived in Stettin [at the mouth of the Oder] by ship, and it was all, there was only rubbish, nothing. The whole placed was bombed: there was nothing. And I had a big accident there. I fell down an air-raid shelter and I was hurt. For a few weeks I lied there on a makeshift bed but then we had to walk again. We moved on and after a few weeks we arrived by the river Oder. And I still had my photographs and my little bundle of things. But they were all full with civilians and wounded soldiers and you had to go on a sort of wooden boat across and the water was seeping and you weren't allowed to carry anything. So a German just grabbed away my bundle and chucked away and so went my photographs. And then we crossed the thing and then we started to walk, hundreds of us, like you saw last year in Kosovo.[3] And so we walked and walked and walked, sleeping in the woods, in some sheds that is how everyone did it and then we arrived in the American zone and I remember, I remember seeing for the first time the white bread. It was white bread and oranges they were giving us.

And then we were parted. I was put in one place and they [the Latvian friends she had left with] were moved down into south Germany. And I stayed somehow in the middle in Westphalia in Germany. There was for a while some camp or big building or something, some big barracks with all the soldiers pushed in and they sorted us out to do some work. I was allocated to go to a German hospital. I was by then 16 already and I was sent to work in a laundry which was dreadful, with the cold water and so on. But I was not the only one; they [refugees] were all working. At this special hospital I was the only Latvian, there was only me from the displaced persons there, rest were Germans. Well, they were displaced, but from north Germany. So after a few years there, in the laundry, though at the weekends I was allowed to sweep, and then after a while I got a job in the office and by then I was fluent in German and so on and I got promotion. By then I was 17 and a half.

Then, while I was working there, it wasn't a very posh job but reception, you know, and I had to register people and nearby there was a big English army. No, an RAF place or something, but they had to come and check the X-rays or do the health checks of something and one day arrived this wing commander or group captain and his wife. And they X-rayed and when I was doing the papers we start talking. 'Yes, I'm from Latvia.' ... And they [the English couple] said 'we are going back to England. Would you like to come with us and work for us for a year when they got back to England?' They had this old nanny from the Isle of Wight and 'would I be the nursemaid to the nanny?' 'Well', I thought 'well, I am quite friendly and probably I am cheap labour too'. In those days you did not think like that but when I look back, probably, or perhaps they genuinely liked me, I don't know. So I came with them to England.

Diana grew up in the countryside, where her father was a forester. Like Elvira, she was born in 1920, and she also trained as a teacher during the war. She left Latvia for Germany in 1944. Unlike Elvira she left with her family, including her mother, but as only single women were accepted as Baltic Cygnets, she had to leave her mother behind, and came to England in 1947 with her sister after 24 months in a Displaced Persons (DP) camp in Germany.

I was born in Riga and my father was a forester. He was transferred more north. Latvia had quite a few forests and they were looked after by the Minister of Forestry and my father was high up. So we were three sisters and we were brought up in the country. There was land and a big house to go with my father's job. And then we went to primary school and then to Riga to grammar school. My mother looked after us. In those days mothers didn't work. There was the big house to look after and anyway nobody did in those days. We had a maid and we had a man that looked after horses.

I was five years in grammar school in Riga in the winter and then in the summer we went home. I finished grammar school I think in 1939 or 1940. We were 19. After grammar school I went to domestic science college. That was in the late 1930s, beginning of 1940s. Then when I finished, I was a teacher in primary school for one year. I loved that. It was my best job. It was back in the small village where my father was. But, of course, the war changed everything. The school was closed. The first time [1940] when the Russians came I was at college. It was dreadful. My father was very well known and I don't know how we escaped deportation.

Germany then occupied Latvia from 1941 but in 1944, it was clear that the Russian front was close and Diana's father decided the family should flee to Germany.

My father decided that whatever happens, although there were bombs in Germany, it was more civilized and so the whole family would go to Germany. Each had one suitcase and that was all. We packed and left the house, the furniture and everything. I was 25 by then and I could see and understand and we had seen earlier what the Russians had done and what they could do.

I was lucky we escaped together, parents and all three sisters. After we left our country we went to Germany and we stayed in Germany. And then the war was nearly finished and we couldn't escape. When the Russians came they couldn't find us there. And they are not people; they are animals. I don't know if it is the same in other places, but we lived in a small village and when they came in they were like animals. They took wedding rings, they took watches; they took everything that they could. I am not lying, believe me. They were terrible and they raped the German women. Even the girls 13 and 14. My three sisters, we were hiding in lofts and everywhere, where we could and I think what saved us was that we all could speak Russian. There we stayed for three or four months, more perhaps.

There were quite a few Latvians working in the fields and when the Russians came, we all gathered and there was a big house and we all went to live there. And then one day, German officials came and said you had to go home. Nobody asked us or anything and we were put in a cattle truck and we were taken to a camp. Then it was Poland, near the German border, we were put in a camp. It was dreadful and there were quite a few Russians as well, prisoners of war. And we knew if we get in that truck and we were taken away we would not get home; we knew we were going to Siberia. They put us all in a cattle truck. It was in February [1945], no heating or anything and it was freezing and we knew we had to escape. And the Russian soldiers with the rifles were going up and down and when they were up, we jumped off the train and disappeared.

It was 1945 when we escaped from the train. We were in the Russian zone. That used to be a German city and now it was Polish and there were so many empty houses with furniture, exactly the same as we had left and so we went in an empty house and stayed. We didn't have anything else to do. If we stayed in the train we would be taken to Siberia. And so we took a house, everything was there but food was very scarce but we found we were near a nursery and we went myself and my sister and we just, a vegetable farm or something like that and so we worked there for a year.

And there was, of course, the Russians there as well and so we lived in the house and we never knew if one day the Poles and Russians come and bang the door and you have to open and let them in. That was nearly a year and then we heard rumours. Because Poland was full of different nationalities who didn't want to go back to Russia. And the Polish government, that of course was Communist, they have agreed that all the Russian citizens, because of course we [Latvians] were then Russian citizens, they are going to collect and send back, to 'home', that's what they said. And we knew if they found us what will happen. Then the Poles sent, not by force but they did everything possible so that the Germans would leave the towns because a big part of Germany now belongs to Poland. And they wanted them to send all back and they did everything possible. They didn't give them work, they weren't brutal but they did everything possible and really we were, we did not know what to do, and there was a special office where Germans had to go to leave Poland.

And one day, we were very desperate, we went in when there was only one person and we said 'we want to emigrate. We speak German' and they said 'where is your papers?' And I forgot to tell you earlier, when they took us to Russian camps they took away all our passports, everything. We had nothing, no papers, so you are nothing. So when we went to the Polish office, they said 'where are your papers?' and we said 'we have no papers'. And in that split second we had to decide whether to lie or to tell the truth and we told the truth, that we are Latvians and the gentleman that was there, he said 'Yes, that is true. They are going to send you all back.'[4] And you know what he did? He said 'you come the next day and I'll give you a big pile of papers and chose one which you want'.

With false papers, Diana and her sister were then sent to a camp in the British zone from where in July 1947 they came together to England as directed labour. Diana was sent to a geriatric hospital in Hitchin but her sister was sent elsewhere.

'Nursing's what in those days a lot of ladies did'

Working in caring roles, particularly as nurses, was a key route to England in the 1950s and 1960s, and indeed in earlier decades for young Irish women. Large numbers of women from Eire and from the Caribbean islands came to the UK to train as nurses.

Mary was born in rural Ireland in 1943 and left for London in 1961.

I was born in Bray, and it's County Wicklow in Southern Ireland. We weren't particularly well off. My father was unwell and so we were often in some hardship. My mother didn't work, no, not at all as I had three brothers and a sister. So, I'd always worked because of the family circumstances, during my school holidays and at weekends. My schooling was a bit basic. It was mainly shorthand and typing but it had a little bit of education in terms of English and Geography and History but very limited. It was mainly concentrated on secretarial skills and in fact, as I completed the course, at the age of 16, I left home and went to work in a learning disabilities hospital as a care assistant.

Two years almost exactly, then I came to England to train as a nurse. Oh, it was part of the tradition, I think. My mother was always very much the matriarchal figure of the whole road, and I used to get involved in both looking after children and looking after older people. So it was a logical thing for me to do, go into something of that nature. And at that point in Ireland to train as a nurse, you would have had to pay for the training so that clearly wasn't particularly possible in my family circumstances, so that was a good driver to move.

It was very straightforward in that I had a friend who I'd made at the learning disabilities hospital and between us we just sort of found the names of various hospitals in England. In fact we didn't apply to very many. I think the first one we applied to, we got accepted which was the

FIGURE 1 *A young Irish migrant arrives alone in London, October 1955.*

Source: Thurston Hopkins.

North Middlesex Hospital in Edmonton, and got immediately accepted and on reflection, I'm sorry. Well, I was going to [apply to] one of the teaching hospitals such as St Mary's where I learnt much later that they were very keen to have Irish people. I didn't know that until much later.

And in Ireland it was considered a very good thing to have a daughter or you know, it was mainly daughters who went nursing in that day because we are talking about '61 when I came over. We took the slow route which was going by the mail boat and whatever, over night and I enjoyed it, I think because I liked rough seas. So it was not a problem, it wasn't a problem.

Four years earlier, in 1957, **Georgina** *had made a similar decision to Mary, to leave home to train as a nurse in the UK. Like Mary, she organized the process herself. Georgina was born in Trinidad and she was only 16 years old when she left the Caribbean.*

I was born in Trinidad and Tobago in a village. We were very poor. My mum was a peasant and my father was too; he worked in the fields as well. He had a cow and he cut wood and saw wood. I have got three brothers, three sisters; I am the last of seven.

I went to high school before coming to England. Because I grew up as the last of the family and my brothers and sisters, they had left school, my mother took me away and I went to a private school. I attended a private school run by nuns. They taught us a lot about the scriptures, about our lessons, about prayers and how to grow up in a decent way. My mother had to pay a fee for going to school which was a small fee. For them it was a lot, but I was the last and there was nobody else. I have good memories of it but remember in those days they were very strict and you get a lot of smacking, a lot of beating and I was very afraid of beating.

I did not completely finish high school. I leave then to come to do nursing in England. As a last child, my mother worked very hard and I always wanted to travel and I've always said I wanted to be a nurse. I was a very spoiled child; I didn't even wash my own knickers in those days, but I wanted to travel and I decided. My family were very strict and I get a lot of beating and it was hard work studying. Because of the beating I could not concentrate, the beating you'd get at school and the beating you'd get at home for breaking a glass, because in those days that's what your parents knew. They were very strict. They were very poor, so everything meant everything.

So I thought if I travel as a teenager, come away to study nursing, I will be able to do better. That is one of the reasons I thought of travelling and as a teenager and leaving home. Nursing's what in those days a lot of ladies did. You were looked upon as either to go and do sewing or housewife or to do nursing. As a woman, it's always nursing, to be a nurse. It was something to be a nurse. This is why I just wanted to do nursing. With nursing you could travel the world and that was one of my ambitions, to travel. I came to a hospital in Essex where we had a lot of Trinidadians and a lot of people from my high school. We were British subjects. Trinidad belonged to the Empire. We belonged to the Commonwealth so we had a British passport. So the idea is that I had to write to the hospital in Essex to come and do my training, who in turn replied and accepted me to come. Then my mother gather all her little pennies and saved which was a big secret to the family because we were very poor. Being the last, the others wouldn't want her to spend all that money on one person to travel, because it was a lot of money and to buy all the clothes and everything to come away.

When I was accepted, my mother was very happy. It was a big secret to the family until everything was done. I came on the boat called *The Venezuela* from Trinidad and I travelled then to London. It was May or March, I can't exactly remember the date that I left. I think it was on 21 March 1957. It took three weeks on the boat, with other people. They were from Trinidad, they were from Guyana, travelling as well to come to study and to work with the government and to earn a living.

I was very afraid, very afraid. The day I went to the port and all my family came to see me off, I cried. I cried because then I was leaving. I just realized what was happening; I was leaving the family. I had nobody and getting on a boat. Looking back there was nobody with me. It was hard but I made friends on the boat and we stayed friends.

The Nursing Council, the Nursing Council meet you. And they take you to the hospital that has accepted you and there you were met by the Sister and the Matron who became your parent. In those days, I lived in the nurses' home and there we had lots of nurses from Trinidad and Tobago, so we all made friends and those who were there before came to look after you as the younger one, as you were brought up that you always respect your elders, that if we did anything wrong. We always eat with our spoon when we were young but when we came, you had to eat with your knife and fork, so they made sure we held our knife and folk properly and eat properly, that other people do not laugh at us. The older ones would come and make sure and told us all the things. We make sure that we dress, because we came from a hot country and we had bright clothes and they will tell you, 'don't wear the bright clothes, they will laugh at you'. And so the older ones came and take care and look after us, make sure we were doing the right things and behaving in the right way and we did listen to them.

*Ten years after Georgina, **Brie** also left Trinidad to train as a nurse. She was recruited through a UK-owned but Caribbean-based agency rather than applying directly to a hospital in the UK. Brie was 19 in 1967 when she left the island. She was the oldest child of nine and had 'always wanted to be a nurse, because I always cared for my brothers and sisters. I was the one with*

FIGURE 2 *Seven hundred Caribbean immigrants in the customs hall, Southampton, May 1956.*

Source: Haywood Images Picture Post.

the plaster if anything happened.' She had lived in England for 40 years, most of them in London, at the time of this conversation in 2007.

I was born in Trinidad. I think in Port of Spain. At the time, well, I would say we were very poor, because my mum had nine children eventually. So I would say we were poor, but we got by. My mum didn't work, of course, housewife, and when she did, as a young person, she did sort of jobs here and there. But she had her first child at fifteen and a half. She fell pregnant. As I say, things happened and so, of course, my mother couldn't finish her education, so she did jobs here and there. My father was a stevedore; he worked on the wharves in Trinidad.

I went to high school, though, and then I worked for a short while. I had to work and I had a job, because, I mean, I was busy doing other things like voluntary work and stuff like that and then, I think, the year before I left Trinidad, I just did a seasonal job with the Carnival Development Committee because I was, sort of, getting fed up looking after young siblings and that and I just wanted to get out. And they were asking for nurses to come to England and I applied. I think it was, well, I think it must have been some agency. I think in my time it may well have been Enoch Powell was doing the, was it Enoch Powell, was it Enoch Powell, the MP? Yeah, he was pushing, I think, at the time. He was Minister for Health.[5]

It must have been through an agency and I just applied and went for an interview and did all the bits that they're supposed to, you're supposed to do, and was successful. I had done an exam in Trinidad to start my training there. Yes, I did the exam in Trinidad but the easiest way to get in was to do mental nursing and I wasn't interested in that at all. I did the exam and, of course, in Trinidad then [in 1966] you were talking about thousands of people doing an exam and they're only picking a few hundred, if you're lucky. So if you weren't one of the few hundred, you were just out. So this is why I plumped to come away, because I just wanted to move on with my life and chose to come 4,000 odd miles.

I had to organize everything, not the agency. I had to get my passport. I remember, the only thing I really can remember, is going down to the police station to get my fingerprints and also I had to go to the doctor's to make sure that I wasn't pregnant when I left.

To pay my fare, I think my mum had to, because I came by ship and that was two weeks, and I think my mum had to ask my uncle for the money and, of course, then it was only 80 Trinidad and Tobago dollars. So it shows how long ago that was, which is about, what will it be now? Was it 80 dollars or 80 pounds? I honestly can't remember. But it was a lot of money in those days.

I did all that alone, but when we got on to board the ship, I just sort of glanced across and there was another girl there and she had the same address as I was going to in Lancashire, so we just palled up then, and that was it. I was on my own.

When we arrived we were collected at, now was it, I think it was Victoria Station. Someone came and collected us onto the train to get to Lancashire. I think we had to get to Manchester and then we had to change to get to Rossendale. And somebody collected, picked us up from Victoria and helped us on to the train and then we made our way to where we were going.

I was absolutely terrified. I did not want to stay. Did not. I always said if I had the money, I would have gone, did a right about-turn. I mean, I'm glad as I didn't now, you know, because it's stood me in good stead and I'm quite comfortable at the moment. But at the time, I remember the day in question, I can remember now what I had to eat, and I can remember crying into it and, of course, when we got to the hospital where we were going to train, they separated myself and the girl who was, who were at the same hospital with me, so that made it even more traumatic.

It wasn't England itself, it was leaving my family, because when you've got a big family, you know, it's eleven of us and then you have to come over on your own, it's kind of hard. But England to me didn't, because, I mean, we learned English history and England to me, what we learned was, the only thing that was different was that we were almost told that everybody was blonde and blue-eyed. That was, well, that's the impression that was given when we did the history but, of course, when I came and realized people had dark hair and brown hair and I used to think, 'well, it doesn't look any different to Trinidad', because, of course, Trinidad is a very mixed community as well, you know. It's very multicultural, so it didn't feel any different, apart from the weather, but I missed my family.

Twice migrants: India, East Africa and the UK

In the late 1960s and early 1970s, as African countries gained independence from the early 1960s, women of South Asian origin who had lived in East Africa began to move to the UK in sizeable numbers. These women, like the EVWs, were refugees, deciding to leave as the newly independent regimes made their lives less comfortable than previously. Then in 1972, Idi Amin expelled the South Asian population of Uganda and these women had no choice but to leave.

Parvani was born in 1941 in Kenya into a middle class family. She left to marry in India but moved back to Kenya with her husband. They moved to London in 1966 when she was 25 and already a mother of one child. Her parents joined her there two years later as Jomo Kenyatta's Africanization policies in Kenya reduced their standard of living and they decided to leave.

I was born in Kenya. My father was a manager in a tea factory. My mother was not working. She was a housewife. We got a lot of friends but it was really very, very a hard time. It was at that time, Africa was very good but we had the hard time over there, but we get lot of food there, lot of money there but the town was so small that you hardly see the people [other South Asians] there.

I've got five sisters and four brothers. My brothers were very educated because they go to Nairobi to have education, but not us, the girls, we never chance to get out to the big city because my mother was very, very backward you know. She don't let us go anywhere. I was 13 when I finished my school. And then because I was the first my family, then I had to stop. So I just help my brother and sisters to grow and look after them and my mother, we don't have a job, we don't know much about it and then after that, when I was twenty-one, then I go to India and then I getting married in India.

I liked in India. I was really surprised that in seven days my mother saw a boy and she says 'yes, okay' and we get married in India. Then after that I go to Kenya again, after my marriage and then my husband start working straight away, got a good job, and I feel I was very, very happy over there because we've got servant, three, four servant and we don't have to do anything and we have a beautiful life. But you know, I used to say that I wanted to come to London because I see the picture and in that picture I see the [Buckingham] Palace, and say 'London must be a very beautiful place.'

When I come here, after two years then my parents come here, all of them, 12 people. Because of Jomo Kenyatta, they do bad thing.[6] They have to come, in one night they decide to come in this country, you know, and everybody come together, leave everything there. They are running after they made announcement and they leave everything, all the things. They just coming on the plane. But at that time I was lucky. I had a house [in London]; I work hard and when they come to me, they live with me. Now they are all very settled here, everybody has got the children, very happy.

In Kenya, you know, when I was thinking of going to go to England but I don't know how to, at that time. My uncle says, he said 'you sign your name then you come here in London'. So I went because I wanted to come to England. I told my husband, 'yes, I will go to India for one year, then I will come to England' but soon after that they announced that you can have a British passport in Kenya. Then I come here with my husband because I was British from there. I had a British passport from Kenya. That was a very good thing, you know.

I just come here, I didn't come by the plane, I come by ship, 21 days in the ship because my husband like to travel in the ship and in the ship we come here. And then when we come here, then I was really missing my parents because there were no Indians here and it was hard work and at that time the weather was so horrible. There was a lot of snow in front of the door and everything and then it was a really hard time.

I come to England because I thought, because I see that in Indian film London must be a very, very good place and the life is very good. But when I come, I didn't like it. I was crying and if my parents was there and hardly at that time you could phone – now you can phone anywhere. At that time there was no phones and so we had to write a letter. It was a really hard time. Then you know, crying day and night and then we had to stay in one room and that room we had to stay and put the sewing machine [for Parvani's first job making shirts at home] in the room and work very hard.

Jaba also left in 1968, in her case from Tanzania. Eight years older than Parvani, she too had lived in East Africa, but grew up and was married in India.

I was born in India, in a village in Gujarat. My parents were very good, very well off. The building where I was born was like a palace. My father had 500 acres land. He was a moneyed man. In those days, in his house, we used to have visitors – white men – for whom we specially had a table and chairs and they used to bring toys for us. I had an older and a younger brother. I grew up in a very well off family, so I can say that I had no difficulties in my early life.

I went to Africa after I got married. My husband was born there – in Dar es Salaam. He had his business there. He came to India to get married and we got married and he went back. I had my first son in India and then joined him after two years. I was in Africa then for about four years and then went back to India and stayed there for four years, and then came here [to the UK]. My mother-in-law and my sister-in-law were in Gujarat, so I stayed on in India after my marriage. Over the weekend I used to go to my in-laws place and through the week I stayed with my parents. My husband was in Africa during most of this time.

They [the British government] were about to pass a new immigration law and in February 1968 they announced that they will pass an immigration law after which even those who had a British passport would have to queue up and get permission to come here. When I heard the news on radio about the new immigration law, we had to act quickly. We had thought about going before, but we thought he'd go first, find a job and find a place to live and then we would all join him. I said 'you have planned and planned, but not done anything and now this law will come into being'. He said, 'I will go to Bombay and I have a British passport, so nothing will affect me.' He went to the High Commission and asked them, and they said 'you will also have to stand in a queue'. I had this – you know – like a brother. He tried and got a ticket and he put him [husband] on a plane and a telegram came saying he had left. He had just taken a tiny case with him for an overnight stay in Bombay to assess the situation, and he ended up going to London.

So, my husband came here on his own and stayed in a rented room and after six months, my sons and I, we all came here. My first feeling was 'why did I come here? This is so unlike my country, what am I doing here?' This place is not like what I had heard about it. I came in October when everything was dark. It used to get dark so early. And all the houses looked the same. And if you look upwards at the trees, it seemed like they were all burnt out, dark and bare. I thought, 'why am I here? Why did I come to such a place? It's just not what I had heard.' When I had heard about London, it was about this grand place.

I did not mix with anyone because I did not know the language and I stayed at home all the time. But we had visitors. It was later, after two months, that I asked one of our sisters[7] here to take me with her to work. She used to work at the laundrette and so I wanted to do so too.

Like Parvani, Jaba found she needed to find employment, although in her case, she decided to find work outside the home.

Bina *came from Tanzania too. She arrived in the UK in 1978, aged 18, as a consequence of her father's decisions about emigration, based not only on anxiety about the Africanization programmes in Tanzania but also his family's composition. Bina trained as a nurse in the UK after her arrival and, it seems, in the face of family disapproval.*

FIGURE 3 *South Asian migrants from East Africa at London Airport, February 1968.*

Source: Bentley Archive/Popperfoto.

So for my dad, we were too many girls [in the family] because we were five sisters and two brothers. Because he had five daughters he had this worry at the back of his head, you know, 'what's going to happen to all of you? And are you going to find good husbands?' And all this type of thing, so he had to move on. Now where does he move? My grandfather had a British passport, so somebody said 'why don't you go over to that way, towards England way?' Some said 'why don't you go to India?' and all this type of thing was going on, but we were never asked where we wanted to go.

So anyway, they gave their passports to see if we were eligible or not and it seemed that we were. So two of my sisters came over first because they were of age, if you like, and they would be fine to come over. So they came over, started working here. My grandfather died over there [in Tanzania] while we were still there and because we were very close my father didn't want to come over any more, him being the eldest. You know the eldest normally takes over the family business and what have you. But everyone said 'with five girls and that it's better if you do go over and things are not improving in the country'. You know with the Africans, you're a little bit afraid, they come and rob your house and all this type of thing happened.

So once everything calmed down he said 'all right, I'll carry on with the plan', my dad said, and we came over. I was just 18 I think when I got here. When I came over, everybody knows that you need to work and learn and play and all this type of thing. And I thought, I've always wanted to nurse, but I never thought I would, you know kind of thing, because over there I wasn't going to do nursing in Africa, that's for sure. My parents wouldn't have let me go out to work over there because girls just don't work over there. It took a bit of cudgelling sort of thing to make my father come round but eventually he did and I did it.

Temporary migration

Georgina, Brie, Parvani, Jaba and Bina all came to stay and made their lives in the UK but other women planned a temporary stay. Typically they came to gain work experience, in for example, the UK banking sector. In the late 1980s, the City of London was expanding rapidly and there were numerous opportunities for short-term transfers. Other women accepted contract work – directly recruited in their own country or applying for work through the aegis of a UK-based agency. Many doctors, like Martine, and other health professionals, including nurses and physiotherapists, moved to Britain already qualified, once again in response to shortages in the NHS, but thinking they would stay only for a limited period.

Martine was already an independent adult and qualified as a doctor when she decided to emigrate. An NHS time-limited contract gave her the opportunity of working in a new area of medicine. Martine grew up in South Africa. She was born into a close-knit middle class family in Cape Town. Her father was an accountant and her mother an estate agent and her older brother is a barrister in Cape Town. She came to the UK in 2000.

I was born in Cape Town in South Africa, grew up there, educated there. I went to the University of Cape Town for my medical degree, and at the time the government had introduced something called Community Service which meant that the House Officer year, there was an additional year that you were obliged to do before you got your registration to practice independently. I didn't have a problem with the Community Service as a concept. I'd worked in the townships beforehand. As a concept I thought it was fine, the problem was, they could place you anywhere in the country and if you didn't want to go there for whatever reason, you would not get your registration. So I was quite nervous to do a House Officer year without registration, you know, without the guarantee of a registration at the end of the line. So I decided to come to the UK for a year or two. I'll get my registration here and then I'll move back.

It happened in a sort of casual way. There was a visiting professor from Scotland come to speak to us [in Cape Town]. He was doing a secondment and we were talking and I said 'that would be really interesting to go to the UK', and he went 'phone this person and I'll get you a contact, that's all you need to do'. Which is what I did and then that got the ball rolling and I got shifted from person to person to department, and finally I sent off my application and I was accepted and that was it. Even entry to the country was easy. You made sure you had your X-ray done and you had all your documentation, but I sailed through that quite easily. I had most of my paperwork and almost all of it and it probably it looked acceptable that I was coming as a doctor. At that point [2000] the UK was desperate for anybody with a medical degree. My experience at Heathrow was very ... because you hear nightmarish stories, I was expecting to be grilled and I think I must have been two minutes as this desk and that was it: 'please come in'.

I'd been to England on a holiday a few years beforehand, but in terms of working here and being away from home and the realities of being away from home, I think had I known, I don't know if I would have done it. I'd lived at home for my whole life. University was 25 minutes away by car, so I'd lived at home. And as independent as you can be when you're living at home, it's not the same, and coming from quite a tight-knit family. I went to a place where I knew no one and I had no family there and it was a huge culture shock. I was thinking 'what have I done? I'm a million miles from anywhere, anything.' I didn't know anyone. I'd arrived in the city just out of Glasgow and I knew no one. But it was a good growth experience. Sometimes I think maybe I should have stayed in South Africa, but I think which ever road you choose, you always learn something from it. But yeah, in retrospect, I don't know now whether I'd have done it.

I stayed in digs the hospital found. They were very nice, and after a few months I bought a car, a little second hand car, it was just great. We worked long hours and this great camaraderie amongst the hospital, and a lot of us were also from different parts of world, so there was a bit of a bonding experience, and it was good, it was good fun, learnt a lot, enjoyed it, got very positive memories but I remember those first few weeks were hellish. You get over it.

Martine did seem to 'get over it' as she was still in the UK four years after her arrival, in a new post near London. Other young woman came to the UK as students and, like Martine, did not intend, at least initially, to remain in the UK.

Li Jing was born in Hong Kong and came to the UK as an overseas student in 1999, aged 26, after completing a fashion diploma in Hong Kong. She was brought up by her father in poor conditions and scrimped and saved to be able to supplement the educational grant she received from her government.

Why did I come? To make my dreams come true. First of all I quite like sitting on the lawn, reading about all the dreams and things like that, and also I liked studying and, you know, the wealth of, the wealth of education brings you not only the money as well as your confidence, your personal development. I saved up my money to come and study, and I got grants from Hong Kong government and saved money for four years to come to study, because, you know, family's not wealthy. They can't really support me, so it's very expensive as overseas student.

Afterwards [post-degree], I was trying to get a job here because I met my husband, then my boyfriend. I met him and trying to stay here, but my heart, you know, was still wanting to go back to Hong Kong. I wasn't really prepared to live in this country. Although I like it a lot, you know, but it's still like things draw you back to Hong Kong, and I couldn't get a work permit. I got a job from Wallis and Company, you know the fashion company, I got a job. But I didn't have a work permit so I couldn't work and so I had to leave.

Eventually Li Jing married her boyfriend who was Chinese but with British citizenship and she was able to return to the UK.

'A little bit of dirty business': moving within Europe

By the time the old millennium ended, new restrictions on migration had largely closed the door to women of colour from Commonwealth countries, although, as Catherine's and Hana's narratives below show, women still came from Africa as refugees. New patterns of migration within Europe, however, became more significant. Young women from countries once dominated by links to the USSR, including the Baltic States, Poland and Hungary, began to arrive in growing numbers as economic migrants after the expansion of the EU in 2004. Other young women, including Marianna and Fitore, came as refugees, both made homeless by the conflict in the former Yugoslavia. For them the journey was far harder than for the economic migrants from the new EU member states. These women were able to go back and forth between the UK and 'home', in a Europe far better connected by good transport links than in the early post-war decades. However, women, like Dominika, who moved to the UK before EU expansion, were irregular migrants working illegally.

Dominika *moved to Britain in 1999 aged 25 and because of her irregular status found life difficult initially. Her entry was arranged by an agency that seemed to be engaged in shady practices.*

I heard about some people going to London and it was like, 'Okay, let's try' but in this time because Polish people, we couldn't work legal here.

Then there was a lot of Polish people telling, 'we will find a job, you have to pay us we'll find you a job, we'll send you the invitation' and all this. But we have to pay, and for Polish people it was a lot of money, £300. And imagine, even now [2005], average is like £200 a month what you're earning and then you have to pay £300 and it's a lot. I decided he [her boyfriend] will go first, and see how it's there, and if we'll lose the money, at least one person will not risk nothing and he will check out there and if it will be okay I will come.

Then he went and this was like Polish, well it was English agency but Polish people, a lot of Polish people out there and after three months I came to England. He paid some money to the people, not to the agency, it was like a little bit of dirty business, something like this, like making money on the people who want to work and they were giving us some fake IDs and things like this. We were paying Insurance Number on somebody's name or something like this.

I had really bad at the beginning. It was really horrible in this agency when I came; it was like everybody was scared, people were scared to say something. I was earning £1.40 for an hour, but I know they were charging no more money for the hotel, the agency and the rest was going to the pocket. And they knew we can't even complain because we were not legal here, we couldn't work you know. After I think one month me and my friends we ran from this agency. I started to, because I could understand English, but I couldn't talk. Then after one month I picked some words and things like this, I was more confident at communicating. Then we ran from this agency because what they were doing. They was keeping you until your money finished, then they were finding you job for one, two days and you have to, they were saying, 'I will take this money, because you don't pay for the rent.' Then you were always minus and you was always working for free. And I said, 'No' and we ran with my friend.

It was really, you know hard times. But I was lucky because I already, I moved to English agency. Then we both some different papers on our names, already but it was like I was paying for the temporary Insurance Number and all this. I had some papers and already I was working on my name, because before I even was working not on my name. And I was working there quite long [cleaning rooms in a hotel], two years, maybe more. Two years I think, but after this I bought visa, student visa and I started to be legal. Half time legal, then I was working full-time, but I have the permission to work for the part-time.

Dominika purchased the student visa but did not register or attend courses, and so her status was still irregular until 2004 when Poland joined the EU.

Nadia, *also born in Poland, came to the UK in 2005 and so, unlike Dominika, was able to find employment legally. As she explained, she was able to move between Britain and Poland easily. 'I go back quite often. I would say every two to three months I am there.' Nadia came to England in 2005, following* *her divorce. She was 31 in 2012 when I met her in a cafe in Oxford. She grew up in Poland with one brother and her grandfather also living with the family. Although she had a BA degree in history and philology, she was working as a bus driver, her third job in the previous two years.*

I was born in a city in north-central Poland, very close to Russian border. I was living there for the first nineteen years and when I was studying in a city in central Poland but just for one year. Then I came back home. And my other migration is to the UK: that happened in 2005.

Growing up, I would say we were not very poor. There were periods when my father was earning quite a lot of money. My mother never worked. When my father was earning good money it was fine but there were some periods when he was unemployed as well. Then, obviously, we were struggling to pay for the bills, to pay for the food. We were not hungry, if I can describe it like that. We were not hungry, we have clothes but we didn't have a car. We had like a two-bedroom flat for five people. So that was that kind of conditions of living. And in the beginning of the nineties there was a massive inflation. We experienced real difficulties and that was especially in 1995. It was the period when I was applying for university and we needed money.

Nadia did casual work during her university years and then was self-employed running a small business.

I was actually the owner of a very small company and for a very short time. I used to have agency which was doing leaflets, doing websites, some advertising agency. Very small business for a very short time: just for one year. The business was okay, I could actually say that. The finances were not the reason for my migration. Personal life I would say was the main reason that I just decided to leave the country, the city, because I was married before and when I divorced I just decided to leave everything and start a new life somewhere else. So, you know, the finances in that small business were not that bad to push me, you know, to go abroad.

I came alone. But in 2004, when Poland joined the European Union, many of my friends just came to the UK and I came alone but I had some friends in England already. I just asked them if they could help me at the beginning. So they agreed and that's how I ended here. I came to the UK without having found a job. I started to look for and also my friends helped me at the beginning. My friend, she was asking around if somebody heard about some jobs. So when I came here, the job was actually waiting for me. However, I didn't even know about it. So that was a surprise on the coach station. When I came, my friend told me 'oh, by the way, good news. You already have a job'. So I was like 'wow! You know that's so easy'. My friend, who worked there [in a retail unit selling ink cartridges], she just asked the boss and the boss agreed.

Many young women from Latvia, Lithuania, and particularly from Poland, had similar experiences. Considerable numbers of Polish migrants moved to the UK in the years between EU expansion and the start of the financial crisis in September 2007 and so were able to draw on a network of friends and acquaintances to find accommodation and a job. Dominika, who had struggled as an irregular migrant, nevertheless found the journey itself was simple. As she explained: 'I got a call from a friend who said an agency had jobs. I just jumped on a bus in Warsaw on Saturday and started work [as a chambermaid in a London hotel] on Monday'. For other women from parts of Africa but also Europe outside the EU, danger and political or personal violence were often the reasons for displacement. Their journeys had more similarities to those of women who left the Baltic States in the 1940s, involving danger and considerable hardship, as well as complex journeys and temporary residence, sometimes for several years, in intermediate destinations before arriving in the UK.

Seeking asylum

Catherine, a Kikuyu born in Kenya in 1978, came to Britain in 1999, well before Nadia and Dominika and under very different circumstances.

I had three brothers and two sisters. My parents had a farm so we were helping in the farm. We went to school but during the holidays we used to help in the farm and help out in the housework, maybe fetching water, fetch firewood, and helping milking and maybe taking care of children, maybe friends who used to bring small children to look after them because we were a bit bigger. I went to a boarding school and it was a missionary school. I became 8 years is when I went to that boarding school until I went to the secondary school. I still went to a boarding school too. Then I went to college. That was a teachers' college so I got my qualification and after that I went to a school where I started teaching.

Then after three years is when I came down here [to the UK]. I felt this was this . . . there was this land clashes around. I don't know whether you know about it?[8] There was this fighting and killings of the . . . you know, if you go back to the Kenyans about 1990s and late 1980s and early 1990s and even at this time there are people who would do the killing and doing anything to harm anyone, they gang up. That was the thing that the churches tried to push away some people from the places, they just moved them from that place where the fights are coming up. They move you to a better place, just for your safety. So if you're lucky maybe they come and grab you and take you to certain churches and the churches, the missionaries maybe, refer you to go to a better place. That was the issue that I came down, just for the safety.

Because they [the insurgents] notice maybe if you're well off, maybe you have enough money, they come and demand for your parents and your parents don't do anything. Maybe they just do the killing, you know, the harming of your family. My parents got to grabbed up, they never . . . they vanished.

So if you're able to escape, you escape and go to a certain place maybe. Then better people maybe just come and grab you and take you to any country, a place where there is safety. There was a church, it was in the . . . it was a church that . . . it was not even in our area, but it helped me. It was 1998, yeah, because they were trying to fight for those who were a bit educated, to move them away and not get caught up because they were talking of the future, to look further for better future for you.

We were sent in . . . is it Derbyshire? Yeah, it was Derbyshire. I do still remember it, grips in my mind. We came on the plane. Ten of us. We stayed maybe about how many months? Six months, eight months, around there. About two months we stayed with a church but later there were people who were just volunteering to give us things and all this and the hotel they had sort of . . . they started being paid by the government and then the Social Services, they give us rooms to stay in. Then everyone will disappear one by one. Most of them went to London.

We were given a visa for six months staying in Derbyshire. After that our visas were expiring and we went to the Home Office. The thing is they sent us to the solicitor in Derby. So they were dealing in our cases. They have granted me indefinite leave to remain. It took ages because it was about 2006.

Hana was a multiple migrant, fleeing Eritrea for Sudan as a child in the mid-1970s, later imprisoned in Somalia and then moving as a refugee to Holland. She finally moved to the UK in 2005.

I'm born in Asmara, the capital city of Eritrea in 1970. My mother exactly she don't know which date, that's why when I came to Holland they said we can take 1970 and then the middle of the year which is 1 July. And there was actually war in Eritrea, between Ethiopia and Eritrea[9] and we have to flee war, me and my family.

I have four sisters and one brother. And my father been taken to prison while I was 4 years old and then he was 40 years old in prison and when we left Eritrea I was 6 I think. He was in prison because he was a politician. He was involved with the revolution and since that time we didn't see him. We fled. My mother fled first with my elder sister to Sudan and then she send us that we should leave the country.

There was a person who was guiding us because he had been given some money and we just walk for many, many days and we didn't know where we were just going, we were just leaving the country. He's from Eritrea who's like smuggling people, because it's not allowed; you have to stay where you are. There was no food or anything because it had been for a while and everything was closed I think at that time. So we have to leave and we walked until our legs, our feet can't walk anymore. We had wounds and my younger sister she couldn't walk, so there was a donkey that we just put her there. And we didn't have enough to drink or to eat. Whatever we had is just a basket that my elder sister was carrying and it have this Ethiopian kind of bread, homemade, and that is all what we were sharing. In days, I think it might have been weeks, there was other groups as well with us. Some of the children were dying, some of them were eaten by animals, but I think we were lucky, we survived.

The family had little money and decided to send an older sibling to the Middle East as a maid.

The only option we had was one of us to go to Saudi Arabia or somewhere where they can work and earn some more money so we can . . . . At least one of us have to sacrifice and leave the family because leaving the family was a big issue. So my elder sister left and she went to Saudi Arabia and she work there. They just smuggled her in a boat from Sudan, the port of Sudan and from there she went. And she also had a big story actually, being in Saudi Arabia, all the lady and all the young girl, she have a lot of stories. But in the end she managed to help us with a little bit of money. My sister in Saudi Arabia she was supporting us but by the time we were in Sudan we never heard anything about my dad. He just stayed in prison.

And I go and look for whatever job. So I was all the time working, cleaning or washing in anybody's house, whatever I find. Then the money they gave me, I give it to my mum and my mum had the money to keep us together. And she always in the evening ask us are we okay and say 'is there anyone who have touched us or somebody who molest us or anything?' She used to tell us that there are parts of our body that we have to be careful with. She say people shouldn't come more closer than this and she tried really in her way to tell us but at that time I didn't understand what she was talking about.

And then life got actually better and better and people started to come from the Eritrean force. They were pushed to go to Sudan, so there were more people coming from my country. I was able to, there was teachers who used to teach the Eritrean Revolution Front and so I started to go and ask them if they can help me. I don't know, it was some kind of target that I want to study and to know what all this planet is about.

Hana managed to start a university course. By then her mother had moved to Saudi Arabia and some of her siblings to Sweden.

Then in 1990, no 1989, I decided to leave Sudan. I have it in my head so I had to leave. I didn't have a passport, I didn't have anything. I didn't have any identity or anything so there have to be a way which is the smuggling and my sister she have to pay. She sold everything she have and I was smuggled instead of going to, coming to Europe, because at that time the Eritrean people were allowed, because they didn't have any country, they were allowed to use diplomatic Somalian passport. So that passport was Somalian. So when I was caught in Egypt with that passport it was my choice to go back to Eritrea which will be the end of me.

And I chose to go to Somalia. In Somalia they directly put me in prison because they say I am one of Ethiopian spy and at that time they really had very big issues going on. Me, I ended there first in prison, but with my big mouth I went and I talked and I talked and I talked and I said 'I'm Eritrean I have nothing to do with this and blah blah, and I have evidence that I'm Eritrean.' And they say 'where?' And I say 'I have it in Sudan, I am from that university and I have been there.' At last they took me to Eritrean office and when I spoke to them and I told them from which area of Eritrea how I left from there and they started actually accepting. And I was in every newspaper that they caught a spy woman from Ethiopia and it was in all newspapers in all Somalia and I was supposed to go to, you know they have like a court and you go there, and they decided what to do with you and you don't even know what they'll do to you.

That was going to be the end of me if I am not lucky enough to escape or to find somebody who would be responsible, who will say that I am from Eritrea. So the Eritrean office they came at last after four weeks and they say, they claim that I'm from Eritrea. And then I applied for a passport being an Eritrean and my dad being a politician I was entitled to so they took, they . . . . My gosh. But during the four weeks that I was there in that prison I was raped, and from there I went back to Sudan because I was pregnant.

I had an original passport which I have signed, from Somalia. Eritrea doesn't, it's not accepted as a government, they didn't have a passport or any, so the Somalian government was allowing Eritrean politicians to have a passport. So I was given a passport and then they said 'where do you want to go?' I was supposed to come to Europe but I thought 'how can I come? I'm that age and I'm pregnant, what am I going to do?'

So I went back to Sudan and I couldn't go back to school or anywhere. I just hung around so many places, in the end I found somebody who could help me signing all the papers, saying the baby is his. And in Somalia I had so many medications, also when I, they give medication to let the baby come out or whatever, it didn't. They gave me injections, it didn't. So when I came back to Sudan it was nearly four month. You can't see it but it is there. So when I came I said even though if I want to keep it, it won't be [ok] and also I don't want to keep a baby who will remind me of all of that.

So I went to a doctor and he says 'You can't do that; the person have to come and sign.' I said I was on medication, I took this and this. Even if

I want it to live it wouldn't be a normal child so they have to do the operation. And I think literally they took it without, I wasn't really, what do you call it, I was feeling everything when they are chucking the things out of my ... it is the most horrible experience. But then from there I took my passport and I put a normal visa and I came to Holland.

In Holland of course when I came it was a bit of a shock. After all that, you expect to come to a country which people will understand your situation or will support you but when I came to Holland it was so shocking. I was put in a camp very far away from any other people. We were just us, all different kind of people and most of them were from white European country or other. There was only one black woman from Somalia where I stayed; it is in north of Holland.

I am supposed to go to Sweden but I had a KLM ticket and usually you have transit in Amsterdam so when I went off transit and they asked me what am I doing, I said 'I'm going to Sweden to my family to ask asylum' and they said 'the rule of asylum is whenever peaceful country you go first that's the country you apply for asylum'. So I was pushed, I had no other choices, only to ask asylum in Holland. And that's what I did.

So it was the most depressive time of my life. Being locked in one place and then what you see is only from the window and you don't have enough clothes or enough warm jackets to go outside because it was, when I came it was October, yeah 16 October that I came; in 1990 I was in Holland. I wasn't able to leave in a month. It took me I think nine months until I came to live in Amsterdam in a room with other Ethiopians and other nationalities.

Hana lived in the Netherlands for 14 years, during which time she lived with a partner who was also Muslim, with whom she started a family. She worked in an accountancy firm until 2005.

I started to put a scarf on and I was more deepened in my religion so at that time I was kicked off my job. And things got really, really tough. First of all they found somebody who is Dutch [to replace her], and also kind of, they didn't accept that I put on a scarf and I'm different, so that was my experience in Holland. So I decided when I was really nearly 37 weeks pregnant, I decided to leave the country and to leave it forever. And so it was the decision that I have to make, to go to Sudan, and I had been away for 14, 15 years and it was very difficult then. Eritrea, I left it when I was a child, I have nothing there, and then to go to Sweden? I am now above 30 and I don't think I am capable of learning another language. So the idea came that I come to England.

In Holland you get stuck. There is a roof on your head, if you just move your head up more than you should do, you just get pushed and you get pushed in a black hole that you never come out of. And after the incident of 11 September[10] it was much worse. All even my neighbours they tried to, they started to treat my children differently and some of my friends in the road they were pulled and pushed and they took off their scarves and pulled their hair on the street and that is while the police is watching. And there are, where my child used to go was the Islamic school, that school had been bombed.

Imagine, you think you came to a safe country to live safely and to have happiness at last in your life and it being discriminated and you know I had to leave Holland . . . my 14 years, I have no history in Eritrea it doesn't exist anymore, so I came and build again in Sudan. I left Sudan. I don't have even, I don't own anything which is as old as my age because I have to leave everything behind and then begin again. And now I've started my life again here in England since 2005 March.

Europe too was not untouched by civil war and political displacement, with the risk for women, as there has been for centuries, of rape. As the former Yugoslavia disintegrated, the resultant wars badly affected Kosovo from the mid-1990s until the end of that decade.

Marianna was born in Pristina in Kosovo in 1973, one of five children whose parents who had moved from Albania years earlier. She came to the UK as a refugee in 1999.

We were not very rich, rich, but we were okay, we were managing. My father was a builder and we had this little shop, like grocery shop and we [the siblings and their mother] used to work there in turns like, who had time going and work there, but it was a really big support for us. After the situation with Serbs and things we went to Albania and we stayed there. I was about 20 then, I think; it was really a scary situation. So many troubles; they're starting to – so many girls got raped and oh things, things, things, people fighting and everyone had guns and it was a pretty scary situation. So the worse thing it was in '98, yeah that's midyear; some time in spring like that it started to be really scary. We left at the end of November I think, '98 we left Kosovo and we went to Albania.

We went there and I remember we stayed in this family. Oh, they were a really nice family and oh gosh, the way from Kosovo to Albania it was so scary, so scary, because so many Serb soldiers. They can come; they used to stay in that road which we used to walk from Kosovo to Albania, and so many things, scary things happened. We could see that so many girls with cut their breasts. We had this big truck and he [father] used to hide me under there and there was a table, but it was so small and he hided me under the table and he just threw the blanket over and I was under there all the time.

In Albania they used to do these camps, because so many Kosovo people were moving and there was no space, no place where to stay, so they were, the army was giving this, how do you call like, when you go camping you get this? Yeah, tents, yeah. And, they were giving them out and making ready for a family but we were such a big family and really needed so much space. So my father just went to ask in the villages, 'someone can rent us a room?' And there was this old couple then, no kids, they had no kids, so they said, 'Yeah just come, you can have two rooms' and we went there, and they were such a lovely couple, really old, but really nice.

In Albania they had these things that they can do, oh gosh how do I say that? Just to go to Italy or come here or France or Belgium, they just pay money and they can take you over. So, me and my brother really wanted to, I never, I cannot imagine myself going back to Pristina, never again, never, only because of bad memories you have there. So we would talk and talk to my father. He didn't want to let us go. I don't know how we managed to change his mind but finally we came here.

It was 7,000 Euros, I think, per person, yeah. And, my father went for a coffee with that person and I don't know what he talked to him about it at all, but anyway he left a date and we had to go to Tirana here [in Albania] and meet him there and there was ... there were about 14 people in there, oh my god, pretty scary, but I was glad my brother was with me.

Anyway we came by plane. We had our passports and everything from him. So anyway we have some friends which they came here [to London] before so they were telling, 'Oh it's great, please do come try.' So they gave us a lift from Heathrow to here and we used, we stayed at their house I think four days and after was with social services, who used to deal with these people like us. It was like a hotel with seven rooms. We stayed there I think for three more months, four, something. And there was, with us it was this Kosovo boy too and I kind of liked him and he liked me and after – well we came here and his brother was in the same town where we came, we came here in Oxford and he came here too, and we saw him in town, in streets and oh we, stopped for a coffee and everything and anyway we got closer and close and closer. Now he's my husband.

Marianna's journey ended well, but for other women escaping state violence or violence in the home, leaving was not easy. **Fitore,** *who also grew up in Kosova, tried to escape domestic abuse.*

My marriage was an arranged marriage. They got me engaged and I saw him [future husband] two times. I was just listening to the conversation when he was sitting in the room and I said 'I don't want him.' They sent me to Imam to make me go with marriage. Then I got married; it was an arranged marriage and I was being violated from the beginning. Lots more, not just violent, physically, mentally. So I've been raped by my husband. I was being beaten up. And I have three children from that marriage. I was 18 and a half when I had my daughter. And three years after I had another daughter and after that I had a son, so it was seven years gap. But I had loads of abortions after my daughter because every time he was getting drunk, just hit me. I had to, so there was no way to, and it was just like with metal needles to break the pregnancy. Every time I have to go to a house because there wasn't a nurse. They just have to put something like mat down and break the pregnancy.

Then my daughter she was about ten, and war came and we have to climb the mountains and we stayed there for two or three months. When we came back everything was gone. So then we moved across to Albania and so we stayed there for some time. It was beginning of '99. Then after that, what I did, I took my children on a plastic boat from south of Albania to Italy. Just a private boat, we have to pay the money. But I didn't have money so I asked someone to pay the money after when I had the money. So I stayed for one week in the south [of Albania] with my three children. Then at night we came across, I think it was 7 September '99 we crossed the boat. It was two hours journey and it was 23 people in the boat and everyone was squeezing them [the children] and finally we got on the side and when we got there, it was rocks, very slippery rocks and very deep water in there, and I fell in the water with Mario [her son]. But I was lucky; I came out, and somebody took Mario. And I came out but I was bruised and everything. I just felt dizzy, but I remember I've got my children with me, I just shake myself. I said 'okay that's it, I have to keep going'.

And it was two, three hours on roads and very, very long journey walking and I had my three children but we have flip-flops and my youngest daughter the flip-flops were falling off and there were two guys, basically they help, and the little [younger] one, he was about 16 this guy, he was with us, he kept Mario on his shoulders all the way. That nice boy he was helping and everything.

Fitore and her elder daughter, who was 14 by then, found work, cleaning for an Italian woman but her husband found her and moved back in. He began to drink and treated her and the girls badly and so she decided once again to leave him; eventually, after travelling though France by train, she managed to find someone prepared to smuggle her and her children across the Channel.

And then we got this guy who came and took us to the lorry. So he came, he took us to the lorry from there, about ten o'clock, eleven o'clock, one o'clock. And he got us in a lorry one o'clock in the morning. It was freezing, 23 December, and the lorry was a lorry with wine. Five o'clock the driver came out and he went around. He was coughing, we can hear everything. He checked, everything was just fine. He didn't open the door because he couldn't think because the people who opened the door and close it, they were just like experts. And he went around and off he [the driver] went at five o'clock and we can hear like stairs, chut, chut, chut, that was the train express. The lorry went into the train so basically when we came out to England. The lorry came to Didcot. When we were going down, because we didn't know where we were, on the hills, those guys, it was four guys, like the older guys, jump from the lorry, because they could jump. I could not jump with my children. And then lorry stopped, I think he stopped for a break. Suddenly we just jump with the suitcases down. He just came out and he was just looking. He was shocked when he saw us jumping. So off we went, stopped by the train station, and there was this guy who knew we were refugees, he knew English, and he took us to the social services. It was 24 December, just before Christmas.

The family were housed in a hostel but only a week later, Fitore's husband found them again.

And he was doing the same thing [being violent] for one year. Then after one year he was doing the same thing, because he was beating my children up. So I phoned the police, took him to court, they said do you want him back the next day I said no, that's it and he's gone. So two years after that they took him immigration, they kept him one year in detention. They sent him back, now he's gone to Spain.

These stories reveal the complexities and difficulties involved in leaving home. They illustrate the multiple reasons for leaving and the different journeys to the UK. For some young women, like Nadia, it was a deliberate decision to leave to improve her income and her knowledge of English and involved a simple trip on a bus from Poland. After May 2004, travel between EU member states was unrestricted and once in the UK, young Polish women were able to work legally. However, as Dominika found, entering the UK without a visa led to difficulties and exploitation by agencies. For young women who left Poland and other parts of continental Europe, almost sixty years previously, the journey was different, involving danger, having to hide, many different forms of transport including ships, railway trucks, walking and begging lifts in carts. However, like the more recent economic migrants from this part of the continent since 2004, for young women recruited as domestics, cleaners and mill hands by the British government after the war, entry was permitted as they were regarded as valuable workers for the post-war reconstruction effort. Nurses from the Caribbean, including Brie and Georgina, were also part of this effort. Their recruitment marked the start of the reliance by the National Health Service on migrant labour, a trend that has continued to the present.

For other women, however, the decision to move was not a voluntary one: political change, violence and events such as famine or floods precipitated their departure and their eventual arrival in the UK was not always straightforward. Unlike the EVWs and the nurses from the Caribbean, women who left East Africa came to the UK as part of a family group. More recently, many women have come alone, often as refugees. They have not only endured difficult journeys but then found that they had to claim asylum once they arrived in Western Europe and initially were denied the right to work.

The stories here, some from decades ago, others more recent, convey the trauma of moving. Even for women who made a positive choice, the journey to a foreign country was not easy. They were often lonely, on the journey and during their first weeks and months in the UK and many were homesick. For women who had little choice but to leave – subjects of family decisions in which they had little say like Bina, or victims of war, unrest and oppression, like Hana, Marianna and Fitore – the journey was difficult, and for the three women refugees, often complex, with temporary, or longer, stays in several different countries before arriving in the UK. They also had to use the services of migration agents or intermediaries, who often demanded money, and sometimes using threats to enforce payment. Their stories also reveal the consequences for women of sexual harassment and violence, including rape, both during the journey, in prison and in workspaces such as the private homes where Hana and her sisters sought work as maids. As several of the narratives show, migrant women often had to find employment or were forced to work, like Latvians in Nazi Germany, during their journey to the UK. Once they arrived, however, waged work became and remained a central part of their lives and is the subject of the rest of the book.

As the following chapters show, migrant women's contributions to the UK economy, often in hard and under-rewarded parts of the labour market, have been immense as they labour in types of jobs that British-born women often reject. Over the years since 1945, despite the significant changes in the structure of the labour market outlined earlier, the working lives of many migrants are marked by continuity. Whether employed as mill hands or domestics, sewing seat covers for Ford or shirts for Marks and Spencer, picking fruit or looking after other women's children, typically women migrants find themselves working in poorly paid, feminized jobs, and disadvantaged by the intersection of all or several social characteristics or differences and so often regarded as inferior as employees to native born women. Their old and new class position, their gender, nationality and skin colour mark them as Other in a predominantly old white country. And as Chapter 6 shows, even the most well-educated and highly skilled women migrants – doctors, teachers and lawyers – found that they were differentiated from other employees and often confined to the lower ranks of their respective professions.

3

Making Things:

Textiles, Toys, Shirts, Seat Covers and Engines

This chapter is about making things, telling the stories of women who were directed into or found jobs for themselves in manufacturing industries. Women have always worked in all sorts of jobs in the service sector – cleaning, caring, and catering, in the retail sector and in sex work – over the second half of the twentieth century, and before. But many women have also been employed in various parts of the manufacturing sector, although in declining numbers since the mid-1950s. Manufacturing jobs declined rapidly over the next half century, from employing almost 40 per cent of all workers to less than one in ten by 2015. Even in 1951, women were more likely to work in the service sector than in manufacturing but one in five women workers was making things.

As well as going out to work in jobs in textile mills, on assembly lines, making and assembling goods ranging from car components to toys and white goods, packing and boxing a wide range of food and drink, women also worked for wages in their own homes. Some of the Latvian women, for example, who on arrival in Britain in the late 1940s had been allocated work in the mills of Lancashire and Yorkshire, in succeeding years worked from home, combining waged labour and child rearing as they started families. Some of the later migrants from East Africa bought or rented an industrial sewing machine, and also started to work at home. Sewing, of course, is regarded as a quintessential women's task, considered a 'natural' feminine talent rather than an acquired skill. Even when it is undertaken in the workplace, it is 'women's work' and poorly paid. As the narratives here reveal, this led to dissatisfaction and to strike action on the part of women workers at the Ford plant in Dagenham. In 2010 the famous strike there in 1968 was immortalized by the popular film *Made in Dagenham*.

In the 1960s and 1970s, the female workforce at the Ford plant was almost entirely white. As Parvani explained, when she started at Dagenham in the early 1970s, 'there were 350 English ladies and only two/three Indian ladies worked there'. The 1968 strike, as the film makes clear, was the impetus for the 1970 Equal Pay Act introduced by Barbara Castle, then the Secretary of State for Employment in the Labour government headed by Harold Wilson. However, the purchase of the Act was limited and, as Parvani's narrative in this chapter documents, significant pay differentials between men and women remained and were the impetus for a further strike in 1984, when the machinists were finally re-graded as skilled workers. The vast majority of jobs remained sex-segregated, however, and Parvani was one of the very few women employed doing 'men's work' – in her case assembling engines.

As the decades passed, manufacturing employment declined. Jobs in the mills of Lancashire and Yorkshire shrank, as workers were recruited from a different group of migrants. Men from the Indian subcontinent, as Brigita mentions, moved into the mill in the 1970s. The British car industry also lost huge numbers of workers. Vehicle assembly at the Dagenham plant, where the women from East Africa found work in the 1970s, ended in 2002. The stamping plant, all that was left in 2002, finally closed in 2013, leaving only about 1,000 people making specialist engines. Plans for new investment and new jobs were announced, however, at the start of 2015, with the prospect of doubling the then current number of employees, but at its peak, in 1953, more than 40,000 workers, mostly men, had been employed at the plant. Even as jobs in large factories declined, though, women still found work making things. Bashira, for example, made toys at home, using an industrial machine provided by the manufacturer. Amrita explains below that she made clothes for old people, working in a community centre with a crèche attached, in a 1980s version of 'putting out', a system of homework that had been common in the textile industry two centuries earlier. Other women went 'out to work' in a range of similar jobs, often on a temporary or casual basis.

Amrita, who had moved to London from East Africa, started work in 1982 and had a number of jobs that involved sewing and knitting.

My first job was assembling car seat belt parts. It was in a factory in Hayes. It was okay. But it was a temporary job, and after three months they told me that they did not need me there. Then I worked for six months in a knitting factory – the work was piecework. The first four weeks were good, you learn during that period. So you get a fixed amount of money, however much work you do. From then on you used to get paid according to the work you did. I learnt that work and spent the next five to six months there quite happily. I made friends at work. Even if you have a good family, you feel like going out and talking to someone. We used to finish work at 4.30 pm and my husband came to pick me up. I often left five minutes early – it was piecework, so there was no pressure to stay on til the end of the day. I found it easy going.

But I gave up this work soon [as she was pregnant]. When my daughter was four, I used to go to sign at the job centre. It was then that I saw this job advertised for a community organization – you had to make clothes for old people. It was 1985. I told them I was interested. The place was in Southall, and the council used to pay you for making clothes for old people. They were interested in giving the job to people who had small children, as there was a crèche there and they wanted you to use it while you worked. So I went there and told them that I knew how to sew. So they interviewed me and gave me the job. I worked there for a year. My older daughter used to go to nursery full-time by then, and I put my younger daughter in the work crèche. I worked 15 hours a week, maybe 21 hours. I went three days a week.

As the twentieth century came to an end, many of the sorts of jobs described in this chapter had relocated to other parts of the world, where women's labour was cheaper. Some had been moved to the countries that migrants to Britain had left behind decades earlier. The textile industry, for example, employs hundreds of thousands of women in Bangladesh, as does the electronics industry in China and the car industry in Eastern Europe. In the late 1940s, however, many of the women displaced by the war and recruited as European Volunteer Workers were allocated employment in the textile industry, a sector already at the beginning of its long post-war decline in the UK.

Spinning and weaving in the 1940s

Jelena was born in a village in Latvia in 1931. As an EVW, arriving in England in 1948, she was sent to work in a cotton mill. She went to school until she was 13 and then left Latvia in 1944 with her parents and her brother. As she said, 'At that time in my life I looked on it as an adventure but now I realized what it must have been like for my mother and father to pack up everything'. In 1948, after three years living in a displaced persons' camp, Jelena came to the UK on her own, after her father, mother and brother had already left Germany.

They started taking people to England. It was 1947 and my brother was 19. They took agricultural workers and nurses. It was called the white swan for nurses and my brother went to Warwickshire to a camp. They would only take single people at first . . . . I came to England in 1948 to a job, mill working; up in North, near Preston, first to a camp. We were all girls; that consignment was all girls. We didn't know by then what work we would be sent to. I had a friend who lived near Stockport, in Marple [in Cheshire]. She came before us to England with her mother.

They were just a mother and daughter and they worked in the Goyt Mill in Marple. She wrote to me and said 'why don't you come up to Marple?' I can't remember what the arrangement was – whether you could just go if you had a job or they allocated you. Anyway I wrote to her and said I would like to go there and so. I was about two or three weeks in that camp near Preston and then I went to Marple.

There were about six or seven of us who went on the train together to Manchester and then we went to different places. I went to work in the cotton mill. It was a spinning mill. We worked in the card room; it was the first where the cotton started coming through and they are quite thick there, these ropes of cotton. I had never been in a mill before. It was quite horrendous at first you know. Noisy, dusty but people were good, you know.

There were about 20 or 25 women in there. There were all these spindles going round and you had to go round putting new ones on and join them together again and when the bobbins get full you had to take them off and put them on again. It wasn't hard, not very, very hard but it was dusty and you not being used to it. I didn't like it, to tell you the truth. I wasn't happy at the work. We got £2 17s 6d a week, that's 57s and six pence. It was good having my own money though. That was 1948.

I stayed in the carding room til 1949. It wasn't very long, maybe a year, and then I went to a weaving mill at Compstall.[1] But I can't remember how I got the job there. I worked in a room where you have shirts or pyjamas and you put the patterns in. The stripes and all the coloured threads had to be put in a certain order. That was much better.

In 1951 Jelena married a Latvian man who was also an EVW and had been allocated agricultural work. Jelena moved to the farm where he was employed and helped with the poultry.

He had a job in Buckinghamshire in a farm and so we moved down there. We lived there for about three years. I was feeding turkeys, well 3,000 hens, and turkeys at only at Christmas. We had a farm cottage. It was okay, nice there. When my son was born, I was still working on the farm, you know. He was there, he was put in a pram and I could take him with me. I didn't have to keep to certain hours as long as the hens were fed in the evening and morning.

Then we moved and I went back to Compstall mill. My mother worked there too but there was shift work there and whoever wasn't working looked after him [her son] and either she or I came to work and brought him with them for the changeover and the next person took him home til he started school.

Brigita was also only a teenager when she came to England in 1947. Allocated to a woollen mill near Bradford, she worked there and in a series of other mills in the locality until 1982. From the 1970s, as an overseer she

*trained male migrants from Pakistan to operate the looms, just as she had
been taught as a novice thirty years earlier.*

1945, the war finished in 1945 and we landed in Germany. In a camp. We
all escaped – my brother, mother and grandmother. I was 15 when the
war ended. In 1947 the English people started people to work for one
year. My mother, brother and grandmother were in Germany but I had to
go on my own. But actually I had a guardian, my uncle who looked after
me. When I came here I was 17. We lived together in Bradford. We came
together.

I came on 20 July and I only worked for about a week and then they
had the holiday.[2] I worked in a mill, I was a weaver; I learnt a weaver. I
were deaf for a fortnight, all that noise and I couldn't speak English, not
a word that was useful in a mill. I knew a table, a knife and fork, good
morning but I couldn't speak, all that noise. I was so lonely. I sat and cried
and I didn't know what I was going to do.

I used a shuttle to weave cloth. In the mill there was quite a few of us
[EVWs] and we stayed in like a boarding house and a lady was looking
after us. There were five in one room. Not allowed fellas. We had breakfast
in the boarding house and we had dinner in the mill – one shilling. And
fifteen shillings we had to pay for boarding house and was it twenty,
twenty, £2 and ten shillings was our living. And of course was all on
ration books which had to give to that woman.

At work we was in a huge room, that was why it was so noisy, about
50 looms, with one person for six looms. You had to run from one end to
the other changing shuttles. And when the yarn was broken, you had to
stop the loom and run in the back and tie the yarn and push it through
the eyes of the needle and get it on again. Mostly girls doing it. There
were two of us Latvians and there was Ukrainians and Polish, and English
of course. The woman who taught me weaving was lovely; she looked
after me.

I worked in that mill for two years and then I went to Lister's mill and
there we didn't have a house. We stayed in, it was not a hotel, it was not
a boarding house, it was like a barracks, owned by Lister's and they had
a bus to take us to the mill and back home. It was more like a camp.
Plenty lived there, perhaps 60 of us, men and women. The men were at
the other end and we were at one end. All foreign – Polish, Estonian,
Latvians and Ukrainians, all these four together. The first mill was shutting
down and that's why we had to move to Lister's. Same work, weaving
and by then I were all right. It was piece work, you had to rush. You had
to work to have a little bit more money. If you couldn't work, you lost it.
I stayed there nearly two years.

My uncle had bought a house by then in Bradford, so I moved in with
them and travelled to Lister's. Mostly he worked in a farm and then he came
to work in the mill as a drawer and his wife worked as a mender, mending

the pieces, both in Lister's. But in Lister's I been working for thirty years. I stayed in there. No other jobs at all, just weaving. But I got promoted. I were teaching people who wants to weave and weaving all patterns, showing all the patterns. Scottish patterns. I was like a teacher. It was difficult again for them to me, especially when they start the dark people coming in and they couldn't speak English. I had to teach them. It was men mostly. Day time work. There were no shifts then. I worked from 9.00 am to 5.00 pm at night. Before then it had just been white women. I worked there from 1950 until about 1980. Then I went to Hill Bros. for another two years.

Diana's job, after a period doing domestic work and cooking in a hospital, was in a factory in Leicestershire making shoes.

I found work in Blaby in a shoe factory, making children's shoes. It was piece work. But you know, I have been through so many things, you learn and you cope. It's a special name, it's called skiving.[3] It's a special tool and you have to work very hard. The leather tops are cut out and you have to cut to make it thinner so if you put a sole it is not so thick, it turns round. Different things, but I learned that. I worked full-time there.

Elvira, like Brigita, was allocated to work in a mill, also in the woollen industry in Yorkshire.

I was offered work, weaving in Bradford. I had seen weaving with frames on the farm but that was different. It was a laugh at first but not easy. They [other workers] were laughing at us. They put two girls together. We put cotton wool in the ears because all machinery working, not like weaving by hand, the noise. But the people were marvellous.

More or less all the people who worked at the factory lived in houses belonging to the factory but it was lovely. That was my first place of work. We were the first people [EVWs] there, not just the two of us but others. Then later on some Polish girls came and they were dirty and awful. We felt quite ashamed. I don't know why but in the toilets they wouldn't sit, if I may say so. Anyway, there were nice people. We lived with a couple who didn't have any children. They were so helpful. She was Irish, Mrs O'Donnell. I can still picture her and she had a piano and I could play there. The man was just demobbed from the army and they had some money and that'd bought the piano.

In the mill there were just the two of us, there in Oxenholme. But there were more with the firm in Bradford. At first we had lived there in Bradford and went on the bus there. It seemed unreal to me but we thought 'it's not for ever, it is just for now'. I think we had agreed to work for a year in a hospital or factory – we could chose – or domestic help in posh houses.

It was women in the mill, except there were some foreman, I think, and men who set what we had to weave, all the yarn. It was fun. First of all because the spools. They shoot through a wooden handle with a bit of leather, through the cloth and when the spool gets nearly empty you have to catch it. The number of times it landed in the middle. First of all we got odd pieces of cloth to weave, to get the rhythm. To catch it you had to stop the machine, the whole thing and it comes out at each end on a little sort of platform or box and you had to catch it there and rethread it. You stopped it by hand with a lever. I don't think they did shifts but we started at 7.00 am and worked til 6.00 pm, I think.

Later Elvira worked in a hosiery factory near Leicester.

Marta, *who had previously worked as a domestic servant, started at Courtaulds in the summer of 1950.*

At the labour exchange they finally agreed[4] that I could go to Courtaulds[5] and there I did shift work. I did two shifts 6.00 am til 2.00 pm, one week and 2.00 pm til 10.00 pm another week and you have a half day free, so you have got your own life, you see. The first job I don't even know how to describe it. It was a rayon machine and there was a great big rack with spools of silk on it and you had to watch when the spools ran out you know, put another spool on it and join up the threads and make sure that everything goes through the machine and the silk sort of winds round, a bit sort of like a huge bobbin. And then that goes to the knitting department where they used to knit. And then, after the first job, I got a second job in another department when the material is already knitted and it's checked for faults and then it goes to the dyeing department where it is dyed various colours. I think there all these sorts of materials were rolled and weighed and marked because the dyes are used according to the weight of the material. So that was quite interesting in its own way, you know, but the shift work, that was the main thing: that was really good. It was no problem to pick it up. It was very simple basic work, unskilled, you know. I think I started off at £4 a week but no board and lodging and then later on I think it got to six pounds. It was quite good.

The work was mainly with other women, there were one or two men but mostly women. My husband-to-be was in the spinning department which was all men and that was three-shift work with nights as well. That didn't suit him, the night work didn't suit him.

'That solder stinks': on the line in the late 1940s

Although most of the EVW women who were allocated manufacturing jobs were sent to the mills, and many of them remained there for years beyond *their required period, a few women found other types of manufacturing employment. **Lina** worked on the assembly line at Plessey in East London, after initially working in the canteen at a reception camp.*

I'd moved here to an engineering factory – that was Plessey. I found that job myself, it was advert in the paper. They came and they engaged me and I survived. It was an assembly line all ministry work, wires and coiling. When I arrived I wasn't married, when I start. I start in first of September and one month I was there. And every night when I went home I said 'I am not going there tomorrow. That solder stinks. I can't bear it' and Pop[6] he said, he said 'go, you will survive'. And then I came home one Saturday and I said 'so many girls got the sack' but they said, 'girl, you will survive cos you are different'. And I used to do something and I was ever so precise.

After so many months they let you do other soldering. They come round and see how you do your work and how you bending the condensers and so on and I call them chocolate bits. And I said I can't do so many an hour, and Pop said 'you can do it'. He always supported me. And I survived. I got married and asked if I can have a week off but I didn't tell no girls, cos I didn't want to know anybody and when I came back it was to a great heap of things. And I said 'what's this?' 'It's all for you', they said. And so I didn't get the sack and I was surviving. So after one month or so the foreman calls me in the office and he said 'I want you to take a section over' and I said 'me, I don't even know the work properly?' and he said, 'I have faith in you, you will do it'. I think it was because I got through the work. And I had 45 girls and they were all English and they were very nice and I was nice to them and after all these years I still have half a dozen or so I know. I used to help them. I didn't have to but in my free minute I used to electrify something or there's something I could help to put in the cans and so forth. There's hundreds and hundreds and I used to do it. There was one girl who was deaf and dumb and she got behind and so. That was Plessey. I worked there '53 to '61.

Manufacturing work at home

Some of the women EVWs who started in the textile mills of Yorkshire did homework for a few years when their children were young. This was a solution also adopted by Bashira, although she preferred to work in her own home because she was unconfident in spoken English.

***Bashira** was born in Pakistan in 1961, one of nine siblings, the eldest of whom was born in India before partition, after which the family moved to Pakistan. She moved to the UK in 1979, when she married at the age of 18.*

I came straight away here. Like when I married. My husband came here before me, like six month before me and his parents before him, one and a half years. They fixed a date when I came here, they fixed a date and then we arranged – invited people, all of their friends, their families and they make a big wedding here. At that time was not any at all people or too many people Asian here [in Oxford] who came new.

When I first came here I was very like say nice, feeling nice, feel happy because you can say it's like heaven, because there's everything different than village and family. But also you miss your part of family, the others, very, very. I was upset sometimes because I missed my family and then also my new family was nice with me, and I was so happy. My husband, my law, all was good with me and I was happy. Only was problem, language, yes, which one I found very hard, the language problem. Because English, I know English. I can read properly but I can't speak. I was too much shy and so only slowly when my children was growing up, well it hard at times. Slowly, slowly, like when I goes outside, I build up with my confidence.

Bashira had seven children between 1981 and 1994, five boys and two girls, and while they were growing up she worked in her own home, making toys. First she describes her current job making dolls but then she explains how she started making toys in the 1980s, after visiting older Indian women whom she refers to as aunties.

They arranged the most kind of work from home, yes they arranged like this, because they benefit for the women. They can work at home with the children. And they arranged a person who are making dolls. One factory they arrange from there to teach dolls, to have a women, then they can work for you, either when they, when they're ready, other than they can work for you in the factory or other than they can do at home.

Then I was joined the class and she show me dolls and she said, 'this is the dolls we're going to make and I'm going to teach everything' and she give me two dolls and I, as part of the cutting material, that make the body first, then dress, doll's dresses and then hair, everything ready like this. I said 'Okay'. I made dolls for her straightaway and she said, 'Oh my God, you were perfect.' I said, 'I see', because I forgot to tell her things, 'I worked at home before and I have two children, boys, I was at work already at home where people was giving at me. . . . Everything, like teddy bear, frogs, horse, elephant, everything.'

It was one was that I continued three years, done this job; this was about 1982. It was about . . . it depends how many hours I spent, I was, I was easier to how many hours, five, six, hours. Because we are a joined family[7] and I was free all day, no problem at that time, so how much I can sit and that's it. And I do a lot because it was fast, I was fast and I was three years do this job.

When I first started this teddy bear making and I was finding it hard because I feel like, at first I feel that I'm going to learn from my aunties and my husband's auntie was doing this and then I was visiting her and said, she was always busy with sewing and sewing and she said, 'Ah, I made this much money, this much money this week' and I was thinking, I said, 'Oh, why not? I start this one at home with the children.' I mean, the children, this whole family together and I feel to start, and I ask her, 'I'd like to learn from you' she said, 'Okay, come to over my house' and I go every day her house, because I was not concentrate fully I think and I don't know how to make. One day I goes there, second day I goes there, third day I goes there, when I got four days goes there, continue new every day and the fifth we can start, we can. 'Oh, look at me. I did a bear in her house' and she's doing straight to me and faster and faster and I even not finish one bear and her there was 12. Twelve bears, and one bear, one bear.

I said, 'I didn't finish even one bear' and she finished everything, one, bear, two bear. She said, 'Look at me, and what I do.' I said to her, I said, 'Oh, I know how to make them. I know how to make, but tell them they send a machine in my house and send the work in my house and I will.' And she said, 'Oh right, okay.' She asked them. 'One of the lady wanted to do this job' and they said, 'Oh right' and they give it to me, a big industrial machine, which I never used before that. I would bring in this big machine and work, one, two, three bears or big, big bags, they sent. They were delivered at my door and they picked from the house and delivered here, drop work in the house and collect.

And then I said, 'Oh, okay.' The first week I was very slow, one bear I think was the first time. I found it hard, and I feel easier then. When my home I start, I feel easier and I found easy. Then I feel like this, I do like this quickly. They paid about, well I think it was, at that time I think fully was, if I do 40 bags a week, £1.50 a bag, £1.50.

And after that I stopped when my third child born [in 1986]. Then after I stopped and then I didn't do anything at all. Then I fully like a housewife, all til my last child born and I was all the time housewife and look after them, and then the last child born [in 1994]. Then he just start school and I start. My friend was sitting in the culture centre, a woman's, there is woman's, Asian women and the food club every Monday. I go to in the group often there for lunch. And then one day they need a worker for the cooking, catering and she said, 'Oh, you can do it' I said, 'Yes I can' and she said, 'All right, you do Monday' and then I start cooking, catering for them. And after this, I carry on; carry on two year. Then I carry on, I thought I need to do some more. And then I start courses like English course, and then dress making.

It was through this dress making class that Bashira was recruited as a homeworker to make dolls.

When this time, this one to making dolls, and they asked, they offered me straightaway the job, second week. The second week they offered me job and they ask 'Oh, can you do job for us in factory?' I said, 'I can't because I've got responsibilities at home, my children, I have to collect my children, I have to drop my children at school and I have to everything doing inside the house and I'm not doing.' And then they give it to me at home, work at home, straightaway. Dollies, I spent a lot of time on dollies and they give the dollies £3.50 for each dolly, and each dolly I spent two hours. They said, 'Each dolly take one and a half hours to make everything' and I was thinking, I spend more, because with the children we had to not account time, because you have to sometimes stop, sometimes do, but you do continues, that I have to spend more than one and a half hours, more than one and a half hours. I said, 'I can't work in the factory but I can work at home.'

Every week I've written how many dollies I make and I made the money. And then they finish. They've given to a contract in China. It was a man goes there and he found more labour cheap. I then start, I start making dress. And then they give me lesson, this time, very big lesson, because when I made my dress and one and a half hours so if I spend one and a half hours and I fully made one Asian dress and you know, people made £8. When I made the dollies and I was thinking how much I spend time on the one of those to make and then I make £3.50 and this dress I can make £8. I continue I think two, three years I made a dress and I stopped.

Bashira then took a childcare course and began to work part-time in a local authority-run crèche in her neighbourhood.

Sewing seat covers: working for Ford

Harshini was born in the Punjab in 1948 but was brought up in Nairobi. The family was not affluent. With two sisters and seven brothers, money was tight and Harshini left school aged 12. She came to London with her family in 1962 when she was 14 and started work in 1966 when she was 18 and just married.

I start work when I'm 18. Between 14 and 18, I'm staying home because Mum and sister and brothers, yeah. I started as a sewing machinist in Manor Park; it's Marks and Spencer's. We're doing shirts, shirt factory, we do shirts. They teach me to use the machine. When I sit on the machine first time I'm really scared, really am scared. After two or three weeks, then I'm all right, then I'm really good, I'm doing very good job, then I make samples for them. I done 12 years over there. I work there 12 years, because he [her husband] find work for me over there. My husband is just working there and then he find for me the work there. So many people working there, so many young girls, school leavers, they work there. Some people come from India, some people come from Gujarat, some people from here.

In 1983, after various casual machining jobs, Harshini began work at the large Ford plant in Dagenham.

Somebody met me, somebody working there, they meet in a pub. We went to pub and they meet there and they said 'a job is there, I bring application for you if you want to work there'. I then applied and I get it. I write the letter for them; then they send me the application; then I fill it out and send it back; then they call me for the interview.

At interview, they test me on the machining, machine test. Then they talk 'why you applied, why you come here, why you work in Ford?' Then I say 'I need the money for my children, that's why I apply. I like to work over here.' That's the things we talked, generally talk this, yeah, then they say 'you take your test in machining'. When I went on machine, then they test me on the machine. They gave me one cushion to do it. She tell me how to do it, she showed me how to do it, then I done it and they said 'oh right, you passed'. I very easy get there, no problem, no nothing but it is different from shirts. Because we're doing only the piecework over there, in the shirt factory. I do just all the sleeves, I do only sleeves. Then over here [at Ford's] we make all the cushions round. It was a little bit heavy. Shirt is not heavy; the cushion is heavy to do it.

When machining seat covers was discontinued because of technical changes, the women who had been employed to make them were offered alternative work on the line. Many of them turned it down as too demanding, but Harshini accepted.

Now I'm engine plant. The machining stopped and I went to engine building. Now I'm in the plant. I'm on the line. I do the oil pump; I put in oil pumps now. It's not difficult work. It's easy, not heavy, no, but still on the machining you had a rest and do the job. In here you work, work on the line, you work hard.

Parvani *was born in Kenya, the daughter of a manager on a tea plantation. She was married in India aged 21 and then returned to Kenya where she was content. Her life there was disrupted by political change (as her narrative in the preceding chapter outlined) and she moved to England in 1966.*

I had a shop in Kensington market at first. I was working in the shop. Not working, it was my shop. And at that time in three years the shop was not doing very well. I need a lot of money, so I thought if I go to work anywhere else the money was not good. So one day I find out the Ford people, they give good money. So I was interested to join the Ford. So I called and I was getting good money from there. So I had to wait one year to get the job in Ford, when I get the job in the Ford. The job was a little bit hard but the people who were there were very good, you know, and everybody want to try to help us and the union was really very good with us, but it was hard work. It was not easy work, you know. You have to do so many bundles and you cannot do this, this, but you do.

The union support, they help us a lot, because they support us a lot and yes, there was a problem about the language because they are like that Ford. There were 350 English ladies and only two or three Indian ladies worked there. And when we get with Indian ladies, we start talking Indian and they say 'you are not allowed to talk Indian because we think you are talking about us'. Because they were surprised to see Indian; they don't know and when you have to fight for that and the report go to union and the union help us. Slowly, slowly the English people get used to us. When they see that we are humble, we are polite to them, everything, then they were very friendly with us and they were very good and still I can say that. Ford was not bad because the work we were doing outside, that is quite hard and very less money. They [Ford] give us the break, after ten o'clock, one o'clock, we got the breaks. So we thought Ford was best for us and we quite liked Ford. But we're very hard workers, you know, that's how you cope. It is not easy. It was not an easy job, it was a very difficult job, because already we work more harder than that before we joined the Ford, so we had a tough life.

So Ford, it was okay with us, Ford was okay with us. So I work there for nearly 15 years and I was quite happy there. Sometimes there was a problem but all the times union was spoken with. That was a good thing, you know. So the union has given us a lot; I cannot forget that union. You know when the strike happened, we want the money as the man was. We want the C grade, we want a grade equal to the man and there was a big strike in the Ford, there was really. I think two months the strike was for that and we all, all the machinists, fight for that and we stay together and after that, we win the strike and we got the money equal to the man. That was really very good.

Then we were getting a lot of money there and they give us discount if we want to get a new car. The time was not too bad, four o'clock you had to go and it was really good, I don't think anything bad for Ford, I think hard work, only hard work, otherwise money was good for people who are good.

I worked as a sewing machinist for 15 years and that was easier for us because they told us, 'you have to make the seven bundles, you make seven bundles. You can make in four hours or in seven hours, it is up to you.' But we do it so fast machinist, we finish at 1.00 pm; the work, we finish at 1.00 pm. After that time we'd go and sit outside, we'd go and do our exercises, so that was quite fun for us. And the people who were slow machinist, they have to work up to 4.00 pm. If they can't finish their bundles, they have a problem. Then Ford ladies go to them and tell them off because everybody's not very fast, you know, because we were very fast and so we finish our job at 1.00 pm and the rest was our time because we finish our job. They want seven bundles, they don't care, even if you work up to 4.00 pm, even if you finish at 10.00 pm, they don't care, you're a very fast machinist so we all said, three, four friends, we make it, we all finish the job at 1.00 pm, then we all free from there.

Only women, men was not there with us [among the machinists], only the older women were together. I think it was a little bit manic, that was more interesting, I think; all the womans, you know what they're like. But I like men to work with them, you know, men from there but from other department. When we go out little bit, we just go and talk with men. We go with men on the machines in the Ford, but people, some people don't like it but I like it, you know. But we were womans and the time went quickly. It was not bad.

As in the textile industry, from the late 1970s, migrant men began to undertake what previously had been 'women's work'.

But you know after that, after that, there were some men who were doing that, on the machine, they start doing this job, you know. We work together; it was nice. The men were, they weren't Indian but they come from Pakistan, I have not seen any English but the men were Pakistani and they worked with us on the machine.

When Parvani was moved to work among men on the press, she found it was too difficult and so she complained to the union.

One time there was one manager, he come and he took me from the machine and put me on the press. Believe me I didn't like the job of that, always pressing and standing, that was a man's job and he says 'no, I'm going to put you temporary, one week only'. Then he know I don't like that job and he was a very bad manager. He put me there and he don't want to bring me to the machine.

I was so upset and I thought that I come here as a machinist and I want to do my machine job, believe me. He just go away and every day he go again 'I'm putting you in the press' and you know what happened? Then I thought what to do, then I go to the union and the union lady was not there and there was a union man. He phoned to the headquarters, say 'the union should come and see this case'. I say 'I want to talk to union, I cannot do this job.' It was 10.00 am and two union people come to the Ford and it was tea break. They call me in the office, 'why don't you want to stay?' I told them in my language, as they was Indian, I told them 'please you put me on the machine' and at that time, at 10.00 am the union people put me on the machine and the manager didn't like it. But I win because I was a machinist over there. Because I fight for myself. Why should I go and do that job? That was a very difficult job, you know.

So the union people help me at that time. And everybody was so surprised that this Indian lady. 'What she is doing?' but I thought I have to fight for my rights. Otherwise everybody was very good, to be very honest.

When she was in her fifties, Parvani accepted an early retirement package. Her son had been diagnosed with multiple sclerosis and she wanted to spend time at home, caring for him.

The time come when they say 'after 50, anybody want to retire? They can have this much money'. So then I thought 'if they are saying that, let me have the retirement'. They pay me £17,000 cash and they give me the pension. Then I thought 'this chance, I won't let it go', because my son is ill, then this chance will come, you know. At that time the £17,000 a lot of money, so I thought 'let me stay at home with my son'. Because of my son's disturbance I leave the Ford. Otherwise still my friends are working there. They are earning a lot of money and they are happy there, but my situation was different. But I miss working for Ford.

As the British economy changed and opportunities in manufacturing work for women shrank, it became more common for migrant women to take jobs that involved packing of different sorts: films into envelopes before the rise of digital cameras, toys or chocolates into boxes, or food for airline meals. Jaba, an Indian woman from Tanzania, was employed in the 1970s by Grunwick, a photo processing firm, to sort out developed photographs. Raksha, Surjit and Saran packed meals for British Airways and other airlines. In both cases, their employment opportunities reflected both the growing affluence of the general population, with more opportunities to take holidays in the UK, and, in growing numbers, abroad. While many of these women had not been employed outside their homes previously, they nevertheless found the courage to challenge the exploitative conditions often found in workplaces that employed migrant women.

'Hard to touch meat': providing airline meals

*Packing airline meals was a job that, as **Raksha**, born in India in 1951, explains, was difficult for women who were vegetarian but which also led to friendships and fun.*

I started work in '69. The other children [in her family] went to school, and I was the eldest [she was 18 at the time] here. So I had to work. My first job was tray-set, you know, the meals on flights. That was my job. I was not used to standing all day, so I found that hard. It was okay. But what can I say? For someone who had never worked before, it will be hard. I found it hard to touch meat, as I did not eat meat. My hands used to tremble when I had to handle meat. I often used to feel sick. And when I was like that, my friends used to take over and exchange their work with mine, so I managed to get through that. It was hard, that job, but it was not that I had a bad time there either. I made friends, and it was not unlike family. We used to get together, have a laugh. I became friends with some women there.

These women who worked packing photos or food are Indian by ethnicity. Many of them, although born and married in India, had also lived for several years in East Africa. Surjit, for example, moved to the UK in 1996, although Saran was an earlier migrant, arriving in 1971. Like Parvani, these women were politically active in the UK. They joined a trade union and participated in industrial disputes in their workplaces. Their working lives challenge common stereotypes about the political passivity of South Asian women workers.

Surjit was born in 1948 in a medium sized village in the Punjab, where 'we had a lot of land, we had several servants working for us. We were very well off'. She went on to study for a BA: 'I was the first person in my village to go outside to study. Other girls used to get married early.' Surjit married in 1971 and had her first child in 1972.

After the marriage, we lived in India from 1971 to 1984. Even at home, we had servants and someone to look after my daughter. My husband's family were well off. They had a transport business in Africa. My husband had five brothers and I stayed in India to get them all married off. You see, I was the eldest daughter-in-law of the family. One by one, they came to India and got married and went back to Africa with their brides.

Surjit and her husband moved to the UK in the mid-1990s, leaving behind a business in India. Their decision was a consequence of political unrest in the Punjab at that time. Life in the UK was a shock to Surjit.

At that time I imagined that this was a wonderful place, where everything would be amazing. But when I came here, I did not like it because I had to work at home and outside. I had never worked outside the house. I came in '96 and started work almost immediately at this factory in Southall where I did packing work. It was hard, I felt pain inside me. When the supervisors said anything, the way they often do – 'do this, do that' – tears would well up in my eyes. My life changed completely. It had completely turned upside down. I had servants there [in India] and here I was working in a place like this. But once we had come here, the work had to be done, and however painful it was, I did it. I worked at that factory and then after a year, I started at the airport and worked there for about six years. I don't work now. I'm almost 60.

It wasn't easy for me. I had to work for strangers, I was that much older [than many of her co-workers] and was married, so on top of that I had responsibilities at home. It was that much harder for me. I had to start work at 50, it was hard to adjust at that age. That's an age when people start planning for their retirement. I had to start with a new way of life then. It was hard, so hard.

I started there in '98. There was a newspaper advert. At that time the women who worked there were all there because they did not know much English and could not find work anywhere else. Some of the managers were Asian, others were English. They were the same. They used to treat the women badly. There was a lot of pressure to work hard. They could manage but I found it very hard to keep up. The managers had no respect for you, they used to talk rudely, you know, the Asian managers, as well as the white managers. Asians being rude to Asians. Sometimes Asian managers are our own worst enemies. But it was much better than the packing job that I did earlier. We used to pack things for Sainsbury and Tesco's and supermarkets like that. And then the warehouse caught fire. So they closed it down, but I had already begun the application process to get another job. I didn't get any redundancy money from there.

Then I came here. From the very first day, I really liked it here. The BA [British Airways] facilities were very good. You could work in peace; there was no rushing around. You could take your breaks. We used to be happy there. You know how a wedding day goes by with all of you talking and working together? That's how it used to be. As if you had come to a family wedding. We used to have this group together. We were all from one district [in Punjab]. We met at work. The women who work at Heathrow are mostly Punjabi. We used to be together as a group. There were also some Gujarati women too.

The conditions remained the same for three years. When BA sold off, there were some changes, but that's what happens. Instead of working at a table, they introduced a belt. You can work at your own pace at a table, but with belts, you have to work at their pace. Things have to speed up. But it still wasn't bad. But they kept asking us to change things, and little by little they kept negotiating. Sometimes we would give in, sometimes we said no. We managed some things but not everything. Two women cannot do the work that used to be done by six women earlier, can they?

In 2005, after the speed up accelerated and the workload became intolerable for older women, there was a strike at the food processing plant, and Surjit was made redundant. She then decided to retire. Before the strike, after an illness, she had already been on 'light duties'.

I was off work for three months and they gave me 'light job'. Picking the leaves of coriander – that kind of job. I still had pain on my left hand side, but I returned to work. I used to work with the ladies at the table. That's why they gave me redundancy, because I had taken that time off sick. But by that stage I did not want to carry on working anyway.

Saran was born in 1955 in Punjab and came to the UK on a 'fiancée visa' in 1971 when she was only 17. Her employment history in the UK includes service sector work, as well as different types of work on the line.

All I knew of England was what my aunt had told me. She was in Punjab but had heard about how things are here from her relatives who were here. She said things were good here. You could get a job, you could do well. So when my mother-in-law came to India looking for brides for her sons, my aunt arranged it. I did feel scared when I first came here. I did not know anyone here other than this one person from my village. I came here on fiancée visa and got married here. There was no one from my family for the wedding, just one person – he is like an uncle to me – from my village. Oh, I cried and I cried. What a way to get married: all alone.

When I came here, life was not bad here. It was not like it is now. It was not hard to find work, things were very nice. I was so young then, everything was different here, and it was all like an adventure. I started work when I came here, in 1973. I had my first baby in 1972. A girl. My mother-in-law looked after her when I went to work.

I first worked at this laundry and then I moved to United Biscuits in 1974, end of '74. I stayed there for a few years. It was the first time I worked. It was very hard, but you get used to that. It was not bad, but I found that kind of work hard. The managers [at the laundry] were okay. The staff were mixed – there were people from everywhere. There was nothing bad about it, but it was hard work.

Then United Biscuits. I enjoyed that job. I was there from '74 to '80. The place closed down in '82 and moved elsewhere. They had started making people redundant over a period of time. And that's how I left. In any case, my second child was born in 1982. After the biscuit factory, I had my second child, a girl. So I did not work for some time. Then in '82 I worked briefly at the same laundry. From '82 to '85. For about four hours a day. That's all that was possible along with looking after the children. So I worked part-time for a few years, til '85. Then I had my third child – another girl.

Then in '89, I had twins – a boy and a girl. My eldest daughter was 17 then, so she helped. When they were two, I started work at the airport [where her husband also worked] at nights. It was getting hard to manage the finances with just him earning. When they went to school, I started working days.

I started as an aircraft cleaner. The other workers were mostly Asian women. So the job was okay. I worked there for two years. Then I went in catering in '93. In Japan Airlines. You spent the whole week packing fish. That's what went into the meals. It wasn't a bad job. I did enjoy myself the two years I was there. But it was too far from home. So there was this catering company which was closer. I started there in '95. Our job was to assemble drinks, papers and things like that and we used to assemble them at the bay where they were loaded on to the trucks [to be loaded on an aircraft]. It was good. I used to earn about £1,200 [in 2005] a month without overtime.

In this country, when both of you work, it becomes easy to run the household and manage the expenses. There are so many expenses here – the mortgage, bills, everything. The difference that it made to me was that I did not have to ask each time I wanted to spend on something. You know when you have to say, 'I need so much money' and you feel you have to say why you need that. And now, when you earn I mean, it's different. You have some money to travel to work, for those expenses and you can spend it on other things if you want to buy something. It feels good, and you know, like, yes, it feels better from inside.

Saran was involved in a dispute in 2005. After refusing redundancy, she was sacked and initially she found it hard to find another secure job.

I started work in November for some time. It was a seasonal job at Royal Mail, for three weeks for the Christmas period. I had worked for three weeks til 22 December at the Royal Mail. After that, they used to call me to work whenever they were short of staff. On and off. Alongside that I had started looking for work. I applied at a lot of places. I had applied at this place – it was a security job – and had completed the whole process but the job centre delayed sending my reference, so I lost that. I went and spoke to them. 'You ask me to find a job, and when I do, you don't do your bit and make me lose it.' But they said there had been some mistake. Whatever it was, after that I had this friend who worked at Alpha Catering. She told me to apply there. They told me that there was no job then, but they kept my application form and contacted me later in March. It was the same sort of company as earlier. Catering for airlines – United Airlines, American Airlines. The job is same. I am a flight packer here. I enjoy my work here. There are mostly Asians here as well. Asians, but not just Punjabi. Some of them are Gujarati as well, and from other places.

Other women who had been employed by catering companies at Heathrow were more specific about the origins of their co-workers. **Jasbir***, born in the Punjab to a family who had had to move from what became Pakistan during partition in 1947, explained the composition of the female workforce where she worked in some detail.*

The women there, most of them are Sikh, from all the regions, some Hindus and only one or two Muslim women. There were also a few white and black people, but not many. All castes. There were also a few Christians, two, three, from Pakistan. I would say, most were Jat Sikhs. Even the Hindus were from various castes. And then there are Pappe Sikhs – they came here from Afghanistan. And a few of our people from Africa as well.

Jasbir lived in a large household with her in-laws with whom she had strained relations.

I had my first daughter in '81 and the next in '82. In '83 I started working. At a bakery, for four to five hours a day. My mother-in-law looked after the children. They [her in-laws] wanted my pay-packet and I wanted to get out of the house for a while. I used to earn £45 a week, and I never saw any of their child benefit either. I used to do everything at home before I went to work – cook, cleaning, wash clothes by hand. They did not have a washing machine at home. So I had to work hard, but I was glad to go to work. It was as if I had been freed from a cage and could spend some time with the girls [her co-workers]. It felt good. I enjoyed the work. I was young; it was not that difficult for me. But most of all, I was glad to get out. The atmosphere at home was bad; anything was preferable. It felt like freedom.

Initially it was hard. I had to pack the rolls, the bread. The bread was okay, but the roll was tricky. The tray used to move like this – here now, gone the next second. I kept missing it and it would fall off. I just could not gather together and pack the rolls in time. The tray was far too fast for me. I did not have any experience. I almost gave up and left. But the other workers were all our people – Indians – though the main manager was white. But my immediate manager was Indian. He was nasty to me. He used to keep saying things, criticizing me. He gave me really hard things to do. I put up with it for two days, then on the third, I said, 'I can't take this anymore. I'm leaving.' I didn't know that there should be four weeks of training. How would I know? I had just come from India, so I didn't know how things work here. So when I had enough of listening to him, I took my overall off and told him I was quitting. I had had enough of putting up with his criticism.

So as I was heading towards the locker, this other manager – also an Indian – saw me. 'What's the matter? Tell me what the problem is.' I told him that I was leaving. That this manager was very rude to me and I would not put up with being treated like that. 'I am only here to work, if you want to get work out of me, you have to treat me with respect', I said. It was a Sunday, so the white manager was not there. So this manager said, 'Come with me. Don't walk off just like that.' He asked me to show him where I was working and I showed him. He said to my line manager, 'Are you stupid, placing her here? She has to receive four weeks of training first, only then can she do this kind of work. Let her work behind there.' 'Sorry, sorry,' said my manager. And that was that. I felt very good. After that, if I ever had a problem, I went to this manager. I had a good time at work after this. I worked there for four years, til after my next daughter was born in '85. I have worked at a lot of places, but my experiences at work have been good.

I was casual there [at the bakery]. They did not make me permanent. The system was like you work for 13 weeks, then they laid you off for a week, then you started again for 13 weeks, so that they would not have to give you sick pay and all that. They told me why it had to be like that. To be honest, I did not know much about what workers' rights are in this country. It was a small world, that bakery. There were just ten of us girls there. A couple were Tamil, a Keralan, a Filipina, two Gujarati and two or three were our Sikh women, I think so. We used to understand each other; we got by with a bit of English. Then in '85, I had my daughter and had to give up work. When I was pregnant, a permanent job came up. 'What can I do now?' said the main manager – the white one – 'if you could have come back now, I would have made you permanent.' But I could not work at that time.

I left and had my daughter. Then I was not well and I went to India. When I came back, they wanted me to come back to the bakery, but I wanted a full-time job. I told them, 'if you have something full-time, permanent, then let me know'. But they did not have anything at that time. So I thought I'd go to the job centre and look for something full-time, something permanent.

Like many women working on casual or part-time contracts, Jasbir had a period when she did several jobs at the same time.

Then this friend of mine said I should talk to them at the hospital and see if they would give me the job from 10.00 am to 2.30 pm. When I went there, the manager asked me if I could come at 9.30. I could do that if I came straight from school, so I said yes. She gave me the shift from 9.30 am to 3.00 pm so I could get back just in time to pick them [her daughters] up from school. Then I had this Gujarati neighbour – we used to talk a bit over the garden fence – she said she had this part-time job going. 'Come if you want to', she said. So I got this cleaning job at the airport in the evenings from about 5.00 pm to 10.00 pm.

So for three years, I did these three jobs – Sainsbury [shelf stacking early in the morning], hospital cleaning and at the airport with my Gujarati neighbour – from '87 to '89, for about three years. In '89, I went back to the job at the bakery, where I had worked earlier. They stuck by me, and kept calling me and when a permanent job came up, they contacted me. The money was good and it was a permanent job, and they used to give extra money for working on Sundays.

Then in 1991, the bakery closed down, so I moved back to the airport. So I applied and got the job. I started work there in '91. Meanwhile, they were reshuffling the departments at work and my place was closing down. They asked me to move elsewhere, but I told them that I did not want to go to the cleaning department where they were trying to get me to go. I had been in the kitchen and I wanted to carry on there, or do packing work. Not cleaning and washing up – that's dirty work. Not as good as what I used to do. I preferred to do tray setting. They said, 'This is what is available: take it or leave it.' I had been there only for a few months, but I really did not want to move to that department, so I refused to go. The manager said, 'Give it to us in writing that you do not want to move departments.' I said, 'I will not give you anything in writing.' I said, 'you throw me out of the job and write that in a letter to me, so I can go and show it to the social security people'. By now, I had started understanding how things worked here, you see.

The union was also involved. I was a member of the union from the time I was in the bakery. I had heard that if there is ever a problem at work, the union sorts it out for you. It is good to be a member of the union. That's what the other workers said. 'T and G'[8] – I have always been in that union. I left jobs, changed jobs, but I always stayed with them and every month the money went by direct debit straight from my account to them. So when the company said, 'We are giving you another job, why don't you take it?' I replied, 'Your contract with me was for tray-set and kitchen work. Why should I change the work I do? I cannot work in the new department.' So they eventually gave me the letter, which I took to the job centre.

So I looked for a job everywhere and went to the job centre as well. Then suddenly, one day, I fainted. I went to the doctor, who told me that I was pregnant. My son was born in '93. So I stayed at home for a year and then I decided to look for work again. At that time there was a vacancy in Alpha. I applied for that job at the airport. It was the same kind of job – catering – so I got it. I chose the late shift. My sister used to come back from work by 2.00 pm. And she helped out with looking after my son. So I worked like that for five years, from 2.00 pm to 10.00 pm every day.

Then my son started full-time school, so we thought the money was better elsewhere, so we decided to move there: twelve of us at Alpha. We all used to work the late shift. Our manager who worked there, first moved. He told us that the work was better there. He gave us the form, and all of us filled it out and went for the interview. All twelve of us – the entire shift landed up there. And our shift leader and supervisor. All of us together. We were a very good team. The pay was better at the new place. Also, they gave us tickets to go to India. You get tempted by things like that, don't you? So all of us left and went there.

Things were not easy for us in the beginning. You know you get more money for overtime. When they allotted overtime, they used to do it by signalling to their people. We never even knew what was up. We saw that we were not getting any overtime. We thought that we were new, that's why we were not getting it. 'What difference does it make?' we thought. 'We will go home. Who wants to work after 11.00 pm anyway?' Then after eight weeks we still did not get any overtime. It was 8–10 weeks and they only gave overtime to the old BA staff. But our supervisor was a clever woman and she had a lifetime's experience of working at the airport. She explained this to them: 'You pay the BA staff £9 an hour and when you double it to overtime, you have to pay them £18 an hour to get the job done. These new staff get £6 an hour and their overtime is one and a half times, so you will get them to do overtime for you for £9 an hour. What's better for you, paying £18 an hour or £9 an hour?' And so it was that we began to get overtime.

The BA staff went as their contracts ran out. But we carried on in their footsteps. We had learnt from them, and we carried on that way. But gradually, the management started changing and we started having problems and we had some differences. Take clocking in, for example. Now you had to clock in at exactly the minute you came in and they used to give us three minutes for clocking in. So if you had to start at six, they would give you three minutes and if you turned up more than three minutes late, they would cut your money. If you were a minute later than three minutes, they would dock 15 minutes wages. And so it went on, through the union, they kept coming to us saying they wanted this changed, that changed. Like sick pay; they did not want to pay sick pay. So if you had taken your sick leave one year, they wanted to bring a rule that you could only take five days off sick the next year. We were not expecting that. You can be sick any time. It is not that you will check out the calendar before becoming sick. Even going for breaks – they even used to tell you not to go to the toilets. They used to tell you to go during your breaks. We tried to, but sometimes you have a problem, you need to go extra times, and then it became a problem. It had become a big problem in the last two years; the managers noted how often you went to the toilet. Even the change-over times. You know how you mill around when a shift ends. You had 5–7 minutes to wash hands, get yourself sorted.

Amrita also explained further changes affecting the workforce.

You had a target for the day's work, and that might mean that you had a few extra minutes at the end of the day. But now, if you exceeded your target, they always found more work for you til the last minute. At BA, sometimes when there were flight changes, at that time, there were so many occasions that we were on our break when we heard an announcement about a change in flight time. We used to put our tea down, un-drunk, and hurry down to complete the work quickly. And when we did that, they would let us go early. But these things stopped in the last few years. So we also told them that if that was the case, we would complete our break and only then report for work. There were times when we had printed the labels and got ready to put them on in the trucks, where the trays were loaded. Now the situation was, why should we do more than what we were being asked to do? Why exert yourself when they don't for you?

In 2005, a dispute about whether or not a stoppage was legal began and eventually large numbers of South Asian women were made redundant or sacked. After nine months picketing outside the firm, Jasbir eventually signed the compromise agreement, although Amrita did not. Jasbir received a redundancy payment early in 2007 and she then began work again at Alpha catering.

I took the money in January, and in February I went to India. I had given an interview with Alpha catering service before I went. You know the place where I worked earlier? Well, I had given an interview there and they told me that there was no job then, but they said they would file my form. In February, I went to India to buy things for my daughter's wedding. I had just come back two or three days before, when I got this phone call saying 'there's a job going, come for an interview'. I went for an interview on Friday. They asked me why I had left the same job earlier. I said, 'To tell you the truth, they were giving me more money and you were putting me in shifts and I had a small child and could not do the shifts. That's why I had to go.' They said I'd have to do shifts now. I told them it would not be a problem now as my son was fifteen years old. 'I don't have a problem with that now', I told him. He told me then and there that I had got myself a permanent job. Then and there. I felt so good; I got so excited that I burst into tears. He asked me if I minded being in the prep department. I had worked in the tray-set and kitchen earlier. I told him that I had worked in prep occasionally, so I had some idea of the work there, and it was okay by me. The work there was mostly cutting food and things like that. It was a good job for me, very good. They gave me a lot of respect that I had come back.

By the mid-2000s, manufacturing employment had declined significantly from its peak in 1955, although women were still employed making and packing manufactured items such as mobile phones.

'The smell there, the plastic': on the line

Catherine, a Kenyan of African heritage, had qualified as a teacher in Kenya but entered the UK as a refugee in 1998. She took a job on an assembly line in 2001, thinking it would be impossible to re-qualify as a teacher.

I used to do, there was this, it was just like picking and packing because we used to do the mobile things, mobile phones, which was okay but the problem was, that was not the type of job I really wanted to do because okay, you just have to take what was there at first. I used to consider myself, 'oh my god, I won't step down because I used to have my own course and I really enjoyed it so' but after seeing it is quite [good] pay, I had to take it anyway because about the course for teaching it would take ages maybe to go to college and all this and I never knew which right channels to do to get through and anyway, you could say speaking to the children in school, how to get the job. Maybe I would have applied and got the job, but the problem is the contact with the children, the language, well for me and the kids. It would be hard for them to hear what I'm speaking about. My colour will still bring a big problem for the kids, yeah and myself, I also never thought I would jump into such a career and how I start, and again the qualification, I have to go back to school which I didn't really want.

So she accepted the factory job.

It was full-time, working at night. I went through an agency and they give me, after a few months, I got a full contract which was okay but the problem was there was this, the smell there, the plastic. The people there were all okay but there was this kind of smell. And some people are given work full-time and some are even given overtime but you can't complain because, you know, they're managers, know who to choose and you can't complain if they don't choose you. Some people they were soft on them and they were hard on some people, especially the foreigners. Actually we had to work more than the other people. We were just about four Africans so we had to work more harder than them. If you go for break, for them [locals], they can go for break anytime, they can go and smoke anytime but you, even going to the toilet it used to be like . . . if you're late it's a hassle but for them . . . but you had to accept it because it's your work.

The employees were okay because they are this kind of people, you work in somewhere like unity, there's no problem with the worker. If they find your work had piled up, they would just come down and help you and sort out. Yeah, they were a friend really. And actually when you don't have maybe a car, you don't have a lift, they will ask you where are you coming from. Maybe if it is nearly your area they just tell you I'll get you from such and such a place, yeah, which was so good.

I worked there til about 2004, so it's about three years. Then the company, it went bust, yeah, so we had to stop working there. By then I had already got my children. I got one kid 2001; 2003 I got the other one, so when the company was closing down I just stopped and relaxed.

When Catherine re-entered the workforce she became a care worker in a care home for the elderly (she talks about this job in Chapter 5), and began to think about trying to qualify as a teaching assistant, which necessitated gaining school-leaving qualifications, in her case through a part-time college course.

Some women continued to find work in the manufacturing sector, however, where wages generally were higher than in the service sector. However, for many conditions worsened and employment was often on a casual basis or as an agency employee, without security and many of the benefits, such as holiday pay and sick pay, that permanence brings. The power of trade unions, so important for many women, as the stories from Ford and elsewhere have shown, also dwindled not only because workers on casual contracts are hard to organize, but also because of changes in the political arena that restricted union actions. Even the car industry, once a source of permanent employment, was affected by new patterns of work, including shifts, casual contracts and working for agencies rather than for the end-employer. Maria, for example, is an agency employee working at the BMW Mini assembly plant in Oxford.

On the blue shift: working for BMW

Maria, born in East Timor in 1985, worked from 2008 for the BMW plant in Cowley, Oxford. After leaving a job as a hotel receptionist, she applied for a job in the car plant, keeping it secret from her husband, who also worked there, until she started work.

I tried to apply in BMW. My husband didn't know about this when I apply and then I tell to my sister-in-law, say 'can you look after my son because I'm going to apply?' And then interview I didn't tell to my husband. He didn't know that I try to apply in there because he talk to me before. He say 'It's a really hard job, blah blah blah, and it's not good for a woman, and the test is really difficult.' Then I say 'how difficult'? I'm just thinking how difficult the test, the peoples always fail something like that. Then I tried to apply and then I got interview, the first interview I pass, I didn't tell to my husband.

Then after that the second test, because they have three tests, until three tests, until I got my uniform and my card, everything, and then I didn't tell to my husband until I'm start working and I'm just hiding my uniform, everything in the wardrobe and I tell to my sister, 'don't tell to him until I'm start working'.

In the early morning when he finished working, I'm already working again and then he asked me 'Where are you going?' and I said 'I'm going to working.' 'Where are you working?' and I said 'Don't need to ask me, just drop me in the place I'm working' and then he just thinking I'm working in the Premier Inn in the roundabout at big Tesco and then 'Are you working here?', I said, 'No, just straight.'

He said 'Where are you working?' and then we pass the bridge and then roundabout and he thinks in the Tesco and I say 'No, just drive' and that's until the other gate and you straight to Lidl, then I said 'Stop here'. 'You're joking? You're working here?' I say, 'Yes, stop here.' He said 'Are you serious, you're working here?' I say, 'Yes, I'm working here.' He just sees my face, 'You're serious? Can you show your card to me?' and then when I'm show my card to him, 'When you apply here?' and he's just 'Oh, okay, after I finish work you have to talk with me' and I say 'Okay, see you later.' He says 'Okay, congrats' and then he just kiss me and hugs me and I'm just working.

Then it's about one year I'm working there. I'm on the blue shift, my husband in the red shift. For example, he's working the night shift, he's finished working he have to drop me, I'm working the morning shift and then he'll look after my son and then when he's start working but I'm not finished he have to drop my son to nursery because nobody looking. My sister-in-law she have to work and she have to look after their child as well. Twelve hours every day and then working for four days because sometimes Friday, Saturday and Sunday we don't working. We start again in the Monday but depends the shift we get because sometimes two weeks morning shift, two weeks night shift before I'm working there and then I'm struggle.

In my lines they have five womans. I mean four womans is foreigner and one woman she's a British. She's older, that's why they put, she's put, it's not really heavy job for her because she's older. She's 68 years and then she's still working there and then four womans, foreigner, with me four people and then three peoples from Eastern Europe and then just me that's from another country.

In working the Team Coordinator he is always come to hold woman's bums, especially for when he want to hold my bums and I said 'don't touch me; I'm married and I've got son and you didn't respect me. I'm come here, I'm working here, I'm not to come here to play with you.' But they treat people, the Eastern Europe people, and they say 'oh blah blah blah' and I say 'oh okay that's fine'. It's a little bit like racist, I think, because they treat people, they play with the Team Coordinator and I'm just, I don't want it.

Then he start, like, give me heavy job and he always take me to different line. Before that he's put me in just one line and then but after few months and he start to move me, another job, another job. Because we have to learn from the basic again to how to do this one, etc. Because the main job I'm doing I already know a few months because every day I'm doing this job but after that he move again and again, again, again. For me it's okay because I need money and I need job, for me it's okay. But sometimes he put me in the main job, in the engine fitment, that's why I dislocate my shoulder.

When I'm working in the engine job and then the men see me and it's like 'what are you doing in here?' Because the first woman working in

FIGURE 4 *Working at the BMW Mini plant, Cowley, Oxford, November 2013.*

Source: Credit Bloomberg.

that line, it's me. Then I say I'm working here. 'Who put you in here?' I say, the Team Coordinator. They say 'oh you're not supposed to work here because woman never come here, just only you.' I say okay, that's fine but if I'm not follow him he will kick me, something like that. I just follow him because I need money. I got son, I have to look after him, I've got parents, I have to look after them. They say 'okay but you don't supposed to come here' and then they start talking to the manager and then the manager. . . . Yes, the men, the older men, because just me is the woman. They shocked because they see me working there and then after that they talk to the manager. I don't know the manager ignored them and then I tried to say to our agency, because I'm working with agency, to make right for staff. And then they say 'okay, we're going to see what you're doing' and I say 'I'm doing my job' and I explain. And then when they see they tell to manager and the manager say 'Okay we will not put her in that line again, she is come back to our line'.

And then the Team Coordinator, he is in the line to look after us like supervisor. After that few weeks and then this TC he start move again me to another job and I say 'okay, the agency already tell to manager don't move me but why did you say to move me again?' Then I say 'okay, I just follow him because if not he will sack me or something like that'. I just follow. He put me again in that line, the heavy line again and the men like this to me and I did like that to them and I don't know, and they said 'oh my god this awful'. I start that one and I already start in here pain and this gets swollen and then I can't do it like that and then I just run to the doctor in BMW and then when I'm there, I think she's not doctor, she's like nurse and she said 'Oh you're not working in coffee shop or retail shop, you're working in the factory, you have to carry on your job because you . . .' and I'm already crying because this [shoulder] gets swollen and then real pain and I can't, it means I can't do any job again and she said 'Okay you take the Paracetamol, you go again.' I say, 'okay that's fine' and then I just follow them.

In fact, Maria had dislocated her shoulder and was signed off sick.

I dislocate my shoulder, because I'm working assembly line. It's really, really hard for a woman because I have to lift heavy, heavy stuff and then my shoulder dislocates and the doctor when I see the GP, the GP say you have to quit the job and then every two weeks I have to send a letter to them and that's until about six month. Until six month they pay me and then after that they didn't pay me but I'm always send the letter to them. I say, 'oh, that's when I go to see the union'. The union didn't do nothing to me, and I say 'okay every month I pay you[9] but you don't want to help me, that's fine'.

Then I'm going to Citizen Bureau and they send me to a solicitor. When I'm going there I need they help me to resolve about this one and

they say 'can you take your statement we'll look your money blah blah
blah?' and they say 'you don't have enough money to pay me'. 'Okay', I
say, 'okay, that means I come here, I thought that you help me because I
don't have enough money to pay you.' I mean I come here to help me to
say to them something like that 'why they didn't pay me until now because
this is not my fault, this happened when I'm working BMW, not happened
like anywhere?' I don't, I just have one main job in BMW and they say
'oh we can't do anything'. I say 'okay that's fine' and then I just stop. This
BMW is good money but it's not worth it for your health.

Over the years, migrant women have been an essential part of the labour
force in Britain's manufacturing industries, often, as these narratives show,
working extremely hard at some personal cost. They were by no means the
docile female labourers of popular imagination but active agents, struggling
to make a living, sometimes involved in industrial action against low pay
and discriminatory treatment and managing the difficult balance of work
and home life through a variety of strategies. Their persistence and courage
in the face of the pains, as well as the pleasures, of waged work, is central in
their stories. But poor treatment is also evident in lower pay than men
received, in exploitative conditions and, as both Parvani and Maria found
working in the car industry thirty years apart, in discriminatory treatment
by managers who moved them into heavy jobs that they were not strong
enough to do properly.

As the second half of the century went on, growing numbers of women
found work in the service sector. Their stories are the subject of the next
chapters. Although service sector work might be assumed to be lighter and
so less physically demanding, many of the jobs involved, for example in
personal care, were also heavy work. Lifting patients, for example, often
without hoists, was not easy, as the nurses working in the NHS in the early
years describe in Chapter 5. Work in the service sector, involving close
contact with patients, customers, clients and students, is also emotionally
demanding work, involving the production of a performance of care and
concern as part of the job. Before exploring this emotional labour, women
who undertook domestic tasks such as cooking and cleaning for others, for
wages, tell their stories in Chapter 4. For these women, working in the
homes of their employers, isolation and loneliness was a consequence and a
noticeable part of their narrative. Furthermore, low pay was the reward for
their labours.

4

Waged Domestic Work:

Cleaning, Catering and Childcare

As feminist theorists have argued, and most women implicitly understand, the boundaries between waged work and domestic work undertaken for love, including housework and childcare, are often blurred. The work done by women caring for their own children and keeping their homes clean is not counted as employment, and so does not appear as part of the gross national product, although it is the subject of a later chapter and is, of course, work in the sense of effort applied to accomplishing tasks, albeit unpaid. When the same work is undertaken to replace the 'free' labour of other women, however, and is recompensed by wages, it is classified as 'work' or perhaps more accurately as employment. Working for wages from home, however, typically is poorly paid and socially isolated, with little recognition and no union to speak up for the workers, as the stories in the last chapter by women who made clothes or toys in their own homes have already shown.

*Here is **Jaba** again, reminding us of the disadvantages of home-work. Jaba came to London from Tanzania in 1968, and worked in her own home in the early 1970s making shirts.*

> The money is not good when you work from home and you also feel good when you go outside. If you work outside, at least you get the minimum wage. But not at home. My work was 'top class' – nothing ever got returned because it was not good. Yet I never got the minimum wage when working from home. Asian women still do not get work outside that easily. Even where they do, the money is no good. Then who will take care of the children? They are responsible for the children.

In this chapter, women talk about the jobs that were once termed 'domestic service' and which also involve working at home, although in this case in the home of someone else. These jobs include looking after the domestic needs of more affluent households: cleaning their homes, doing a range of tasks from laundry and ironing to looking after children. This sort of work used to be regarded by economists and labour theorists as 'residual', likely to disappear in modern societies, in large part because it was assumed that so-called labour saving devices would reduce the time and the hard work of keeping homes in decent order.

As so often, this prediction about the future turned out to be wrong. Currently, numerous forms of waged domestic service are increasing in the UK, not necessarily undertaken, as was more typical in the nineteenth century, by young single women 'living in'. Instead workers of various ages, employed in different ways, now do domestic work for wages. Their employment contracts vary from an informal or casual arrangement with a 'daily' who cleans for a few households for cash in hand to women working on the basis of more formal contracts, perhaps with large transnational cleaning companies, as well as, in a reflection of the past, nannies and au pairs. Some are young but not necessarily so, as the narrative by Anya later in this chapter shows. For women living in the homes of their employers, the distinction between work and home is once again blurred, inserting the wage relation into a space more typically associated with love and affection rather than a monetary exchange. There remains significant continuity with the past, however. The poor pay Jaba identified extends to paid domestic work too, which is often even more exploitative and lower paid than making things in the home. The hours 'on call' may be excessive and non-negotiable when the workplace is also the home of both employers and employees. A woman making shirts in her own home at least is able to stop work when she decides to, assuming she has earned enough that day. Young women caring for children and doing housework for their employer have less opportunity to decide their own working hours, as Marta and Natalija found in the 1940s and Flora in the 1970s.

In the early years of the Baltic Cygnet scheme, domestic service was one of the sectors to which women were allocated but the arrangements proved to be difficult to enforce. Young, often well-educated, women from the Baltic States resented employment as servants and often broke the terms of their employment, moving elsewhere, sometimes with, but also without, the permission of the local labour exchange where they had to register monthly in their first few years of residence in Britain. As well as in individual homes, waged domestic work, including catering and cleaning, is also performed by migrant women in institutional settings, such as the canteen where Lina worked when she first came to Britain in 1947.

'Now nobody wants to do the cheap work': forms of domestic service

Lina was born on a small farm in Latvia in 1924. Her father died when she was three and her mother had a hard time, running the farm alone and bringing up four children. Lina's first job in England was in catering, first in a camp kitchen and then in a canteen, in both places catering for other displaced people as they arrived in the UK.

I arrived here to England in 1947, to Hull; 21 April in England and 23 [April] we were already to Hull. The first transit camp, men and women, all single. First of all I was in the kitchen. Three Latvian girls and there was Estonian girls and a boy and so on, and some were in the office, some in the kitchen, some in the canteen and after a couple of days the manager came and I said 'I haven't done nothing' and he said 'I know but I want you, I want you to go there' and I said 'I'm not going. There is no Latvian girls there is only Estonian girls' and he said 'but I want you to go there'. So okay I went there and I was split from them. I was in a restaurant or canteen or whatever and every second day came 500 people from Germany. They slept only one night but we had to feed them and there was food that was really very good and we were making packs of sandwiches for people who were going to the different places. Those camps were all over Britain and later those people were transferred to the jobs, mostly the farm jobs because that was cheap labour even in England, and factories. They needed doctors but no doctors, only jobs. I can't tell you about the nurses, 1,000 girls, cos I wasn't one of them. I was in the second lot for the camps and that. For the first five years we had to go to Piccadilly to put a stamp [register as an alien] but after five years we were free as a bird: 'you do what you like and go and find a job'.

I was working there from 1947 until end of August and then they closed that camp because the majority of people who wanted to come to England had already come and then later on those people who brought their families over came through Tilbury. And at first it was hard but gradually, gradually things picked up. . . . After the camp in Hull closed they distributed the people all over because it was Ministry arrangements. We could not go and look for jobs ourselves because the five years. You had to stay here and that is that and be more or less controlled. After the camp closed they sent four of us – two Latvian girls and two Estonia – to London and here was one camp. It was in Canning Town and we were working there. I was in the canteen serving food, collecting dishes up and that. We got 35 shillings, 5 shillings was for upkeep. We lived in a barracks but the barracks was nice and clean and we didn't need to clean it ourselves. We were doing the shift work and those days it was different as it is now. Those days labour was cheap and it was plentiful but now nobody wants to do the cheap work. Who is going to do so for that money? But, of course, times change. It is over 50 years ago now.

Natalija came to England with her mother and father, each applying as if they were unrelated single people, who then managed to find work together. She was born in Riga in 1930, the daughter of a policeman, and had left Latvia with her parents in September 1944 when she was just 14 years old. After working as directed labour on a German farm, at the end of the war the family were housed in a displaced persons' camp in the British zone. Natalija's early working life straddles domestic labour in an institution and private households, farm work and cleaning in a hospital.

Then we started to think of emigrating, England was one of the first places. The first scheme was young women to go to hospitals. We arrived in England in 1947 April. Officially we came as three different people, as there were no families, but they did try to keep you together. So we came to England. We arrived in Hull and then taken by train to Market Harborough, just outside Market Harborough. It was sort of army Nissan huts, men in one side and women and children on the other. But we met at meals time; the meals were together. One hut was like a dining room with long tables.

One day we were called into the office and we were offered a job all three together – my father to help in the garden and my mother in the kitchen and I had to be in the dining room to serve the people with a meal and to clean afterwards. And it was, it was an agricultural college for the ex-servicemen. There were sailors and pilots and soldiers after the war who wanted to go into farming or didn't know what else to do – a very mixed company. Well, there was fun. Not understanding English, I had my dictionary under one arm. They joked but not cruelly. They were nice. I was still only 17. It was very funny sometimes. Generally they were not nasty, I can say. The only nasty person there was, that was the housekeeper. My mother was in the kitchen, washing up, preparing vegetables that sort of thing. We started to work at six in the morning and very often we didn't finish til ten at night. There was not much time off in between, half an hour after lunch in the dining room, that sort of thing. I remember it was about six weeks.

If she (the housekeeper in charge) had been more understanding, a different person, it wouldn't be too bad. But we decided to look for something else where we could all be together. We couldn't move from agriculture into the town but we could move into another place in the country. Of course, we had to have permission to go from the Labour Exchange; it was called that then. So we went there and said 'yes, we would like to go somewhere else'. They gave us one of those farming magazines with jobs in the back. There was one we thought sounded nice. It was man in a garden, woman in kitchen and a maid and it was very near. It was Leicester and we wrote and they wrote us back and invited for an interview. Already I could write a letter with a dictionary and the letter went several times on the paper til I thought it right.

We went for an interview. It was a farm house but the farm, we gathered, was sold because the father had died and the mother and the unmarried daughter lived in a cottage type of thing and I think they just lived from whatever they sold as the daughter didn't do any work and they didn't go out. . . . I think they were a bit strange, at least the daughter you know. They had very nice cutlery and things, silver trays, and their cats used to have their Sunday lunch on the silver tray, outside. And if it was windy they put cotton wool in the key hole so that the wind doesn't blow on the cats. They were otherwise quite nice but we couldn't stand it there. Mother done the cooking and I helped her with the vegetables and things and my job was to clean the house and to scrub the back stairs. I can't remember what we were paid, as a family. We lasted about three months there. That was all we could stand.

We found another job but that was in Kent. There again a farm was looking for a man in a garden, and a wife in a house cooking and a dairy maid. So I thought 'right, I can milk a cow'. We went for an interview . . . and we got the job and we came down. We lived in the big house, my parents had one room, I had one room and on the same floor was another guest room and the main bedroom. And on another floor, downstairs was a sitting room and a dining room and we had a separate dining room. Because there was another girl who was working on the farm as well, an English girl. We arrived there and had a lovely front garden but a cow was on it, eating the grass. It was an absolute shambles and my father said there would be plenty to do.

The first morning I had to be up at 4.30 am and into the milking parlour for 5.00 am. The first morning the farm owner came with me and introduced me to a couple of chaps and Rosemary [the English girl] and the foreman, he pointed to a cow and said 'you go and milk that one' and it went quite well, you know. That morning I milked four cows. But it was very, very difficult to begin with. There were nights when I was sitting in bed and crying my hands were so sore. Mind you, after about six months I was really looking forward to milking. I could sit down. By that time it was about twelve cows each morning. And then we had to clean up and feed the little calves and clean their sheds out, then prepare for the afternoon feed. We usually finished about half past five but we had two hours lunch time and whoever was on duty in the evening as there were several cows that needed milking three times, not just two times, so those days you were on much later. But we had a day off every week. The only thing was on your day off you had to go in to help with the milking til about ten, half past nine. And then every month we had a weekend off – Saturday and Sunday. I had the same weekend off as my parents but I usually went to London. By that time there was a Latvian book shop in

London and usually I went there and then on to the pictures in the afternoon. I went mostly by myself although sometimes I met people there, other Latvians.

It was a very, very nice place to work there. His wife, she was perhaps a bit tight but as she had nothing to say – the last word was his [the owner]. He said 'I want this for lunch or I want that, all this and so much cream or something'. He was very generous and from the very first day when we arrived, my mother cooked, I don't know what it was, and he came into the kitchen to carve the meat and she put two plates out and he said 'where are your plates, where are the other three?' and we all got the same helping. It wasn't 'we eat first and you get what is left'. And usually they had about between 55 and 60 milking cows. Then they had chickens, they supplied eggs, they had about 15,000 chickens in various fields. So you see there was plenty of eggs, plenty of milk, plenty of chicken to eat. Once a week I had to make butter, turn it, turn it til it comes and then make it into little packets; half pounds. On Friday the owner takes some packets to London and comes back with beef and fish and things like that, you know. Still everything was on ration books. So the food was, you could eat practically as much as you wanted when you wanted. I remember then that my wages were £2 5s a week but with the food and everything else as well. We always pooled the money together. If mum needs new shoes or dad needs this but with me being the young one, I was spoilt.

We stayed there nearly three years. It was getting too much for mother. Housekeeping can be hard work, all day on your feet. So we looked again in Kent and found something not too far away. Again in a house. I was a maid and Mum was in the kitchen and father was out in the garden. There was another gardener who was also Latvian. But that was again, that was a house where they expected you to work from early hours until late at night. They both were business people. He has advertising, perfumes and soap and things and the wife had a bakery in Soho, famous for its pastry and things. Very rich people, but slave drivers. Most peculiar family, they weren't sort of nasty or anything but there was something. I always laughed with my mum when I had to do the bedrooms. Working in a pastry thing, she [Natalija's employer] never wore an apron or anything and the dress in the evening was covered with flour. And most things needed hand-washing, so that was me, sort of thing. Oh, she had clothes, she had about half of this room with dresses and shoes and things and then in a small room she had, I counted, she had 14 winter coats and three fur coats. And in a bedroom, little chest of drawers with some underwear in and that was falling to pieces. I just thought if people would know what Madame has underneath. You just thought that a person with so much money and so much clothes on the top would have some decent underwear. I always said to Mum, 'mine is much better than hers'.

We lived in the house with them, again in two rooms. We never really had any privacy. We lived there about three months. It didn't suit. It was mother, she couldn't cope. Her feet used to swell up in the evenings and her feet were so painful she sometimes found it difficult to stand or walk. So we went to various places, on a farm that was what we were looking for but nothing seemed to suit. . . . Then we met some people in the Latvian house in London and they knew that a hospital in St Albans that needed some people and would we consider hospital. So went there and my father started to work as a gardener in one hospital and my mother and me in the other. We had rooms there and there was other Latvian people working there and the next hospital was where my father was and he had a room there. We started there, but there was vacancies at father's hospital so we went there. My parents had a small rented place outside the hospital but I lived there in the hospital. I was doing domestic work and my mother was working in laundry and father was in the gardens.

Marta's first job in Britain, after three years in a displaced persons' camp in Germany and a short period in a transit camp in the UK, was as a domestic worker in a private home.

Then, it was 1948 and a friend of mine had come to England a year before me, in 1946 or 1947, and she was very happy here and she said would I like to come. And I said I would but the authorities wouldn't let me come because I was 17. I was underage; 18 was the earliest age people would be taken and I was 17 but I looked 14, quite skinny and small. And this friend said she might make arrangements for me to come over here and I didn't think anything of it; I didn't think anything would come of it but all of a sudden I had a letter to say I was to come.

The lady of the house came to the hostel and took me along to see the place. I suppose I was supposed to say whether I liked it or not, but what did I know? I could speak some English. I had learned it for three and a half years in Germany. I knew grammar really well but to speak took more time. It took me another six months in England to get really fluent. Anyway, so I was taken to this large, beautiful house in its own gardens in a little village. The house was beautiful, there was a cat and a dog and everything seemed lovely. So the arrangement was that I had every Tuesday afternoon off and every second Sunday afternoon, but I was told that on my half day I had to be out of the house. If I stayed in they expected me to work, you see, so I went out.

To begin with I was in the kitchen and then the parlour maids, two left so I was promoted. At the time when I went there were two parlour maids, a cook, a part-time secretary, a part-time laundry woman and two gardeners, a large staff and, well to begin with I was supposed to have set hours with two hours off in the afternoon. Start at seven and then two hours off in the afternoon but there was so much work I could never get it done; polishing and cleaning and never ending work so in the end it just happened that I couldn't get my two hours off in the afternoon, I could never get all the work done. The housekeeper told me what to do. The lady of the house gave her instructions to the housekeeper and she told me what to do. People were nice enough to me but how shall I say, the lady of the house, she was very nice for about the first six months but then I couldn't do anything right. My wage was £2[1] plus board and lodging and then later on I got five more shillings. Well, £2 a week isn't much. I remember I bought a coat and it cost me £16 so it was saving up for quite a long time. And coming from the camps I hardly had any decent clothes so I had to buy everything like from scratch, shoes and dresses and whatnot. All my money went on that basically, on clothes, what little I earned. It was not much.

I resigned the job and in those days, there was a, like a government office, like a job centre and you had to go there to get another job, a labour exchange.[2] The thing was that in my papers I was registered as a domestic worker and in those days they thought that if you are a domestic worker, you have got to stay a domestic worker. You have to do that, you are supposed to be, I don't know, maybe not qualified for anything else, I don't know. But anyway at the labour exchange they wanted to put me into another house like that, in service, but I didn't want to do it anymore. I thought there was absolutely no personal life, you know, you're totally you know sort of doing what they want you to do, the hours and so on, so I didn't want to do that.

And they had to give a little card to take to the future employer and they didn't want to give me this card and again I was at a loss, I didn't know what to do. I was desperate. How long had I been in the country then, about 18 months and I didn't know anything. I didn't know the laws, I didn't know my rights, I didn't know anything and also in domestic service in those days there were no trade unions, people could ask you to work any hours they liked. And in this house I worked from 7.00 am basically until ten o'clock, well not exactly, let's say 9.00 pm when the washing up was done. I had my meal breaks, you know, coffee at 11.00 am and then lunch and teatime, but you are tied to the place. You can't say 'I am going to my room for 15 minutes', you couldn't do that, it wasn't done and you can't. People never complained. If you didn't like it you left and tried to find a better place. But there was no union and you couldn't say I am not going to do it, because you are there and that's it. You are in service you see. So when I finished there, I thought never again because basically you really do have no life of your own really. I was completely on my own, except that there were two more Latvian people in the house, doing the same sort of thing. The man was a butler, and the woman then took over my job in the kitchen. They were older people. It was tough. Then, at the labour exchange they finally agreed that I could go to Courtaulds.

Vieda also left Latvia, when she was just 15 and a half, and came to England already engaged in Germany by the parents of 'little Fiona and little Mark' as she explained in Chapter 2. Her post was nominally as a nursery maid but she was expected to do all sorts of domestic tasks.

So I came with them to England [in 1946]. I had some papers, displaced persons' identity papers, birth date and so on. I came with them and we moved from one place to another because he moved with the RAF. First we arrived in Sandwich and her mother, the children's mother, was a Lord and Lady. It was in this big white house, and land and mushrooms. The nanny arrived, very strict and uniforms and all. And anyway we lived there for a while and then we moved to Andover, because he moved his stations from one place to another, and then near Winchester.

I had a room up in an attic or something like that, my little room. It was cold and so but I only slept there. It was just after the war and everyone was still on rations too and even if you were Lord and Lady you had to save and so on. But there were all these functions and parties and so on. RAF people. They had a cook. I had to help the cook and sometimes the nanny and I would go and pick the mushrooms in the fields, sometimes get the Brussels sprouts from the garden and whatever. I think they paid me 30 shillings in a month. I got my food and I had half a day a week [off]. In the end I said 'I want to get on'. And they did help me because they drove me to Salisbury and I met the matron and I said I wanted to do nursing.

Scrub the dishes and polish the floors: hospital domestic labour

Ruta also left Latvia aged 15 to work, despite the official minimum age of 18. She was allocated to domestic work in a hospital, which in her case led directly to nurse training.

I volunteered to come over to England as a domestic worker for the hospitals. Father said 'you go to England for one year and earn money and you keep that money and then come back to Germany and you can study then'. That was the arrangement but the camps were breaking up and then my parents came over to England and my brother and they went north. My brother worked in a factory and my father in a camp in a place where they were keeping these displaced people and he was looking after the rooms. No-one went back to Germany.

I had come on my own with a group of volunteers and I was put in the Fountain Hospital, a mental hospital and I had to scrub the floors and wash the dishes and polish the wooden floors, light the coal fires. You go into a place and light the fires to keep the place warm. It was in Tooting. There were four of us [doing the work], two elderly ladies and a friend of mine. We kept together. But her sister came over [from the DP camps in Germany] and was sent to Bradford and she wanted to join her. So she left me alone and I developed the housemaid's knee because of scrubbing and all that work and I lost a lot of weight and was crying a lot. I didn't like it all. And there was an old German doctor and he kept talking to me and he saw that I had all the education. I showed him my papers and so on and he said that he would try to help me that I could do nurses' training. So I, before my time, before a year was out, I was already a student nurse. This German doctor helped me.

Illona followed the same path.

We [Illona, her mother and a friend] landed in Hull, 29 May 1947, on the Westward Ho! scheme[3] and we were taken to a transit camp and we waited for jobs. It was about three weeks we were in the camp and then my mother, myself and a school friend of mine went to Leeds General Infirmary, worked as maids, you know domestic staff. And it was difficult. It was an old hospital and we lived in domestic quarters and the nurses lived in another, you know, another wing, and we weren't quite allowed to go there. They were a bit higher and it was, well, like a caste system: matron, and the hierarchy and sisters and nurses. It wasn't said but it was understood that you hadn't to get any contact with nurses and everything. And it was difficult to go on your knees on these stone floors scrubbing, and crowds of students coming. And one stepped in the bucket once and upset all the water. And it was, you know, I don't mind working, but it was very hard. You felt repressed and in hospitals you had to work Saturdays and Sundays and later on when the people in the factories, they had Saturday and Sunday off and the Latvians developed a social, there was a choir and a dance group and a theatre group and you couldn't join in because you were always working.

  The girls doing the domestic work they were all, well there were three Latvians and I think there were three Estonian women and of course the English, they lived there as well, but some were, you know, simple-minded. They were only for domestic work and all and it was a bit, well, you couldn't hold conversations with many of them, nothing in common. I mean I am not a snob and, of course, the English. I have learned English from the age of eight all through school, but it was a different language when you land in Yorkshire, it was much broader than now and it was difficult. Mind you, I asked if I could go to evening classes at college and our shifts were changed. . . . And then, I was so longing to study something, you know to have higher education, and on Sunday mornings I had to take a tray of breakfast to the dispenser and I asked this man 'what are the chances to study pharmacy?' and he said, 'well, girl, if you have no money, you have no hope to study in England'. And, of course, at that time we didn't know there was a world organization of refugees, you know to help you.

Anyway, I went to see the matron and asked if I could train as a nurse there. And she said, 'What and all your friends in the domestic staff.' But she gave me a list of hospitals where you could train and I asked one of the nurses which is the most modern one and she said Bradford Royal Infirmary but it is very, very strict. But I didn't mind that. So I applied and I had to sit a little exam and in my English. And I had good marks and so I was accepted in Bradford Royal Infirmary and I didn't work the full year in Leeds Infirmary. And the atmosphere was quite different; you could talk to anybody and you were friendly with porters and so, and matron was nice. Matron was half Norwegian and half English, a real lady, you had to respect just to look at her, you know, and it was nice and I trained there.

Eva was born in 1928 in Riga. She lived in a camp in Germany until 1947 when she came to England to work in a hospital. Her initial work trajectory was similar to that of Ruta and Illona but unlike them, she did not complete her nursing course.

In 1946 already there was this campaign that young girls could come to England to work in the hospitals. But I didn't come to England then. I came in 1947, in April. I was one of the last ones to come to hospitals. My parents stayed behind. It was a sad parting. When I came to England in 1947, I will never forget that day because it was Princess Elizabeth's birthday. That is 21 April. We were coming by boat, lots of girls together. So we were in London. I don't know whether it was in a hostel or something. I can't remember that any more but we slept the night and there came the welfare officer, you know, ladies who would offer us jobs now. 'What part of England do you want to go, and what hospital?' but what do we know. We got friendly, I got friendly with another two girls who were sisters and from the same camp I came with another girl.

In London with these welfare officers asked where you like to go. And they needed four girls for this mental hospital and we were four and they said 'it's in the Midlands' so we thought 'oh well, in the middle that would be good, that would be best, not far away from anything'. You don't know anything, you see. But now we registered in this hospital outside Warwick, but we had no idea. And then we are talking among ourselves and said 'I wonder what mental means?' you know. We didn't know what mental means. It was all in English and it was not so much at that time. So my friend had this what do you call it, like a little book to look in? And she looked and she said 'aagh' and we said 'oh god, we don't want to go to a mental hospital'. And so we go to these ladies and we say 'we don't want to go to a mental hospital' and they say, 'no, don't worry, you not going to see anybody, you are not going to work with patients' and they explained to us a bit more. They are old people and we said 'all right. We will go.'

Oh, it was the best thing we could do. It was a lovely hospital and me and my friend, you know who came from the same camp, we worked in the ward where you know, you have a little nervous breakdowns, you know, where they bring people in. And we were polishing floors and serving meals and making beds and you know, we were ward orderlies, we were not domestic help. One up it seemed. Later on we just found that out. And the sisters they worked in cleaning the rooms and tidying the rooms for the nurses in the nursing homes, and we thought we were in paradise. We each had a room, a nice little room. We had a basement where we were just the four of us and a bathroom and a sink in your room, hot and cold water, all the time and then we had a separate, like a sitting room for us, the four of us. And the surroundings, it was April you see and that year it was a very nice summer and all the fruit trees were in flower and it was lovely. When we worked in the ward we could see all the fruit trees in blossom. It was a really nice place. It was three miles from Warwick and when we had our days off, naturally half day, I had a Thursday half day. What about Sunday? I think I had a Sunday always off and we could go to Leamington.

We wore a uniform, they provided it and they paid us ten pounds a month. Everything included; nothing else to bother about, only what we wanted. So my friends wrote to the sisters and somehow got to know about this hospital and about us and in the end, you know, we ended about 12 Latvians girls. We were really lucky. And matron, in those days there was discipline you know, you know where you are.

And then, I think it was 1947 we started work at the hospital, 1948, 1949, I think we had to do two years. The agreement was for two years. The matron, the sisters, they all told us that we are not really the lower class people. I am sorry to say that. We couldn't fit in so we kept to ourselves mostly. We learnt English there, the hospital provided us with a teacher there. And after two years the matron said, 'Now, whoever wants can do nursing'. It was marvellous. Well, I never liked hospitals. A mental hospital is more interesting, I wouldn't have minded that, no, but in those days as well there were wards where old people, like they have nursing homes now. In those days there were a lot of old people in mental hospitals, people who maybe didn't have relatives to take them out of the hospital and they lived there for years and years. And some of them were bed patients you know and they had all sorts of awful things, you know, and I couldn't do that sort of thing. But my husband proposed and we got married in 1949 so I only went to the lectures for about six months. I would have given it a go because it is a very interesting subject but we had to go in all wards. So, in 1949 I gave up the nursing.

Eva's husband was still working as a miner in the first job he was allocated to in the UK. Soon after he left and together they took over a large derelict building, which they converted into bedsitters that they rented to single Latvian men and then to migrant couples of different nationalities.

Valda *was also employed as a ward orderly from 1947 but in Scotland rather than 'in the middle' of the country like Eva. She managed eventually to move to Chesterfield where there was a larger community of displaced people.*

They started what they called the white swans or whatever to come to Britain to work and so I came. I was first in Scotland where I worked in an isolation hospital. There were hospitals first. There was one lot who came before Christmas and then a second lot after. It was 1947 I think when the big snows were on but it was a beautiful summer. It was a small hospital and we were quite lonely. There weren't many Latvians around but we found out where and used to go visiting. It was two or three hours by bus really to meet some people. Then we found out that we had some friends living in Chesterfield and we managed in the end, we managed to get permission from Labour Exchange. We couldn't move anywhere without permission.

In Scotland I was a ward orderly, partly nursing really. We were called ward orderlies but we helped with the patients, it wasn't cleaning or that. We had to wear uniforms. It was much better than now with all these managers, everyone liked Matron. We lived in. I wouldn't say it was hard work. The first month, though, I worked in laundry there. We had to accept, you know, what we were given the jobs and later on the matron just gave us different jobs and so on. I enjoyed it really. I had never been very keen really on hospital work but I had to do it and I did it. I wouldn't do it again if I can help. But the conditions were good. It was a small hospital right outside a little place. At that time you know the TB patients used to be in hospital for years and years. The patients' relatives, they used to ask us out to tea, to visit them. I still correspond with two or three people. And some church people found out we were displaced persons working and they used to ask us out to tea.

I had learnt English at school but language at school and to start speaking is two different things. The first night we arrived and we were waiting for supper and the girl came in and she said 'do you like fash?' We just looked at each other and we didn't know what it is fash. They brought us kippers! It was very hard with the different dialects really, it was hard. We didn't have any classes in the hospitals but we picked up ourselves whatever. We were all right really but it was just the loneliness. We wanted to see more of our people so we got the permission and we went to Chesterfield in 1950. Managed to get there, the same I worked in a hospital; first a ward orderly again. And even on night duty we had to be in charge of the ward, we were allowed. They were TB patients, they weren't really ill. In hard cases, the night sister was there. We were on shifts. We used to do nights three months on a time. I think you got used to it. We lived in the hospital there too. Occasionally there was an odd person who doesn't like a foreigner, but it was all right, couldn't grumble really.

'I didn't come to England to be a slave': working as an au pair

For many young women the route to the UK over the post-war decades was through employment as domestic worker, often to look after children as an au pair or a nanny in an employer's own home.

Flora, who was born in Colombia in 1952, left when she was 22 to become an au pair. Like many of the women from the Baltic States before her, her post-school education had been disrupted but in her case by revolution in Colombia rather than by an external war.

I was born in Colombia, in South America, in time, by car, 14 hours away from the capital, Bogota. The financial situation was very, very poor. My father ran his own small business. He was a hands-on man; he learned the trade of blacksmiths and artistic metal. He worked with wrought iron and all the metals really but initially his main job was making horseshoes for the farmers, in the farm where we lived. And then as he moved to the city, he then started designing candelabras and street lights, hotel lights and he was trying to compete with industrialized world around him, which made life for him economically unbearable at times. He was bringing up a family of ten children, more or less unaided really because my mum would be looking after the kids at home.

I'm the eldest, eight sisters including myself and two brothers. I did up to diploma level, high school. I went to university but the universities were on strike and we couldn't really [study]. There was a year of revolution by the time I was trying to do something. But I was always interested in learning English. Well, I learned English and French at high school and was always interested in English history. My cousin wanted to come in England. She found out that the British Consulate was issuing visas to students like us with interest in learning English and coming to England for a couple of years, with student visa. So I then took that opportunity and I came to England.

It was very difficult because it was the first time that I have to leave my family and I remember crying a lot because I could see what was going to happen, how it was all going to be different. So it was heart-breaking but I just felt that I needed to be economically independent because the system hadn't worked in the way I was expecting it. There were not many opportunities for developing your professionalism unless you came from such a wealthy family that they could pay a private university and I was not in that category. By then my family was growing up and my father's business was going down.

They [the Consulate] had like an au pairing agency and I think it was through the British Consulate, through an au pairing agency that would allow us to be in families and to be au pairs to help out with light housework, take the children to school and so on. I couldn't leave before I was 21, so I left just short of my 22nd birthday [in 1974]. So I left, and I was supposed to be meeting up with this English family at the airport, which was quite difficult because my English was not really too fluent. I understood more than I could speak and as I started going to English conversation classes I got more confident. The family I went to become an au pair, this family arranged for me to go to English classes and I think they paid for everything. And it was a very nice family; I was very happy with the two girls that I looked after but they started changing.

They started expecting me to be a domestic and being paid as an au pair. They started being very mean with food. If you had a shower or bath they said that it was expensive and started restricting my freedom. If I had any time to do my homework, they would send the children up to say I should be playing with them and every day there would be more tasks for me to do. So initially the first week or so they were really lovely, very welcoming and they invited other au pairs, Spanish that we can understand each other, but gradually it was less and less and less. The tasks that I was supposed to do, they started increasing. Like I'd have to do the cooking and get up early to do the breakfast; I have to do the polishing of the silver and I have to do the ironing because apparently there was a domestic lady there. It seems to me that I replaced her but I was led to believe that I was only just going to be as an au pair and the letter was very much as an au pair. I said to these people, 'I don't understand why you let this change. This is the letter, this is the contract and all these extra things are not in the contract.'

Then they said I couldn't go to English classes because I have to do more housework and then I couldn't have my evenings off because I have to babysit, then I couldn't have weekends off because there would be a number of excuses. And I got more and more disappointed, more and more disillusioned and I said, 'Really I didn't come to England to be a slave.' My main purpose was to get to know the culture, to know the language and then eventually to go home in two years to teach there, but I was never prepared to come as a full-time domestic and I said 'I am not paying enough either', because I was, the first earnings I had was £5 a week and then I said 'how can you expect me to spend weekends as well? My friends who work weekends, they get more money'. So I think when I started challenging them, then they put £5 up to £7 so I would also stay there weekends.

Flora, like Natalija, wasn't prepared to put up with slave drivers, and so she left and, like Vieda and Ruta before her, trained as a nurse. In her case she returned home for her training and re-emigrated to the UK in the 1980s.

Women migrants, typically, are young when they decide to leave, or have to leave, their own country for the UK, with decades of waged work in front of them. Many young women from the countries that joined the European Union in 2004 came to Britain as it permitted new entrants to seek employment immediately. They often took poorly paid domestic servicing work, in some cases hoping to improve their English and then to move into better paid employment. Beatta, from Poland, and Karina, from Latvia, both found work as room cleaners in a large London hotel, employed through agencies, rather than directly by the hotel.

'The guests, they don't see us': agency work in hotels

Beatta was 24 in 2006. She hoped to attend university in Poland but she had three sisters still at home and the family needed financial help and so she decided to look for work in London. Beatta's English was very poor but she was working in a team with other Polish women and, indeed, had been recruited through an agency owned by Poles.

Why I came to London? Money, money, money. Yes. I came together, two friends, she go back to Poland and I stay. I find job in a few days, through friend who works in same hotel. He give me name of agency. [At the interview] she asked me why I came here, how long I want to stay here and she explain me what I have to do, and if I have some problem or something I can call to her.

I start and training is three days, and then I clean rooms. I wake up, it's 5.00 am and I clean body and everything and go to the work. I walk – 15 minutes. Then changing uniform and go to the trolley and everything put on the trolley and go upstairs, taking the list [of rooms to clean] and going upstairs, cleaning rooms. And 10.00 am go meeting, breakfast and later it's cleaning room again. Sometimes it's not many, sometimes it's very more rooms and no time, 20 minutes because I'm near end. Should be 30 minutes [to clean each room] and finish at 2.30 pm. Sixteen rooms is usual. But sometimes when we don't have the empty room or free room to clean, or we don't have something, hand towels or whatever, we have to wait for this and then we are nervous because we can't clean and then are just waiting, and so finish at 3.00 pm, 4.00 pm. Most of the time I have 16 rooms [to clean] and more. And sometimes takes longer to clean. Very dirty room, one hour is cleaning this room because everything is oh my God! Family, it's one room and family, the children, many children and all the rooms, it's oh my God!

Sometimes the supervisor ask me 'you more rooms, you want?' Maybe sometimes it's busy, they ask help. And sometimes I can say if I, don't know, feel bad or I am tired, I can say 'I don't want to take it extra rooms.' And now I work sometimes in the public area and I clean the room sometimes in public area, so it's okay. But if we are sick we have to call one hour before and they don't pay for this day, no.

The guests in hotel, they don't see us. For the room service, they like them more, and the same with the tips, we clean their rooms, we do everything and they give them plate and not us. We have maybe £1 sometimes. And, oh my God, I'm tired. I have headache. Sometimes in the room when it's too hot. And I have sick skin, even if you use the gloves you have. And I have to look nice, good. Broken shoes are something no good. My uniform clean, not too much make up, hair spiky if short. I have to look nice, even if nobody see me.

I am sad. I am very, miss, oh my God, I go home on holiday. Then I am very happy. I miss so much for the Poland, for my family and I don't know I want to stay here for my whole life.

Karina was born in Riga in 1982 and came to the UK with her older sister and her twin sister in 2003, a year before Latvia joined the EU, and so they were working illegally for the first year. Like Beatta, Karina had hoped to go to university but her family's financial circumstances also prevented her starting a degree course.

Me and my sister want to study somewhere to get a high education but it's impossible, it's too expensive for my mum in our country, it's impossible. And no jobs, it was too difficult, not too much money of course and we decided to go here in the UK, to try, at least to try. Actually we ask her [mother] about that but she didn't have enough money. But she said 'okay, I'll find money, if you want you can go, because you will die here. It's boring for you, I can see that because you want to do something'. And then she said 'okay, I'll find the money, we will try go sort it out and you will go as soon as possible'. And we are here. On 23 March 2003 we came in England.

Karina and her sisters paid an agency in Latvia to arrange their move.

It's like our friend of our friends, she was trying to send her husband in England and she said, 'you can go there, it's good agency, good woman, pretty'. So we went there, she said 'you have to pay too much money but 100 per cent work, accommodation, everything'. We said okay, 'too much money but we will pay, then we have guarantee'. We paid £600 there [in Riga] and here [in London] we paid £250, £250 more. She said £150, but we paid £250 because in UK agency they said, 'we don't know anything about £150, you have to pay £250. If you won't pay, you can go outside'.

We didn't want to go outside to sleep on the bench in a park, then pay this money. And because of that we didn't want to go back [to Riga], because of this money. Because our mother, she found this money, she took this money from the bank like loan. We didn't want to go there and see it just like that cry, no, we decided to fight.

After a struggle to find accommodation, Karina found a place to stay with a group of other young Europeans from both Latvia and Estonia. She also found work, like Beatta, cleaning hotel rooms.

I have been here two and a half years already. We didn't know but we were working here illegally actually, because our agency, they said in my country, 'everything is fine, just pay money and you will go there'. We came here, we were in shock. We couldn't go back. Mum, she paid too much money for us, then we have to work. It was all terrible and on from May 2004 we got the job, almost one year we were jobless. Before May 2004 I didn't work at all. Then a friend, we didn't know him like very good, he just lived in one house with another school friend and sometimes he called to us. 'How are you, did you find a job?' We said 'no'. He just said 'you can go to this agency, maybe they can help you'. And we went there. They said 'of course, go to hotel to clean rooms, a room attendant'. We didn't have a choice. We were happy at least this one. Yeah, they agreed and we start working there.

This guy, my school friend, he said, 'you can go and work at least one day a week when it's busy in the hotel, you can go there. It's illegal but you can go there, at least £30 a day or £20 a day.' And maybe twice a week, once a week we went there, it was busy but it was of course illegally. They said 'you can clean the rooms and just go' and they paid £30 cash. From the beginning it was terrible, I couldn't walk, my feet, it was horrible, my arms, everything. But we had to do that, we need money, we earn every penny.

Three month more I was jobless again. I was trying to find hotel job. It was easy to find hotel but everybody wanted to see student visa or work permit; nobody wanted to take me. They said they can't take anybody from European Union because our country join the European Union in May 2004. Until this time nobody can take people from European Union until May 2004. And three months we had to wait again, and thank God my friend, our friend, he gave us this number for agency. We went there. My sister, she start working there in end of April and me in the beginning of May. In hotel; I was cleaning rooms. One and a half year I was working there as a room attendant.

It was just a small agency we worked for. And then manager in hotel, housekeeping manager, she said that one of us, me and my sister, we were trying to do our best, we were trying to be the best maids and we were the best and she said one of us will be the supervisor, floor supervisor. But our agency was too small, me and my sister, maybe two or three people more, very small agency for big hotel. They couldn't give us better opportunities than clean rooms. So I left. But I was happy there because everybody trust me, respect, it was like very big plus for us to be somebody there, to become somebody there, so they were very nice.

I left my agency in November and I couldn't find a job for a month. I left my agency 4 or 5 November and then got my job here [a branch of a large multinational chain of hotels] on 21 February 2006. I was staying at home; it was boring but what can I do? I was trying to find something but it was impossible; it was Christmas time. I found it on the internet, I was sitting on the internet all day.

I am floor supervisor now. Like before I was cleaning rooms, now I am checking rooms. The girls, they clean rooms, after that I'll go and check how they, if they need something wrong or mistakes, dirty towels or . . . and I have to check that. It's like a promotion. And now I work for the hotel and not agency. It's much money but holiday too. They pay me for holidays, big plus for me. At the moment and after three months I will be a hotel Club member. It's good, then I can stay in the hotels for £16 per night, it's very nice and too many things that is better than agency. Agency they pay minimum £5.05, that's it, maybe holidays, I don't know about holidays but I don't want to work for minimum anymore, I need more. Now £6.31 and I think it's better than £5.05, at least not minimum, it's better than minimum wage.[4]

I work 39 hours a week, not too difficult. I know my job very well. I know how to teach other girls to do the same, to respect their job duties. I'll try my best, I know how to do that at least. Some of them, they don't want to listen. They have to understand that if don't want to properly do their job, they will lose the job. Some of them don't speak English at all, they speak Russian as well. I can explain in Russian but some of them, they're rude. They can say 'you are maid as well, you're a floor supervisor never, never, never; you can't show me what I have to do'. Okay, I am not going to shout, I'm not going to be rude. 'If you don't listen to me, you have to listen to your manager, no problem. If you don't want to do what I'm saying, it's your problem. You have to do that because I know much more than you.'

We wear a uniform and must look nice. It's very important because in the hotel many guests are very rich or very important for the hotel because they are our guests and when we are working in the hotel, the hotel is like our home. We have to welcome our guests, our customers in our house. Like if you come in my house, I will try to do my best and you have to feel comfortable, to be like a home and if the guest, they will come in our hotel and they will stay at least one night, they have to feel comfortable that everybody can help them, to be friendly. It's very important and if you are tidy, your clothes are tidy, you are fresh smelling, it's very important for us. If our guests are happy, we are happy.

I don't see guests much though because when I go in the room it's empty, but if the guest needs help I have to ask him 'do you need anything, how can I help you?' Or if I have to speak, I will speak, if he will ask me something, I have to answer and I will answer but it's like he needs, like we need to make him feel happy, so he feel friendly, that I am his friend. If he is angry, I have to make him like calm down, 'everything is fine, it's not a big problem. If you have any problems, we are here to help you.' That's it. Because I'm trying and one time I am trying to put me in staff place and guest place, 'If I go in a hotel, what I want to see from the staff?' I'm trying to show the guests what I want to see and I think it's good.

In this part of her job, Karina is moving beyond the routine 'dirty work' aspects of cleaning hotel rooms, into affective or emotional work, where she uses her own ideas of appropriate service to soothe fractious guests. Other kinds of domestic work also involve emotional labour and caring for others. Here childcare is the most obvious example: another quintessentially feminized form of work, also typically undertaken by young single women, like Flora, although not always. Older women also migrate, though in smaller numbers, to take up domestic employment. Both Jane and Anya, from Brazil and Estonia respectively, came to the UK in the new millennium to work as nannies. Atypically, they were both widows in their fifties.

Jane was born in Brazil in the 1950s and had had a long career in the financial sector in Sao Paulo. In 2005, however, when she was 53, her husband died and she decided to leave. Initially an unregistered migrant, she met and married a Brazilian national living in Britain and applied for a visa to stay. Looking for employment, all she could find was hotel work.

I was very tired in this time [after her husband's death] and I went to travel agents and I bought one travel for 40 days. I went to Spain, Italy, everything alone. And finished here [in England]. And I didn't come back, I stayed. This is July 2005. June or July I don't know, I'm not sure. Of course, I knew a lot of Brazilian people here and they could find a job quickly here in London, but I was illegal and I said 'no, I can't do it because it's not good, to stay in a country illegally'. But I make a lot of friends and I found my second husband. I knew him from Brazil and I meet him here. And he knows that I was a widow now. And we start together and we fall in love but I have to come back [to Brazil] because I haven't money to stay here more time.

And I come back to Brazil and 2006 we married. He was here and I was there. And I went to the papers to the Home Office to come here but not illegal. First I went to Italy to meet my husband and I stayed there two months and then I came to England again and I start to work in a hotel. Very hard job. Room assistant, it's a very hard job but I couldn't speak English at this time. And I started to work there in September 2007 and I work until February 2008, when my visa arrived, the Home Office gave my visa. Sixteen rooms per day. In five and a half hours. It's crazy. I said 'no, I'm not coming back to the hotel' and I tried to find another job. And I start to work in a hospital in August. I work now in a hospital, domestic assistant. It's only four hours, my contract in the agency is four hours every day, yes. Champion pay £7.50, something like that. Champion is agency. I have a contract with Champion, the hospital, no. We have to work in the hospital minimum one year til they give contract to NHS. But I clean good, they like me, I work every day. So I work some weeks 40 hours, some weeks 45. It's good because it's good money. It's good money to live here. It's not too much but it's good. And the best for me is where there are British people, not only British people but Brazilian people and people from everywhere and we speak English, this is good.

Of course, I work all my life in the office, not using my hands. My mum joke with me all the time: 'you moved to another country to clean and you never clean your own house'. It's true; I never do it in my house. But I have to do it. Here I can work, I love this country, it's because I work. I'm not dead. I'm feeling strong, still strong. I work 10 hours per day. I still work, strong. And I am alive. In my country it's not, when you are 40 years and you leave your job, doesn't matter which kind of job, you are dead because you can't find another one. It's difficult. And here no, it's very different. They don't prejudice, there isn't and you can work and do everything that you want.

Despite this, Jane argues that in many ways life is better in Brazil.

I think here, not only here but in Europe you don't live a good life. But in Brazil it's a good life. You stop work on Friday and you go to the pub to have a drink and then you go to the beach Saturday and Sunday and you come back to work on Monday. It's very different and they [my daughters] don't want to come here. Come to visit me, yes, they want but to live here, never. My mum is alive, she's going to be 84 years and she went to a gym and she make walking on the beach every day. Every day one hour, an hour and a half. It's a good life.

Nevertheless, Jane was in the process of seeking indefinite leave to remain.

Anya is Estonian by birth. Like Vieda, she came to work as a nanny in a private home but unlike Vieda, she came to the UK in 2004 when Estonia became a member of the European Union. She was then 57 years old.

By then, there is a huge problem of unemployment. Families have left because of the lack of jobs. They have left for either England, or Ireland, Holland, anywhere. Whole families are leaving. I had a very good, caring husband. He passed away in 2002 – he had a lung cancer. In 2004

I retired. I was 57 and I decided to go abroad because I felt lonely. While my husband was still alive, we bought a house, an old house in a village. We had to repair it although my husband didn't want it, maybe because he already felt that he was not in a good health to manage it. But we women can make men agree. And he was such a good husband I can't say anything bad about him. So in 2004 I retired. I spent autumn in the village and when winter came there was nothing to do there.

So in 2004 I dropped in an agency [in Tallin] to see if they could find a job for me. So I was offered a nanny job in Switzerland. I loved it there. I worked in a family with a five-year-old girl. The mother was Russian from Rostov and the father was Italian. There were constant conflicts in this family. The father tried to take away the child from the mum, and the mum tried to hide all her weaknesses, like alcohol drinking etc. She didn't pay me in due time. It was a difficult family. So I came back to Estonia after a year of working with this family. They asked to come back but I didn't want to go to this family again. I worked there 24 hours because the mother was barmaid. After this job I went to Switzerland to work as a nanny next year, but in another family. It was also a very difficult job because I had to deal with a hyperactive child, some health conditions, you know.

So I came back from Switzerland and I was offered a job, through the same agency, in 2006 in London. So I decided to give it a try. It was a family. This time I had a boy, three month old. And I normally work from September til May because I have my house in Estonia, my garden. I like picking wild berries so I want to be there between May and September. So, this family, they found another nanny for this period but in September they called me again asking if I could come and help. You know, because the nanny they found was not very good. She liked alcohol, liked going to parties etc. so they wanted to get rid of her. So, I went to London and spent another nine months there. Then I got another job through my friends which was just for three months and now I work with a little girl.

Normally, I start when parents leave for their work and til they are back from work. So it's about 12 hours a day. I don't cook or clean, just childcare, and same responsibilities in all families I have worked with. It's not difficult. I can't say it is hard. I am strong physically even if I am 71. But of course, sometime it gets difficult if a child plays up, starts getting his first teeth, and with toddlers. So, in these cases I get tired easily as there are more responsibilities, and with toddlers you have to follow their every step. And the conditions are, and were, always good, no conflict. All families were young parents. The only thing I can admit is that I have a touchy character. Well, I always try to do my best, but if I am criticized (it happens sometime!) for doing something, like, for example, I didn't wash an apple with soap or something else, I am touchy.

In Switzerland people were very friendly. They would always say hello to you while passing by. But in England, it's different. If you touch someone, say accidentally for example, you must apologise. I was once criticized for not doing that. But I just didn't notice how it happened. And nannies, we were very friendly to each other and with English people as well who were there [in parks for example] with their own children. They liked talking to us, asking about my work and children with whom I worked. I had lovely children to care about. I socialize though only with the family I work with. But when I worked in London I met a woman from Estonia at a playground. She also worked as a nanny, and she was from a city nearby. So we socialized together, went back to Estonia together. It was great. And when I retire, I will go back. I get pension in Estonia, because I have a very good record of service so I have a good pension. And I plan to live in my village when I am tired of working as a nanny.

As well as jobs as nannies in other women's homes, childcare is also provided by childminders who work in their own homes and by nurseries and crèches, funded both by charities and government, and in the private sector.

Taslima, from Bangladesh, first came to the UK in 1997 just before she gave birth to her first daughter. She was married in 1995 aged 17 to a man who had lived in the UK since 1991. When she was interviewed she had been working part-time during the school term in a crèche in a local community centre for several years.

[In] 1995 I got married, and then '97 I came with my husband in this country, and then my housewife life started. And I've got three children, first my daughters' born and after that my son born in 2000. And then my father-in-law came, and I didn't study at that time. I was busy with, you know, my family. My husband, he has to work in full-time, and my father-in-law came. I had to look after him. He's an old man. Because I did study in my own country. I did my A levels, and I want to, you know do something; my plan was I wanted to do something. And after that, 2002, I was, you know, free a little bit and I went to learn English. And then I, you know, I decided to do like the childcare, that I can find a full-time job. And then I start NVQ Level 2, and then Level 3.

And my teacher she said 'you know you can apply for job'. When I finished my NVQ 2 she said 'you know, with the NVQ 2 qualification, you can apply any places'. And I said okay. And then I applied for the, you know, crèche worker job. And I apply you know, I did work three days, Tuesday, Wednesday and Thursday, like this is a part-time job, not full-time, because I've got three young children. So I can't do the full-time job.

The crèche worker job is only during the school year and during the summer no, but I can apply for the crèche worker, you know, in the private nursery. But you know in the holiday time, my children they've got holiday as well, summer holiday, and I don't want to go outside and they will stay alone. And again I need to pay the . . . childminding money, and when I calculate this I say no, only to give everything to the childminder. I decided not to do that in the summer holidays only, you know, only during the term time I'll do that.

And after a bit, they [the centre's administrators] say 'you can apply for the administration job as well' and I say okay because they say only three hours. They say they gonna pay me you know good money. I say 'okay, no problem'. I need to, you know, receive the phone calls, say if some Bengali men or women, because this area, most of the people is Bengali, our community. You know I can, if they bring one letter, I can read through the letter and I can explain them what like interpreting, what the letter saying. And like if it's the council repair section, I need to phone them and then I can help them. And some people come for photocopy, I do the photocopy, like tidy up, these kinds of work in the administration.

You know, I'm really comfortable with this job because the childcare is very, you know, stressful work. With the children, you have to look after them, feed them, you know. Now I know the child protection things, the child abuse things, we can't do anything with the child, you know when they're crying you have to not . . . every time what they're saying and which one is good for them, activities, these kinds of things. But I prefer the administration. I like the childcare as well but only I feel comfortable with the administration.

Waged domestic work divides into two different types, as indeed does unwaged domestic labour (discussed in Chapter 7). The first is the monotonous, repetitive everyday work of keeping homes and other buildings, including hotels, clean and well-provided with, for example, clean linen, washing and mending clothes for the occupants and sometimes providing meals. Although mundane, these tasks may also be done with love, care and attention. The second type of waged work, however, always depends on emotional attachments between the providers and receivers of the service. Looking after children is a labour of love, even when paid for, or so the parents buying care for their children believe and hope. It is also demanding work. As Taslima concluded, caring for others, especially when they are small children, is stressful and yet, like many jobs undertaken by women, it is under-rewarded financially. The assumption that women are 'naturally' caring, empathetic and in tune with others' needs, as well as willing to do the often messy work of looking after not only small children but needy, vulnerable, sick or frail elderly people is widespread. It influences the job descriptions, the pay and, above all, the gender of those who do the sorts of jobs described in this chapter as well as the work of nurses and elder care workers. Nursing and other hospital-based occupations and less professionalized caring work in 'homes' are the subject of the narratives that follow in the next chapter.

5

Body Work:

Nursing, Occupational Therapy and Caring for the British

For many years nursing has been a well established route for young women who come to the UK either to train in the UK or have left their own country as already-qualified nurses to take positions in British hospitals. The latter route deprives countries that often can ill afford it of qualified medical staff. As the last chapter revealed, some of the women EVWs trained as nurses in the 1950s, once they were released from their more menial tasks as domestics or ward orderlies in hospitals. Georgina, from the Caribbean, whose journey was included in Chapter 2, noted that for women from the islands 'nursing's what in those days a lot of ladies did'. Young Irish women and women from the Caribbean who came to be trained in the UK often found, as Brie and Bina explain, that they were directed into a lower status professional route than white British-born trainees. This restriction affected their entire careers.

As the post-war decades passed, nurses continued to come to the UK from a widening range of countries to become an essential part of the expanding workforce in the National Health Service. Migrant women were not only nurses – some women trained as occupational therapists or physiotherapists; also female-dominated occupations. Other women, perhaps with fewer professional qualifications or qualifications that were not recognized in the UK, undertook caring labour in homes for the elderly. In the earlier post-war decades, almost all patients and residents of care homes, especially elderly people, were white Britons and, as the narratives reveal, racist attitudes and behaviour were not uncommon. Senior staff and colleagues also had ideas about the new nurses based on stereotypical assumptions about their attributes and aptitudes.

'We did clean then': nursing as the NHS was established

Vieda explained in the last chapter that although she came to the UK as an EVW to work in a private home, by 1950 she had applied to start training as a nurse. Here she extends her story.

I met the matron and I said I wanted to do nursing. The time goes on and it doesn't look I shall soon go back to Latvia, but once I have my profession I can do anything then. That was 1950. I was 20 by then and, now, yes, from the beginnings, not straightaway, the preliminary stages, because for so many months, I forget, I had to stay with the matron as her maid in the hospital. To brush up or something. That was the rules or something then. Not as now, not many foreigners, after all I was still displaced person. If you wanted to go and work in TB units you could go anytime but I wanted to go and do proper training.

So, then after a while I went into preliminary training school and so I did my training in Salisbury. I lived in a room in the nurses' home. I had my food and uniform but you had to have your own stockings and food. It was mostly English girls and Irish, and one black girl and in the TB unit there were two Latvians. I don't know where they came from because it was quite different work and living conditions, and so, well yes, I did my training there.

After I finished my training I stayed for a while, first as a staff nurse on an emergency ward and then as junior sister. I was by then, I had been nearly three and a half years, was not so quick. I think I got some silver medal; they gave me a medal for some good nursing. I quite liked my job. In those days nursing was different. You were more, it was not so much machinery about, so you had to do work as well as nurse. Nowadays all the bandages and things come nicely packed up but then when we were on night duty you had to wash all of them and sterilize and put in drums and all the instruments and all the sinks. It was quite different. But we didn't know any difference and from one point it was a less infections those days than when you read now that in hospitals with all these sterile machines and so there is still a lot of infections. I don't know why.

And then I left there, left Salisbury and I went to work in Bournemouth in a private clinic for a change again. A little bit you know, sort of after a while when you are young, you want to move on or something, yes and but I liked my time in Salisbury. Except for one time when I was on night duty and the cathedral bells, oh, the nurses' homes were very close there and at six o'clock, nowadays I would like, but when you had to sleep, oh. Salisbury is a quiet little place and once they accept you, it is a nice place. I met people through the nurses and their parents and so on. Oh yes, it was not anything madly exciting or so but as nurses we were always invited to the officers' mess and so on.

Then I went to Bournemouth, to the private clinic, and sometime after I was working there, I was taken in to my future father-in-law, convalescent after an operation and there I met my husband when he came to visit him from London. He was London-born and English yes, and then after a while, I think I worked there two years and then I got married and came to live in London.

It was 1956 or '57 by then and then yes, when I married I stopped working. I looked after children and then house. But then later when the children were older, I started again as a part-time, only three hours a week, at a little local hospital. Then in 1976 he [her husband] died and I had to go back. Well, I was already working three hours, so I went back full-time.

Nursing is a well-established route to migration for women from Eire. Considerable numbers of young Irish women moved to Britain in the inter-war years, and they continued to do so after the Second World War. In England, they found that they often had to struggle against commonly held prejudicial attitudes of the English.

Aileen, the daughter of a policeman, was born in 1930. She moved to the UK in 1949 to escape a job she found tedious. As she explains, conditions in hospitals at that time were often poor and nurses were at risk of catching infectious diseases from their patients. Her route to qualification was more complicated than Vieda's had been.

I got an office job in the social welfare department in Dublin and it was incredibly boring. It was just paperwork and filing, very tiring and dull and I thought I would join my sister [in Southampton] as a nurse; I would do nurse training. I had never been in a hospital in my life, even as a visitor, so it was a bit of a leap in the dark.

At that time at Southampton Hospital, they had an annexe, Broadlands, and some of the upstairs was converted into wards for patients from Southampton, which, of course, was a very big port and a lot of sick and wounded people. And the nurses' home had been burned during the war. We had a very mixed lot of patients. We had a few TB patients and we had patients with syphilis, diabetics with gangrene, some very poorly people indeed and then some young acute people. There was one man there who was dying of TB and I don't think I'd ever been in contact with tuberculosis. So after I'd been there for six weeks I started to feel quite unwell, but nobody took much notice. And after a couple of weeks I started having breathing troubles and I had TB. So I was transferred into the hospital and I spent ten months in hospital. Ten months later I was going home and the doctor said to me, 'if you look after yourself, you'll have a few years with your family'. At that stage your life expectancy would reach 30, if you were very lucky, if you got teenage TB.

I went home and I didn't enjoy this kind of waiting for my demise and my mother used to worry terribly about me. I got so fed up that I decided I'd speed up the process. So I started going on my bike doing all kinds of things but the funny thing is, instead of getting worse, I got better. Two years later I was well enough to think about going to work again. At that time my sister had finished her training so I went to Leicester [where she then was], and I looked for a job at Leicester Royal Infirmary which is quite a good teaching hospital.

It was '51. So I applied at the Royal Infirmary in Leicester and I passed all their IQ tests and things. Then they saw my X-rays and the matron said to me, 'we'd be worried you'd be ill again, we can't employ you', and I was very upset about this. I was in tears as I was going out of the hospital and the assistant matron came along to me and she said they had a big polio, this was 1952 actually, they had a big polio epidemic at the isolation hospital and they're desperate for staff and they'll take anybody! So I moseyed along right away there and suddenly I was in training in infectious diseases.

We had a lot of children, all those polio patients,[1] and their recovery or not hinged an awful lot on nursing care. They would have antibiotics for any infections and the nursing care was paramount. Some patients, who nearly died, recovered; some sadly had some degrees of residual paralysis but on the whole they were doing fairly well. And at Leicester as well we had a lot of TB patients, acute TB, which we treated both with surgery and medication and nursing again. They did some very extensive surgery to help and we did get very good results. As TB and the infectious diseases were phasing out a bit when we had trained, we went over to all cancers, chest things and we had a lot of all kinds of chest diseases, which we treated. That was the 1950s.

We did clean then. We kept everything clean as we went along. We cleaned bedpans and toilets and everything; we had to serve meals and keep patients comfortable with a blanket bath, all the kind of things. Then later on we used to lay out the bed and in the isolation hospital, the polio nursing and all that was very, very acute and as well as what was regarded at that time as an infectious disease, so keeping clean was important.

And I stayed there for over three and a half years. I used to work in the night sister's office; we would look after the senior bits of the hospital overnight. We did the Florence Nightingale bit of going round and then I wanted to do my general training, when you were considered to be a proper nurse, an SRN,[2] and I went and did that, ENT and paediatrics, all the orthopaedic training and it was three full years.

Even though she was a 'proper' nurse, Aileen found she was treated as an inferior by some of the hospital hierarchy.

When I went to the first hospital [in Southampton], I asked if I could move in on the Friday night. And she [the matron] said 'move in Saturday morning.' I said 'if I move in Friday night, I won't have to have the flat for another week. I can give notice' and she said 'you Irish are always coming along wanting somebody to put a roof over their heads. The last Irish person I had was a man and he got drunk and he was arrested' and I said 'well I don't get drunk, matron, beyond the odd glass of sherry, so that is unlikely to be an issue'. So they weren't always nice, the senior staff, they would be quite ... and they used to say, 'the fools, the flirts and the failures and the Irish'. It never did us any harm. You have your successes and you have your disappointments and heartaches, but then you have your wonderful recoveries too.

In 1958, I moved down to a London hospital and we had a very big load of foreign staff there and we all got on extremely well. Jamaicans, girls from all different parts of Africa; we had a few Greeks and a few Italians, you name it, we had it. And our patients were all different nationalities. Some spoke French fluently, and a lot of Arabic, very good English and we got by. We did some very good nursing, corneal grafts and all the usual run of the mill things. We had a fair bit of tropical medicine too, the skin ward, we had neurology and everything. We never refused admission to a member of the Merchant Navy. We had a bit of problems there with the Russians because it was the height of the Cold War. They didn't want their personnel to stay in the hospital but then Yuri Gagarin, he was the first guy who went into outer space [in 1961], he was in London so we asked them [Russian patients] about Yuri Gagarin and then forever after we were friends. There was a Dock strike[3] and unfortunately it had very bad effects on the dock folk. So many ships came in that were affected by all the political and industrial upheavals. And then I got married and I had four boys.

I didn't work until my youngest boy was five in 1972. I couldn't get a job. They weren't very keen on part-timers. I would have been very glad to do one night or something but instead I actually worked as a cleaner. It was a big come down from being a senior night sister but you have to be versatile. My husband had two jobs. He did driving instruction and he was a chief engineer in a chemical plant, so we got by. I cleaned a fish and chip shop. I used to get up at five in the morning, get back for about eight in the morning. My husband would go to work and I'd take the children to school.

I went back to nursing in 1972. I used to do 9.00 am to 3.00 pm five days a week and I did some night duty. I did that for quite a few years and then I did day nursing at the acute hospital. I used to nurse accidents and big operations. At that time we were doing bypass surgery, femoral bypass surgery which there again was very good work.

And then I think I was about 57 years old, and I nursed quite a few elderly patients in their own homes. It was fine as long as you liked them and they liked you. In fact my sister and I worked together. There was one little old lady and my sister did her day duty and I did her night duty. She [the patient] was very happy. What they hated was having different nurses. Then I went onto work at the nursing home which I was there for about eight years, then that closed down. That nursing home closed down and I thought I'd retire but they headhunted us from different homes and I only stopped when I was 75.

I found with the older people, you had the mindset maybe of an older person and understood a lot of things, which you can't understand really if you're young. I was amazed at the old people and their experiences, their sense of humour, everything about them. Some people consider old people a waste of time but my goodness, they aren't. Demented people get very agitated and if you can give them reassurance and sometimes they're worrying about things that can be helped by listening and understanding. I think nursing, if you don't like it, you'll never be good at it and I think graduate nurses, now before they go to university, they should actually do some practical time in hospital to see if that's what they want to do before they start. The trained nurses now are being turned off and they spend so much time away from practical nursing, they haven't the continuity or the knowledge. It takes years to kind of learn so much. I think that caring is a very misused word. You have to know how to care and then you can do a lot.

Some of my friends are nurses; some are people I worked with in the 1950s but I do get very lonely now [after my husband died]. And I get very frustrated. You miss work terribly. And if I could do anything at all, I thought that people like me went round to schools and colleges and maybe had little talk and answer questions, to would-be nurses, to see how they felt, that would be useful.

'We thought we were doing the SRN': nurses from the Caribbean

Aileen trained as an SRN, a qualification that many of the young women from the Caribbean expected to achieve once they had completed their training in the UK. However, as they explain, it was common for them to be directed onto the SEN course, a two- rather than a three-year qualification, as the SRN was.[4] Like Aileen, they too often experienced discriminatory attitudes, and worse, from both co-workers and patients.

Brie came from Trinidad in 1967, aged 19, to start training as a nurse.

When we left Trinidad, we thought we were coming to the student training and then to discover we were doing pupil training and that was, that was annoying, because student was three years, the pupil was two years, but I don't think they told us that at the time. We thought we were doing the SRN, and when we came we were doing the SEN. So that was a little bit of a con trick. They hadn't explained that in Trinidad. I didn't know the difference between the two before. Well, we were quite annoyed, but, I mean, of course, we were already here and we did it. It was a mixed group of white nurses and black nurses. I can't remember how many of us were in the group at the time that came from overseas. But the majority were, you know, local girls. The training was quite intense, very good training. I must say it was a very good hospital. I enjoyed it thoroughly. I passed it and everything and was getting ready to go and start [in London], because I left Lancashire and, you know, got a job in Mile End in London, East London and then, of course, I went on and did my [qualifying] exam in, I think, it was Plaistow, passed that and as I was about to start the course discovered I was pregnant. So I just had to abandon doing the [SRN] training and just carried on working as an enrolled nurse, which I still am today.

Then, of course, I had my baby. By then I was married and we had moved to Hertfordshire. I had some time off, having her. And I think when she was one year old, which would have been in '72, she was born in '71, I went back to work in April '72 at Amersham General Hospital. It was fine. The only thing is, I started talking to a sister about starting my SRN and she really put me down and said 'what do you want to do that for?' I will never, ever forget it. It was really hurtful. What did I want to do that for? I'm good as I am, and all this nonsense. And of course when you've got, at that time of your life, when you've got children to take on and somebody says things like that to you, it does knock you back, so I never just started that again.

As a SEN though, we had responsibilities. We always worked almost like a senior nurse. We were in charge of the ward. I think in most hospitals that I've worked at, even to this day, you're still working, you're in charge of a ward, so, you know, that was a responsibility. And it was very physical work, lots of lifting. I've got an awful bad back from that. Even when I started training, I mean, when I started training you used to lift up people that were 25 stone and had to get them up the bed. There was no hoists and things like they have in this day and age. And sometimes it was sad just seeing all the, you know, the diseases and illnesses but, you know, you got by. I suppose most of the time it was, if somebody died but, and of course, if it was a young person died, it was quite heartbreaking, but you had to get up and get over it and move on.

Perhaps more difficult to deal with was the lack of respect from other staff. As well as the sister who discouraged Brie, she found doctors also tended to dismiss black nurses.

FIGURE 5 *A nurse from Jamaica working at a hospital in Eastbourne, May 1952.*
Source: George W. Hales.

To this present day, I find the doctors have no respect, as a black nurse. Absolutely none. They would bypass you and maybe talk to somebody else who's more junior to you than actually speak to you. And I just had to learn to live with it. The white nurses are treated differently up to this day and age.

I think my worst problems, really, was when I moved to Wiltshire. Things started off pretty nice when I first started because I was in a little cottage hospital. And because I wouldn't conform to the way they were treating the patients, it just turned nasty, and I had a rough time working there. That's where my worst nightmares started. It was awful. The staff, well, some of the staff, I should say, were horrible. I was told once to do something, so I thought I had to do something about that, and so I had to write a letter because that's the only way I thought I could be able to do it without getting too emotional. And when the person in question was on night duty, I went in and just asked to speak to her with the sister in charge of the ward at the time present and I just told her in the letter that I'd written, and if she did it again, I should report her to the Race Relations. And, I mean, I shouldn't have let her get away with it at that time. But I'm too kind a person, so she got away with it. But it was awful.

Where I am at the present moment, it's, all I can say is it's all right, but they're looking for the institutionalized[5] things that go on and I just have to giggle about it because if you get upset, you know, it does affect you mentally and I don't want to go down that road. And as an older person, I've given up. You've got to give up and let people do what they have to do, but I just tell them like it is. If I'm not happy, whether it's the doctors or whoever, you know, I just say, 'you know, you're just out of order'. They choose, if they choose to speak after it, because I've had run-ins with the doctors and they stopped speaking and I thought, you know, that's up to you. I'm not bothered. And whenever they choose, they're ready to speak again, I'm very civil. You can get problems with the staff as well but, as I say, I just, if I'm not happy with something that's going on, I just tell them it's out of order, you know, and leave it like that. If they choose to, want to speak, it's up to them. If they don't want to speak, that's up to them. And if you're going to get problems with the staff, you get problems with the patients and you just tell them. They can be nasty, call you names and stuff like that. They apologise when they feel like it, you know, and that's it. But, as I say, you've just got to let it go. You get mad, I come home and have a moan at my husband, and that's it, finished and done with, because I'm too old to be coping with taking on problems like that. There is still discrimination but I just try to shut it out. If it really upsets me, then I'm going to say something about it, and that's about it.

'It was discrimination in a very subtle way': Indian nurses

The differential treatment of applicants was widespread as women of Indian heritage as well as from the Caribbean reported. **Vijaya,** *who was born in Kenya and grew up in Uganda, came to the UK at the end of the 1960s.*

I came in 1968 to escape an arranged marriage. I had interview at Birmingham and I was accepted to start the training but the letter didn't state what training I was doing, enrolled training or RGN training, but because I had a plan for RGN[6] training, I assumed that I would be doing RGN training. It's only the day when I started, I realized, because the same student, pupil group started on the same day and I was in the group that were doing enrolled nurse training and not RGN training.

And there was nothing I could do; they wouldn't let me change over. They said I had failed my entrance exam, since I hadn't been informed before, and that was the reason I was being put into the enrolled nurse training. There was about 20 of us in the class and there was only two white people; all the rest were immigrants on the enrolled nurse training, and the RGN training, there was about 40 or 48, there was only about three or four foreign nurses, all the rest were white nurses. And that went on all the time but you couldn't pinpoint and say, 'yeah, this is why you've done this to me'.

It was very frustrating, because it was discrimination in a very subtle way that you couldn't do anything about it. Anyway, I carried on with my enrolled nurse training because if I stopped my training I couldn't get the visa, so for that reason I had to continue doing my training. But I did very extremely well in my nursing training and then I was, I worked about six months after I qualified on the paediatric ward and then I applied to do RGN conversion course. The person who was head of education, she was the one who was quite prejudiced, she was away on long term sick so I saw the deputy who was a very nice tutor I knew through my enrolled nurse training. I found out from him that I never had entrance exam for RGN. And he said, 'would you be interested in doing it?' So I said, 'yes I would like to do it'. So I did my entrance exams in the absence of the education head and I passed my entrance exam and I got into RGN training.

'It's a good thing to be kept on your toes'

Bina, also of Indian heritage, was born in Tanzania in 1959. She too trained as an SEN a decade after Vijaya. As she explained in Chapter 2, her father had traditional attitudes towards his daughters and she had to persuade him to let her train as a nurse. In the event, as Bina discovered, nursing was invaluable when her marriage broke down.

I was just 18 I think when I got here. . . . Well, first of all because I'd missed out on my GCSEs[7] back in Africa because we came over, I thought I need to get something in my hand before I start working. So I did college when I came here and took all the usual subjects except English. I don't know why I didn't take English. So anyway, because I could speak a little

I didn't think I needed that sort of thing, a certificate in it. So anyway when I started applying for the nursing posts you needed English on paper, so one hospital accepted me as a RGN[8] but then declined because I didn't have English. Well that's what I thought it was, they never told me sort of thing, so anyway I did the enrolled nursing. I thought, you know, blow, whatever, I'll just do what I can. So I don't know whether that was a mistake or not, you know, just doing the SEN to begin with, but I didn't want to rely on anybody and I thought, 'Here's a chance for me to do it and let's go for it.' You didn't think then too much as you do now, just coming over and everything hits you at the same time. An offer of training sounded glamorous sort of thing, so I just took it on. I think of it as positive, not negative. I could have moved on at a greater pace than I did really but I don't think I would make a good manager. I'm more a hands-on person anyway, so even if I had moved on it would have been less and less patient contact and more and more management.

So I went to Kingston and did my training for SEN over there, which is a two year as opposed to the three. That took me two years, I studied in '78, took me up to 1980. The people I trained with, I think they came from the Caribbean, some Afro-Caribbean, there were some of those girls but not Indian. There were some in the hospital but I didn't come across them sort of thing. Then I got a job in the same hospital working on a surgical ward and vascular, that sort of thing, which was quite good because for a first job it had a lot of responsibilities which was good to start off with. And there was an Irish sister there who kept us on our toes; sometimes it's a good thing to be kept on your toes, I think. So I did four years of that; so that took me up to 1984, coming up to 1984 I thought, what do I do now sort of thing. I thought 'I've never been to India, everybody's saying how good it is, it's different from everywhere else, why don't I go there, have a little adventure.'

So I left my job in '84, end of '84 and went to India for three months, just with a visa for three months. I liked it there, so I increased my visa to six months and then further to 12 months sort of thing, so I was there for a year. I was just, you know, visiting places, got to know a lot of people and they said you know 'why don't you come and work here?' And all this type of thing. I didn't have enough experience there to be working elsewhere. So, anyway I saw my husband there and I thought, this is something to start off on and what have you, but I came back without anything happening at that time.

I came back, did some agency work near my parents, in a hospital. I did that for a while; then they took me on as permanent on the same ward, and in the middle of everything I went back [to India] and got engaged and came back and got married and came back, all this type of thing.

I moved to Nottingham after he came over from India, you know sort of thing, sponsored him over, in '88. I was working in Nottingham, doing full-time, with internal rotation and all this type of thing. It was the hardest job I ever had. It was a neuro ward, so very, very hard, especially changing from days to nights and all this type of thing. And I think I did experience a little bit of discrimination in that hospital. Just back-biting by other nurses and that. I don't know whether that's classed as discrimination or not because that can happen anywhere but it just makes you feel as if it is because you're a different colour sort of thing. Most nurses were white. One or two were black but nobody Asian. I only once had trouble with a patient. Only once when I was left in charge and there was this African woman who didn't take to me because I was maybe Asian, and she complained and all this type of thing but management knew why sort of thing. It wasn't made a big deal of. I think that woman was discharged home. She could be discharged home sooner rather than later, so she went home and that was that.

So anyway he [my husband] comes over. He's not able to find a job because he's not very forth-going kind of thing, with the language and everything. So eventually he found one but he just wasn't getting used to the lifestyle and what have you. After that I had my daughter, and because he had friends there he moved over to Northampton. I stayed in Nottingham; we had marital problems and so he moved there and I stayed here.

After a period out of the labour market when her daughter was very young, Bina went back to work.

I found a job, instead of doing a refresher course in nursing again, which was a little bit costly, I didn't want to do that, I just found the first job that I was able to get and it was only Saturday nights sort of thing, just to bring a little bit of money in. So I did that for a few years and then I found a job. I wanted to go into primary nursing, primary care nursing, so a GP practice was appealing to me at that time because you don't have to work weekends and evenings and with the family and everything and you know, you have set hours, although I was only working part-time with my daughter going to school and what have you. She was younger then.

So I found a job in a GP practice, just to train me up. So I was on a lower scale to begin with; did that for a few years, then they took me on as a treatment room nurse, giving me more responsibilities. I could have only taken up practice nursing if I had experience behind me, a certain amount of experience. So I've done all the different things, straight after qualifying. The job I do is coming into use presently, all the other things, you know every so often you'll make use of them, because I've done ENT[9] and I've done neuro, so you get anything come into primary care, so you just don't realize when you're using the skills but you are, the experience rather.

I do some of the chronic disease management because there's a lot of that. There didn't used to be before, like looking at blood pressure problems, people who are on medication, finding people who maybe hypertensive and that sort of thing, the basic nursing duties you know, ear syringing, wound care, taking smears. The chronic disease management I'm doing more and more, the heart disease register I've just taken on at the moment, people who have had heart attacks or have angina or had triple heart bypasses and things like that, and I've been trained up on the stroke clinic as well, so those are two new responsibilities for me. And I also look at the practice's emergency drugs and all that kind of thing.

At that time I was still an SEN so I thought, if I want to do practice nursing, I want to do RGN. So I applied for the course at one of the colleges here and did that at home. I mean, you had to go to college every so often, but did it at home. That took me about two years and I eventually got the diploma in RGN. Having got that I could now move on to bigger things. The place where I was already at didn't need another nurse, so I had to look for another job. I did that and in 2003, I found one where I am at the moment, so it's a pretty nice job as a practice nurse, 20 hours a week. So, I'm in primary care now, so I'm not at the bed side, if you know what I mean. You see the patient for 10 minutes and that's it and most of them are able, whereas in hospital you're talking to them, you're building a rapport with them until they go home, and patients stayed longer then than they do now, they're just shunted out now.

On top of that, because we were still having real problems, you know marital problems, I found a second job as a self-employed person, sort of a nurse, going to do insurance medicals, so I'm doing that as well. That's just ad hoc, when you get the case you go and do it. So it's a good avenue to explore because I actually retired from the NHS when I had my daughter with the back pain. So I can only do a certain set of hours in the NHS without losing out on the pension. So in order not to do that, I'm doing the 20 hours and doing this where I'm not going to be losing out, but it's enjoyable as well. You're travelling and going to people's houses or work, wherever they want the medical done. You get travel expenses for the case, depending what's been asked for on the case, and you get paid separately for each, so I mean one case would be worth £40, the other would only be worth £23.

I saw an ad in the nursing bulletin, RCN[10] bulletin and I thought, 'well I need more money now, let me see if I can apply' and I got it. It's a bit jittery at the moment because I'd never done self employed before sort of thing and it's a bit harrowing to be doing something, with the tax and everything. Not the job but the taxing side of things because you've got to pay your own tax and national insurance and all this type of thing. Anyway it's becoming easier now, but we're now divorcing. We've both found rental properties and so I need the money. But I'm never going to go back to a hospital in this present state of culture. They are so short-staffed in the hospitals, and the shift work especially. I don't want to go back to that, so this [being a practice nurse] is ideal, eight to five or nine to five or nine to six, whatever it is, but at least you're coming home in the evening and no weekends, so I'll definitely stay in the practice nursing arena.

'I've never thought to call myself as an immigrant': the NHS and travel opportunities

Whereas the Baltic women thought of themselves as refugees and the women from Ireland, the Caribbean and elsewhere as economic migrants, other women who nursed the British saw their migration in a different light. Some like **Adele** *came because they wanted to travel, never intending to say in the UK permanently, nor, as she explains, thinking of herself as a migrant worker. Adele was born in Timaru, South Island, New Zealand in 1948 and qualified as a nurse in 1969. Less than a year later, she gave up her post to travel.*

I've never thought to call myself as an immigrant, migrant worker I suppose, and a lot of people do come over to earn money to send home. That was never a priority with me. Really I came on a working holiday but wanted to be totally self-supporting which is what I did. So I never, you know, if I was running short of money I would just take on extra shifts or do some agency work. I always kept myself, you know self-sufficient.

I worked for about six to nine months but I'd always wanted to travel and there were four of us during our training who were going to travel together. But if we failed [the final exams] we wouldn't go and unfortunately that happened, so my travel plans had to be put on hold. Then my cousin wanted to travel, she was very keen to see the world, so she and I then went overseas, came overseas. We decided to come to England because my grandfather on my mother's side was Scottish, so we wanted to start off over there and we had Scottish relatives, and perhaps work and travel from there. We originally came over by ship but it took us six weeks. It was much cheaper to travel by ship than to fly at the time – much longer but a lot cheaper.

So originally I planned, my intention to travel but to use my nursing to help me to travel, to help fund my travel, it was called a working holiday permit. Well, it only lasted six months at a time, so you had to keep leaving the UK and go to the continent and then come back into have it re-stamped. I think I did that three times. I was very homesick at first, especially in Scotland because although I had relatives there it was very, very cold and I had never experienced that sort of cold. And I was homesick. It was the first time I'd ever been away from home and I was as far as you could get really, and it was winter and it was just very cold and I think that made me homesick but I settled.

I got a job straight away when I came over, in the Edinburgh Royal Infirmary which was the big teaching hospital there, and I worked there for seven months, so that was November 1970 through to June 1971. I was very lucky because I had this flexible registration because of the standard of the hospital I trained in. There was a fixed number of beds and the right number of training hours, so my training in New Zealand was accepted over here. I became a staff nurse, working in a general medical ward. It was mainly people in for investigations, quite a high percentage of elderly patients, quite a heavy workload but I really enjoyed it because the nursing staff were very, very good.

It took a bit of adapting because it's just, I mean nursing basically is the same everywhere, but it was just the procedures were done slightly differently and there was different emphasis on parts of their, you know, how I'd changed, how I had to change but I adapted. It was just a matter of getting used to the new system, but I felt my training stood me in very good stead because there was things that I did that perhaps the English or the British nurses didn't do. Basically we learnt from one another really. At first though, a lot of them couldn't understand what I said and I couldn't always understand them either, particularly patients.

I was there about seven months and then I travelled because that was what I was doing. I would sort of work and then travel for say a month to six weeks, and then I came to London next and I did some agency work in London just whilst I was looking around. And then I became a staff nurse for the cardiac surgery unit in the Brompton Hospital. I absolutely loved that, I really did. I've never experienced that sort of nursing before. It was quite high powered and completely different to what I'd ever done but it was good and I learnt a lot. I was there for six months and then I moved across to Dublin, I moved there, maybe because I'd met an Irishman. It wasn't just that, because I wanted to go to Dublin, and my friend and I, my girlfriend and I went over and we both worked over there for nine months. And this time I worked in intensive care again because I had the taste of this by then. I was enjoying it. It was a general intensive care unit, patients following surgery, collapse and trauma, by sort of extending nursing experience there.

I was always on a contract but as long as I gave a month's notice, I work for as long as I liked. In those days it seemed a lot easier. There weren't as many nurses applying for the job and quite often I would just go to the local hospital and if there were any jobs, sometimes I'd get an interview that day. Now it's very much different; you've got to apply, you know formally in writing but there seemed to be a more relaxed attitude to it then. I used to carry my references around with me so if anybody wanted to see them they I could just produce them at short notice.

Adele married in 1977. Her husband was a quantity surveyor who moved jobs several times in their married life and so Adele continued to be mobile.

I worked in a hospital in Coventry for a couple of years. I was a staff nurse for two months but because I felt a bit more settled, I became a ward sister. So I had my own ward, a cardio-thoracic ward and I was there for three years. I had a very, very good team of nurses. I was finally able, I'd taken on a more senior post and I was able to put into practice all the things I'd learnt and it was a very busy ward as well because we were connected to an intensive care unit and we were the set-down ward, where patients were having heart bypass.

Then my husband's job moved us on. We moved to South Wales and I worked in intensive care there and I just had a staff nurse post because there were no senior positions going at the time. Then I changed to accident and emergency which I'd never done before. I just fancied the challenge and I stayed in accident and emergency for 15 years, so that was the longest I've ever been anywhere really.

My daughter was born 1984. I only took the maternity leave and then went straight back. I worked shifts so I was available, and also my in-laws who are local helped out as well but I never relied on nursery or anything like that. When I first went back to work, I did drop down to two days a week, and my husband and I sort of worked it out between us, and then I gradually increased my hours when she went to nursery and then, of course, when she was at school, until I was back up to doing my four days. I found that my work was very flexible, it was good. I'm now down to three days a week because I'm hoping to retire next year. So I'm keeping my hand in but I'm looking to sort of change my work–life balance a bit.

Nursing has changed too. When I first trained you didn't have all the hoists and things that you have these days, so it was all very much nurses having to lift the patients, and we were taught various lifts, but it was a very physical job, it really was. Things have improved and now of course you've got sliding sheets and lots of techniques. But it is still an emotional job, particularly working in intensive care and accident and emergency, because we have people brought in in cardiac arrests who we often lose, who die very quickly. Dealing with bereaved relatives can be very traumatic both for them and for us as well.

'Go for nursing and get a job': nursing in three countries

Parnal, who grew up in India, came to the UK as a qualified nurse in 2002. She worked first as a nurse in India and then in Singapore before she was recruited by an agency to work in a London hospital.

I was born in India, Kerala in south India, in 1974. I did my secondary school-leaving exams when I was 14. After than then I did my pre-degree courses. The pre-university course, it was for two years. After that two years I worked myself in a pharmacy to get some money to do my nursing studies, 19, when I was 19. Well, it's, my mum decided me because when my sister . . . all my sisters done their degrees and postgraduate and then they didn't get any job. So she said 'no, you go for nursing and get a job' and that was my family situation at that time. So she just pulled me.

Nursing school, it's three and a half years, in Kerala so I was at home. And I worked there for another two years. It was a nice period. Then I went to Bangalore. First time I am being out of my home town is when I was twenty-two, no twenty-four. I worked in a hospital, it's the cardiology unit and I was living in a hostel. Then after that I went to Singapore for one year. One of my cousin's brothers was there, so he helped me to get there. He paid all the flight charges, the agency[11] will send everything, so when I went there I paid it back to him. And I paid around what is equal to £1,200 to the agency.

I didn't stay long in Singapore. The Chinese are awful really, so we won't get the promotions. It was mostly Chinese; I was the only Indian girl there. The Chinese were there and then the Burmese girls were working as help girls and Filipinas, a lot of Filipinas. It was really nice [to live there]. It's very nice, very clean, less crime, yeah. But the pay is not bad, when you compare it to India, but there's not enough to make up a life there and moreover during that time they were not giving any permanent residency there so we can't bring our family there, so when I got the chance I came here [London].

So, I got selection in Singapore. Then I went back to India for my marriage. It was agencies again. And then matron came out to Singapore and had an interview. The first interview the agency is conducting, the second interview's conducting by the hospital. So they hired me. It was in cardiology. This time, the hospital, everything they paid, everything, even they pay the flight charges also.

And then I went back to India in February, I got married and it was May. In India it's all arranged marriage; it's only twice I met him before the marriage, the first one was for the engagement and he came to my house to see me. So 2002 I got married. It was May and I came here 2002 July, after two months and after two months my husband joined with me here.

Parnal had expected to start at the hospital with other young women but found that she was the only person picked up by the hospital driver at the airport.

The only thing there was nobody except the driver where I thought the hospital, somebody's coming and so the driver, he just picked me and he just dropped me there. Then I came to the reception and they asked what was the name and so they led me to the accommodation place. There was some problems with my work permit, so I was a bit late. I was supposed to come in June so I was late for one month. In the Home Office they lost my work permit and I don't know what's the real problem. The others from Singapore, all Filipinas, all were Filipinas. And there was one more Indian girl also. There was one more Indian girl was there, so we used to go out just to see the shops but when we compare the prices we were shocked. We always first time, we always used to compare the prices in pound and in rupees.

I started work after two days. Yes, after two days. Because all the other girls it was fifteen days induction programme which I missed so they can't do an induction programme only for me, so I started work after two days and that was my adaptation period for three months. So after that I got my pin number. It was in December, end of December I got my pin number.[12]

It is different nursing here because in India all the basics, relatives is doing the care and here I can't see relatives for everybody. The relatives, families they are not; they are just leaving the patient in the hospital and they will come and just visit the patient and must decide either they will take to the nursing home or to the house. There's not much of relations here, this is what I can see. So if my mum sent me in the hospital in India, I'll be there, me or any of my sisters. Family will be there for twenty-four hours. We will give all the care except the medications or injections but here in all the wards. No, all those things are done by the relatives in India.

It is really nice working in cardiology. Because it's a speciality unit, the staff is much better than other units, and the patient usually comes in an active state. So that once they are discharged then we can see the patients coming in good health and it does make happiness, you know. And the other units, like the chronic units, like the stroke, we won't see the patient is getting better. For six patients, there will be one nurse. Three, usually three, sometimes four, nurses all together. And during the night it is two staff and one health care. I prefer night because I got two kids. During the night they are paying extra, and if it's the weekend, if it's Sundays or Bank Holidays. I work in main with women but there's one man. He's Filipino. There's one more Indian girl, three black girls, and all others are Filipinas. And in the CCU,[13] Filipinas mostly, and two black, some English are there, I think three or four English and the remaining are Filipinas.

If I work days, I arrive at 7.45 am and hand over. In the staff room, that's where everybody will be. That will last for fifteen minutes. At hand-over time, they will give the name of all the patients who is in the ward and they give the person's condition, past medical history, and when the patient was admitted, all this. After that we will go to the ward, to our six patients, each bay. There's three bays each contain six patients. So we will get the hand-over of previous day's patient things and what the patient is waiting for, any complications, special medicines, so hand it all in the bedside. And after that we'll do the beds and we will do the washing and all those things we'll do. Then after that we'll go for the waste, then ten o'clock. After that we will do the observations, like pressure, temperature, that kind of thing, then the medications. Then by that time the doctors will come for the rounds. There is only senior sisters they will let on the rounds. And then we hand it over if there is anything special to note and that's our main things during the day time, like the morning time. Then the dinner break is one hour, so go have the break, then again the medication is, again the observations. Then family will come and we will answer their questions because three to eight is visiting time, so that time the families are allowed to come. And then just again the medicines at four o'clock. There will be patients that have got surgery, we need to take special care for those patients. If anybody is going for anything like angioplasty or angiogram or anything they need to prepare the patient.

Night is quite easy because most of the patients will be sleeping unless there is an emergency, so it is quiet and will go for our breaks usually. We are only allowed for one and a half hours but sometimes we will take two hours break; three peoples will be there so that one can have break. By six o'clock, from six o'clock is busy time. Six to eight o'clock is busy. We have to run to finish our work. Actually we can start the work early but we don't want to wake up the patients, we are giving consideration to the patients and let them sleep. So six o'clock, from six o'clock we have to do the observations, we have to do the medications, we have to do the blood CCTs, we have to do the right things, all those things. But not all the time we are working. Sometimes we will go and sit with the patient and then we'll talk to the patient.

They [patients] are giving us, to us, they are, they give us no problems at all. Some days where it's difficult, well that time I think, she's a patient, she will have her own problems as well. Sometimes they will misbehave. Some days they will shout, but whatever, he's a patient. Families also sometimes you know … maybe just because the families are more worried about the patient who's admitted. Often they will say … some days we won't imagine those things that they will say that to the nurse. So then investigations will come, so it is better to avoid that situations. So I am calling my seniors. It's seldom it is happening, the bullying and things, it's very seldom. And that time, if we can't manage the patient's family, we'll call the senior sisters but very seldom. They said there is some racist problems but here there is never.

I'm planning … I'm looking … because some of my friends are in US maybe after two years I'll think of going to US. My friend, she is living in Florida and she said the place is the same like Kerala, the weather and, you know, she said we can buy a lot of land there. Here we can't it's so expensive. And she said, is same as like our Kerala. There is a lot of our language; there's a lot of us there, Indian families, you know. I'm on a work permit here now, I'm not allowed to do other work [than nursing] here.

'I knew it would be very different here': working as an occupational therapist

*Travel was also the motive for **Meg**, a farmer's daughter born in Georgia in the USA in 1978. She 'always knew I wanted to work in the medical field, just because I had that matriarchal desire to help people'. Like Parnal, Meg found her position in the UK though a recruitment agency, although as an occupational therapist rather than a nurse. In the year that she worked in the UK, she discovered that her job was not quite what she expected.*

I started off doing a pharmacy degree and then got into chemistry, and then occupational therapy. After that I graduated in May of 2001, and then I went with a friend of mine to go and travel. I travelled to the Cook Islands in New Zealand, and Australia, because I went with a girlfriend and we had these names to go to of people in Australia.

So I did that for about six months and then came back home, got settled back in and worked for two years as an OT [occupational therapist] in a neuro rehab facility. I worked there for two years, got some experience and then after that I worked for an agency in the States that pretty much contracted me out. . . . I did that for about a little over a year. I spent three months out in Washington State, around Seattle, and then I spent three months in Baltimore and then three months in South Carolina, and then about four months in South Carolina, so I did that and that's when I decided to come over here, and then I came over here [to the UK] in August 2006.

When I was working for the agency before, I had everything packed. My mind was to travel and I was enjoying travelling, and I talked to a girlfriend of mine, who is also an OT, to come over with me. We decided to come over together. So I just decided basically to come here because I've never travelled in Europe. I like to travel and I decided that I can do this before I actually went back home and settled down into my career, but I mean, it's all the experience too. It's just an experience to come over here because the health care system's so different, and it's been very interesting to come over here and see the differences and learn. I've learnt quite a lot since I've been here too.

The job back in the States kind of depended on where I was placed. Average [hours] I would say between 7/7.30 in the morning 'til about 4.30 pm and 5.00 pm in the afternoon, depends, because I moved around so much, it just kind of varied to where I was. It was 40 hour weeks but sometimes I would end up having overtime because that's just how it works, you know, paperwork and patients to see, and then of course you would switch weekends as well too, so sometimes overtime there too. And if you look at it pounds and dollars, I actually made about almost twice as much back home as I do here. But actually as long as I knew I had enough money when I came over here to survive and to be able to travel and do the things I wanted to do, I was happy with that, because I knew when I came here, money wasn't going to be the pushing factor to come over here, just the sense that I would get some living here.

I knew it would be very different here in that even that it's the same language and culture and everything would be different. One thing I didn't realize is actually how many cultures there are here in this area. So working with different cultures was something that was new to me. But I didn't realize quite to the extent but it's different cultures here than what's back home in the States, so that was interesting and I didn't expect that. I kind of came with an open mind.

I didn't know to what extent to exactly what to expect here. First of all the training's different, whenever you go to a school, I feel like with our training, the medical, the scientific side is looked on that we actually dissect cadavers and have neuro-anatomy and physiology and anatomy classes, whereas here they don't tend to focus on that that much. It's not as in-depth, it's touched on some subjects but it's not as in-depth. Back home, it's more like physios. It's more like rehab-orientated and we're actually like moving the patients a lot and getting them up, whereas here, it's more like we're more like social workers . . . it's not focused so much on the medical need, or the rehab need of it, as much of it is as the discharge planning.

As Parnal had also found, once Meg arrived she was expected to start work almost immediately.

I actually arrived on 14 August with a friend and we lived in the dorms behind hospital initially for the first six months we were here, which is right by the hospital. So we arrived there, unpacked and then pretty much came to work the next morning. We lived there until about the beginning of March and we now live in a flat. We share a house with others, in the city. We decided to be closer into the city to just experience it.

For the job, we wear a uniform. These uniforms, they're uncomfortable, the trousers are very uncomfortable. I'm more comfortable in my own clothes back home because that's what I could wear back home, you know, just business/casual kind of dress, and to me that was more comfortable than actually having to wear a uniform, but it is beneficial in that you don't have to purchase clothes for work. And it does help in as far as identity in the hospital. Everyone's used to a uniform here and since it is such a big hospital, it's better that they can identify you as being an

OT instead of not recognizing your face every time on the ward. I understand why they have to wear to wear them but the actual uniform itself, I would prefer to wear my own clothes.

We are all women, there's actually no men, none. It just tends to be that way. Even back home OT is more of a female-dominated career I would say. I guess it's just the nature of the actual career but I've seen more men in the profession back home than I have here. It because I think that the career is based on a home function; a lot of it's based on like looking at what you do back home. It's like domestic things like washing and dressing. Of course, we have to assess patients to see if they need any help or if they need any equipment to make things easier, this type of thing, and we look at domestic things as far as having kitchen assessment and I think that that maybe is looked on more as being domestic.

Typically how the job works is, we are assigned a ward on the hospital and being on the medical/surgical team, the wards that I'm assigned are more of the vascular wards, like people who have had amputations or they have any vascular problems, surgical issues, so I tend to deal with a lot of patients that are in wheelchairs, which I have to measure for and order and properly fit them to see what they're going to need here and when they go home. So that means I have to teach them on the ward about how to use the wheelchair as well as the family too. We would get referrals from the wards too, from the nurses or the physios, or sometimes we refer ourselves if we see that the patient has a need for OT. So we have a referral chart, we go up to see the patient, do the assessment, the assessment consists of questions about how they were doing before, how their house is set up, so we can get some kind of idea of what it's going to be like when ever they go home. And also we assess them to see how they're moving around, how safe they are and how cognitive intact they are to make appropriate decisions. Cognition plays a part with safety too, so we assess them on the wards, right on the chart, the paperwork goes in, we continue to work with them, if we feel there's a need for rehab, that we need to continue working with them to make them stronger, to make them safer, to make them more independent in any areas, from self care to mobility to transferring on and off different surfaces, to like domestic areas, home safety, then we continue to work with them on the ward until they go home. Or if they were to go to another facility, we may have to refer them to go to another facility. In the meantime, there's always lots of paperwork and liaising to be done with Social Services or the family, to make sure that everything's set up and everyone's on the same page.

The Social Services will be involved in getting the care package set up for carers and it would be involved with any kind of community needs, safety needs that were to have when they go home, that type of thing, and the family needs to be aware of what's going on and they have to be involved as well too. And then whenever a time comes to be discharged, sometimes we go out to the patient's home to actually go and do a visit to the home, whether that needs to be us just going out to take measurements, to take a look to see what equipment would fit where and to recommend to the family how it needs to be set up for the patient to be safe, especially if they were to go home with a wheelchair, this type of thing, you really need to look at safety factors there that limits the patient, especially in houses in England, they're very compact.

Parts of the job are not dignified. I mean, being in that we have to go in to wash and dress assessments. You actually see the patient. I have no problem with it, you're so used to it in this profession, the surgery side, you may see blood, you may see something that's infected, you may have somebody who's incontinent, they're not able to control their bowel or bladder and you have to help them get that cleaned up, or help the nurses. A lot of times going into people's houses, you walk into any kind of situation you could imagine, whether it's dirty, there's bug infestation, there's faeces on the floor. And part of our job, if it's something that just needs to be cleaned or arranged when we go on a visit, then we're the ones, if the patient has no other family support and no one to do these things for them, then if we're able to do it physically then we will do things like arrange furniture, clear things up, at least where they have a path and it's safe for them to come to. I don't mind doing it because it's a help to the patient. I mean, I know it will benefit the patient, that's what my job is. It's not what I learned in school [at university in the US], no, but it goes with the job. . . . Sometimes I feel like this job here could be someone who was properly trained, and was bright enough and smart enough and responsible enough to carry the job and the workload, that pretty much anybody, whether they've got a degree or not, if they were the right type of person, could be trained to do the job.

I usually work with the middle aged to elderly. I have had probably only about a couple or three patients that have had an issue, mostly men, with me being a woman, you know, telling them what to do or just going through the whole self care, they would prefer a man to actually work with them in that setting. And not harassment really. If I have I wouldn't say that it would be common here and there, it wouldn't be anything that was like a full on sexual harassment issue. Of course, you get patients, some patients it's because of their diagnosis, it's like neuro patients or something, got a brain injury, they can be very sexually inappropriate anyway, whether they're male or female. So that's happened, of course, and those types of comments you tend to disregard because of course you know that they're not capable of knowing the difference and what's appropriate and what's not, but actual colleagues, no. I have had some patients that have been inappropriate that it wasn't based on their diagnosis and you just have to be firm but if it's ever to a point where you're uncomfortable with them, then again you would get someone to come in and help you.

If you need help, you always go to your colleagues for help, whether it's like physical or emotional or like any kind of support, emotional, psychological, any kind of support, I feel like as far as this team and other places that I've worked, that they're really good about offering any kind of support if I need that, whether it be on the ward or if it's that I have to leave a situation, I always try to be professional about it, if I have the patient screaming in my face, I say 'okay, now's not the time to discuss it', and then let the ward know that there's an issue, and then if I felt like it's something I couldn't handle or needed some advice, I would come down and ask my supervisor about it, or my manager.

In a month it'll be a year that I have been here. . . . My reasons are just come and work here; probably different than families that decide to come from other areas of the world. Most of my finances are going into travelling but I plan to go home [to the US] this September. This is just a year that I've decided to have just for myself basically and then when I get back home, I have decided to settle down and be more career-orientated.

'Embarrassed to tell people I work in a nursing home': institutional care work

As well as working in hospitals, many migrant women are employed in care homes, often those that provide residential care for the elderly. Here many of the same intimate bodily tasks undertaken by nurses, nursing assistants and by occupational therapists as Meg described, are performed by mainly unqualified workers.

Catherine was born in Kenya in 1978 and completed a teaching qualification in Mombasa, after which she taught at a primary school run by missionaries for three years. Because of unrest in Kenya, the mission sent her to the UK in 1998 on a temporary visa. After six months Catherine was given indefinite leave to remain in the UK. After working in a factory for three years, she moved into the care sector in 2004, working as a care assistant, a job that is unregulated and requires no formal credentials.

We knew the English but the English was not. . . . We couldn't understand it: the English from white people. So it was like you want to ask for something, the language barrier because you can't communicate. You want something, yes, you want a paper but the way they pronounce the word paper is not the same as we do it. It is English but the communication was too hard for us so you had to remain silent because you want to express yourself but unless somebody's very patient, who really, really wants to understand you, that was the only time you could be understood.

The worst of it, you know, it's a problem, the colour. When they [residents in the care home] see you they just wonder what are you doing in there. Yeah, it used to take time. Those days, most people were not . . . too many people weren't black. I think they were not working around here. They're old people you know, they're very old. They just wonder what are you doing and they just shout at you 'don't touch me, don't come to my room'. They send you away before they come to understand it. Although they appreciate what they do to them but later, you know, dementia. But you had to take time and you understand them too.

When you get to work, give them breakfast. After breakfast you have to get . . . no first you had to give them a bath. Wake them, give them a bath, give them breakfast. Okay, you have to play with them some games. After some games you have to give them maybe a cup of tea at break time at around 10.00 am, 11.00 am. After that take them to the TV room or help them to maybe meeting, helping them to brush their hair or do just silly things and then we give them lunch. After lunch, we just changing them their diapers and all this, tidy up, take them to their rooms. They can all have a nice afternoon just watching and all this. At around 3.00 pm we take them to their dining. They have their tea and then at around 5.00 pm we leave the work. Maybe other people come in and they drag them up and give them dinner, take them to bed.

Farah, *of Pakistani heritage but born in Kuwait, also became a care worker in the UK. Like Catherine, she was a graduate but the combination of motherhood and poor spoken English restricted her job prospects.*

I was born at Kuwait in 1966 so I received my early education over there, not really like intermediate, then I backed to return to my own country, Pakistan, and from there I did my graduate. My parent was a civil engineer over there in Kuwait and we used to live over there because there was a lot of facilities and many Asian people work into the Arab countries in Middle East. So when my father was retired then we came all of us to Pakistan. I have five sisters and one brother. I have an older sister and then there's me and then all of them are younger than me. I was 19 year old when we went back. In Kuwait, they are well off because my father was in a good post so they were well off, lots of money they had.

As soon as we returned to Pakistan I took an admission in a college for studying Political Science over there. For two years, it took two years to do the graduate at Islamia College, Peshawar. Then I married to my cousin and as they were British-born so I had to come here in 1991. I met him before because we were cousins and keep coming and going and we had friendship. When our parents arranged our marriage we were quite happy.

I came here after three months. First place we moved to Bradford because my parents-in-law used to live in Bradford. There we know a lot of people, loads of people. They were from same village as we are in Peshawar that's why. Friends of family, relatives, so it was not a strange place for me. And as I lived at Kuwait so I know how it will be, I have a little experience.

And then after one year we moved here because our relatives lives in here so they have told us that Oxford is a better place for education and employment. And I personally like Oxford, so when I came in here I liked it. Just for invitation I came here to see how Oxford is and I found it better than Bradford. And whenever I apply for job I got it straightaway.

I did work in Bradford which was cleaner job and I had to work hard to get this job here. When I came in here I apply for care assistant working in a home through the Job Centre Plus and I found it very, very hard as well. When I came in here I went to college as well, just to improve my language and speaking, spoken skills. My English, it was not that good as it is now. I was educated but our accent was like American-style accent because the books we read over there like American-style. And here the British people speak very fast English and it took me ages to understand them and everybody said that your written is very nice, you can speak well but why don't you understand them? And it took me a while to understand them.

Soon after I have my daughter [in 1993] I applied for care assistant and I got that job. And I worked as a care assistant for two years and afterwards I got a job in Matalan as a shop assistant.[14] Care assistant was in a nursing home: personal care of the elderly people. Sometimes they are very shouty and so I didn't like that. Because they were like, because of their medical condition, like some of them had Alzheimer's, some of them had no sense of thinking, they do not know what they are doing. I worked I think approximately 25, 26 hours. It was my choice. If I wanted to do I could do full-time but as I had a baby that's why I couldn't give much time to do the full-time work. My mother-in-law, her grandmother, looked after the baby.

I was so embarrassed to tell people that I am working in a nursing home so that's why I kept it a secret. Not from family, no, but from friends, yes, because in our culture it is not nice to work in an elderly people home because we have to provide personal care and everything which is not allowed to do so. I said I worked in a shop.

Some of the other staff are like discriminative type of people, yes some of them, but not all of them. Because when I was there, they give us the job which they don't give to other people and their way of communication with us is quite rude, it's not like other people.

After some years working as a retail assistant, and two longish visits home to Pakistan, Farah re-entered the care sector. This time she found a more fulfilling post which, as she explains, brought her contentment.

Then what I did one of my friends said that 'You are very good at benefit and you have like skills in three or four languages and I am leaving job in here, why don't you apply?' I say I never worked as a social worker. But when I applied and give them my CV they called me and they give me job for three months trial to see how am I doing because I never, ever worked as a Social Services and Benefit Agency related to this job, I never worked anything like that. And they found me good in everything, in running a group, in filling the forms and in other things as well. And if I am not sure about anything then I always asked my colleagues and my manager and all of them were very helpful and then after three months they gave me contract.

I used to work 16 hour but my manager and myself I found that it is hard to work 16 hour a lot with a lot of people so they offered me five more hours which is 21. It was 2000 then and in 2003 I did an Access course which is a Social Services type. And here my duty is for Asian community. We have to fill in their Disability Allowance form, Attendance Allowance, Income Support and all type of benefits. If a carer come here, come around, say we would like to arrange an appointment with GP, can you call the doctor? Then I arrange an appointment for them, sometimes I go with them, visit with them to the Job Centre if they are stuck in something for interpretation or to give them advice according to their point of view.

Sometimes I make home visit to fill in the forms if they cannot come to here because of the cared for person, the person they are caring for is not well enough or they don't have someone to look after him, then I go over there and fill out the forms and do the official work, whichever they want me to do. Also I run a group of the ladies, for Asian women carers, every Thursday one to three o'clock. And we organize trips to Birmingham, but not only Birmingham, London and wherever they want us to go, so three, four shopping trips we organize. Give them a break and chance for them to do shopping because many of them are carers so their husband cannot drive that far and some husband has heart problem and other problems so they cannot take them or drive them. That's why we organize shopping trips.

This group was started in 1995. And I took over in 2000. It's still existing and people are very interesting carers to join the group. Sometime we do the cooking classes, to tell them how the healthy food, not to eat junk food all the time. We can make curries healthy and other things healthy as well. Sometimes we call speakers from different departments like someone from meditation. And someone from Social Services, which service is existing now and how can you use the services, access to the services. That's what we do here in the group. Sometimes we don't call anybody and they can share experience with each other. So try to be thankful and say I got enough, not too worried about what you haven't got. This thinking makes lots of difference to me. Not only group benefits but it is for me as well.

I don't know how to say, Allah blessed me this place. These people [co-workers] are so nice people. I am out of words to say something good about this place. Sometime I think I was very patient in Tesco's, I was very patient in the nursing home so I am rewarded for that and I got a place in here. I am more than settled and everything is fine. I enjoy my job. I am ten year old now in this job, so they know I am very happy. It took a while to settle but eventually I am settled now. I will say I am still Pakistani but I am under the blessing of the British government.

May is also a care worker. Born in Thailand, the daughter of small rice farmers, after leaving school, she worked for several years as a hairdresser. She married and had two children but was then divorced. She then married an Englishman whom she met in Thailand and came to live in the UK permanently in 2009. Her children stayed in Thailand with her ex-husband but she stays in touch with them.

I met my boyfriend in Thailand after I divorced. So I have two children and my ex-husband. My marriage with my husband is ten year, maybe more than ten years. With my boyfriend we got married in 2008–2009 [in Thailand] and he bring me over. We do visa everything, my documents everything being correct. I met him in 2006 in Thailand and I like to come on holidays to England. He did visa, everything, gave me money for everything. I came then on holidays for try, for learning together about six months. Then in 2009 I came to stay.

My first job in the UK is a carer. I started in June 2009. When I'd been in the UK for two months and after that I could find a job. And my [new] family quite supported me, take me everywhere I applied to a job. And I am lucky because my father-in-law knows about the manager in a care home, this care home where the job was. And I got a proper job. I am not very good in English and I learn a lot from old people and I like it and I feel comfortable with them. I am happy.

They give you learn, they train you two months before you start. You have to follow the team, follow about what they were doing because you don't have any basics. You have to follow them, what they are doing, keep an eye on them, learn. Something good you learn it, something bad – quiet and don't tell them.

You have to learn for three months and then you go to this manager to be interviewed about how you feel. 'You like the job or not . . . you happy with the residents or not, you happy with your colleagues or not?' . . . everything. Yes, I am like 'I am fine and if something was wrong I didn't copy this; I copied good things.' And after that you have training about how you move them, safely moving, handling, something like that. After training they give you a feedback form you have to report every three months about how you feel. And after you work for one year you have something to offer if something is different in your mind in your opinion to tell them something is good or something is bad. They give you a choice if something is good, do they need to include something or not? I said fine.

You start from early morning. You knock into their door and have to say 'good morning. Today, what time do you prefer to get up? Do you want to get up now? You like me helping you?' It looks like a house, a lot of rooms like. It's quite big company. Some people buy their own wheelchair, some people can't work anymore and they can't buy a wheelchair. I don't need to hold them when they need some helping, you have two people to care, it's like double care and single care. Single care is like for a person who can walk, they can move properly. When we are two carers, it's for people who can't move really.

It's 45 hours per week. And I start from seven o'clock to five o'clock for two days and seven o'clock to two o'clock on Wednesday, and after that I have to work on weekend on Sunday from four o'clock to nine o'clock. It's overall 40 hours per week but they give you 45 hours just in case if some carer gets ill and they contact you and ask if you are available. If not they ring another carer. They ask 'do you want six hours more or seven hours more?' Other carers are Philippines, Thai, Poland, Bangladesh: a lot of international coming. We try to learn and understand together. I very much enjoy. I like the environment. I can learn about my English I can speak with original old people there. I enjoy myself, I enjoy everything. It's easy for a carer, more easy than a cleaner.

I never worked as a carer before. I am a hairdresser. I still do hairdresser for the residents as well, for old people as well. As a hairdresser I work when I have a day off. Like today, I have a day off, I go to the care home for two hours. It's a different pay. The person pays. They pay themselves, not company. They get pocket money. The manager looks after their pocket money. He contacts me if someone needs a hairdresser because they can't have any valuables. They keep their money in a safe for them.

These migrant women – working as nurses, therapists and carers – are an essential part of the labour force. Without them it seems clear that hospitals and care homes would not be able to provide an acceptable level of care for the many people in the UK who are sick or who, in growing numbers, are ageing and require support. The stories here spell out in almost excruciating detail some of the intimate and often undignified aspects of the daily tasks that women migrants perform, often for low pay and relatively little reward in terms of support from co-workers or from their patients and clients. They also document the changes in the general health of the population and in conditions in hospitals over the post-war decades, as well as changes in general attitudes to women of colour. The epidemics in the 1950s mentioned by Aileen, including TB and polio, are largely in the past, although TB is now returning among homeless men and women in some of Britain's larger towns and cities, sadly often among new migrants who have been unable to secure employment.

As the stories show, women decide to migrate for a range of reasons, sometimes connected to family circumstances but also to larger-scale events such as civil war. For others, migration was combined with a desire to travel, as well as to work. The stories reveal the connections between employment, marriage and child rearing, and ways in which these are combined as well as showing the sometimes unexpected routes between different types of work taken by these women, as they change jobs over time and in some cases do two jobs at once. The often, though not always, more straightforward career paths of women in professional occupations are the subject of the next chapter but many of the same dilemmas about combining paid work and domesticity and motherhood face these women too.

6

Brain Work:

Banking, Medicine, Scientific Research and Teaching

There is a tendency to assume that all migrants who come to the UK are from poverty-stricken backgrounds, anxious to find any sort of work to support themselves, and sometimes their dependents, in the new country. However, skilled migration is also an important component of the flows of people into the UK, often of professionally qualified workers who hope to gain further credentials or experience that will improve their career prospects. Some of these migrants come on short-term contracts, others for longer periods, and many remain in Britain for longer than their initial intention. Women bankers, doctors, and academics are among highly skilled in-migrants and their working lives are the subject of this chapter.

Banking was, until the crisis of 2008, regarded as the leading sector of the UK's 'new' economy, a knowledge-based industry par excellence and one that offered its key employees large financial rewards and often an exciting life, albeit paralleled by long hours. It is also an industry in which women are the minority among employees, sometimes subject to unequal treatment, if not outright discrimination and harassment. Women are also a minority, at least in the most senior ranks, among lawyers, hospital consultants and university researchers and teachers, although in all these professions women's representation has increased noticeably, especially since the 1970s. As more and more young women attend universities, particularly in the more developed economies of the world, they are gaining the credentials necessary to enter the professions and other well-paid occupations.

The women whose stories fill this chapter are more likely than many women migrants to come from what was once termed the Old Commonwealth – those countries with a largely white population – and from the USA or continental Europe, although they do not all come from developed economies nor from these parts of the world. One of the common threads in these narratives, which differ from the working lives recounted in previous chapters, is the greater likelihood of working in a male-dominated environment and the challenges that this involves for women.

'The brokers are the beasts': working in the financial sector

Caro is a senior sales executive in an investment bank in the City. She came to London in 1978 after taking banking exams in Canada and started work selling bonds. Her reflections in early 1993 of the macho and sexist workplace culture of banks over her 15-year working life now seem shocking, although still not uncommon as later stories reveal.

I wanted to be a forex (foreign exchange) dealer but I didn't get that job. Forex really is the animal farm of the world, where the brokers are the beasts. One of my interviews was at 7.30 am which was unheard of then, way before people were getting in at 7.00 am as they do now. I got a job as an assistant, selling bonds. I'd no idea what bonds were, but like a lot of people you just fall into these jobs. There was a huge recession then [in the late 1970s], high interest rates and a bear market[1] in bonds. I do sales and so I have a lot of customer contact. There are all sorts of clients out there and some are horrible. One of the luxuries of being older is you don't have to speak to people who are rude. At the beginning you are given the dross, people no-one else wants to speak to.

After working for a US-owned bank, Caro moved in 1987 to a more old-fashioned, or what was then sometimes referred to as a gentlemanly, British-owned bank.

They were a bit surprised by my aggressiveness here. I suppose it has worn off. I'm perhaps a bit more genteel now. But it's still a world where you have to be hungry for success. It's a basic hunger and wanting to do it. Does the excitement pump the adrenalin round your blood system? Outside critics talk about bankers as parasites of the economic system, but money has got to be moved around. The excitement of moving markets! When people criticize speculators, they forget it's not the forex dealers who've got the muscle. The people with the biggest muscle, with huge amounts of money, vast amounts of money, are the pension funds. So it is probably the pension fund money that's driving sterling down.[2]

In describing her working day, something of Caro's aggression is evident in
her dismissal of some of the fund managers she deals with.

I get in about 7.50 am. Long gilt futures open at 8.30 am. The pit closes
at 4.15 pm and then opens again until 6.00 pm or 6.30 pm. I don't run a
book – I'm sales so I'm purely an agent with clients. Most of my clients are
insurance companies and the IMGs (Investment Management Groups)
who manage pension fund money. Lots of UK fund managers don't get in
until 9.00 am or 9.30 am so a lot of them still keep gentlemen's hours,
having their second kipper in their club and things like that. People are still
having their soldiers with their boiled egg if you get in at 7.00 am.

As Caro explains, her clients are mainly men, although there are growing
numbers of women working in sales.

My clients are mainly men, although I have had some women clients.
These days there's quite a lot of women on sales but not so much on
trading. I think possibly it's because you're speaking to clients, rather
than just sitting there, making prices, running the book. It's possible that
women have a few more social skills, communication skills and social
skills. One of the putdowns in the market is 'Oh, she's just smile and dial'
and I suppose if you took it to extremes, that's just what it is, but you
have to have the technical skills too. Being a social charmer is not enough.
But anyone in a trading room has to be able to assert themselves. If you
are not aggressive, you get walked over. I mean, the bullies go for the
weakest person, never for the strongest person. They go 'oh, there's a little
chink in the armour there. We'll have a go at that and see if we can open
that up and make that bigger.' They either find out that they can, or find
out that they can't and move on to the next person. If you allow them to
do something, you just dig yourself a grave basically. I mean about being
a girl. 'Get the coffee.' 'No.' You just say no because you are there to sell
bonds not to get the coffee.

Being asked to get coffee is not the worst of the problems women working
in banking in the 1980s had to face.

The trading room here is actually quite genteel. It's certainly not the
worst. You've got to go to the money brokers, the forex brokers to get the
worst. They have blow-jobograms in the office in full view of everyone
else but if you react badly they'll go for your jugular. You just have to
take it with good humour and tell them they're being silly, being boyish
again, you know. They don't do it to me; I don't get attacked a lot these
days. I am not the target but I have been. I've had a condom on my
phone. I got in one morning and there was this condom on the mouthpiece.
I dropped it in the bin and found another handset. I think he was

disappointed because I didn't burst into tears and rush off to the loo. Artistic sensitive people of this world wouldn't fit in. You have got to have a thick skin, and also be a team player.

The work culture is full of tension. It's a basic animalistic sort of job. People get very wound up and have to be able to release tension. I can blow up, have an argument with someone which last 30 seconds and that's the end of it. You can't have simmering raging. Some people don't understand when I am shouting at them what I am doing but that's the way I learned and I think it's a great system. You can have good rows with people and know you are still buddies with them.

I don't do as much entertaining clients as I did when I was younger because I can't stay up so late at night as I could ten years ago. Then I could go out dancing til two in the morning and still get up and do a proper day's job. I still see my clients quite a lot, but not in the evenings. Occasionally I do, but that's probably through choice and now I chose not to. The City's a fun place to work. You earn a lot of money. It makes you tough and independent. You become quite a strong person in all sorts of ways. Everything is possible. You see the upper limits of the horizon. You always go for the higher reaches. You don't settle for what's just there.

Kate, *a New Zealander in her early thirties in 1992, is a team leader in the systems section of the same City bank that Caro works for. Kate provides support for traders, and often works extremely long hours.*

I came to the UK in 1982, after my degree. I wanted to see Europe so I worked in wine bars, things like that. I started doing temporary work, in a back office of an American bank in foreign exchange settlements and after three months they asked me to join permanently. I got involved in testing a new system and so transferred out of the back office settlements department into the systems department as a trainee analyst. I stayed there for four years and ended up running the project. Then I left and moved here [a British owned bank].

I am now the project manager, looking after high risk management products. If we are working on major implementations, a typical day starts at 9.30 am, dealing with programs, users, working specs and testing, and I don't leave until 8.30 pm or 9.00 pm, and often come in one day over the weekend. Once implemented and in the maintenance phase, I usually leave around 6.30 pm or 7.00 pm.

The users of the system are pretty much all men. Traders are generally okay. I get on very well with them. But there is what I refer to as the boys' club. They are sort of quite young and they go out and socialize, and so there is an element of, you know, camaraderie, that boys will have together but women, you know, you can't be one of the lads really.

In our department, there's a very distinct split into boys and girls. There's a group of about ten men who hang around together all the time. So the women decided to also do things together. You know, lunch, go out after work. I find it helpful being a woman though, in my technical job. There's times when it's quite useful to take people unawares. They are expecting a man to come down and deal with a query. I show up, so it puts them off guard a little. Maybe I get a bit more sympathetic response though there are times when it works against me, particularly with the older men.

But there are disadvantages. There's always that label 'you're an emotional woman'. I get that a lot. If you are at all strong and forceful, if you raise your voice at all, you're immediately labelled as emotional. If a man does it, no, that's being assertive. It happens all the time. The perception of a person who is noisy and aggressive and direct is very different. My style of management is forceful and very direct. I've just been involved in discussions with a man who works for me. He does not like my style of management at all. But I think that's because I am a woman and he thinks I should be sweet and, you know, and sit back and all of that, whereas if I was a man, he'd just be getting on with it.

But the users [traders] are very emotional too. They are very demanding in terms of getting solutions to problems immediately. They can be very emotional – lots of throwing tantrums. You just have to let it wash over you. You have to take the point that they are very upset about something which has gone wrong, some part of the system that maybe we should have made sure wasn't going to go wrong. You just have to forget about the emotional stuff and deal with the problem. I typically wait until they've calmed down a bit. Then I talk to them about what is a reasonable expectation in this case. I find the particular group of users I have got now a bit difficult. I walked down on to the trading floor the other day and one of them said something like 'oh, here comes the blonde' which is not something they would say about the guy who worked for them before me. But that's an element of that boys' clubbism, you know and it just try to ignore it, or, if I am feeling particularly jaded, I'll make some sarcastic comment. But I wouldn't be able to work for them if I said something like 'that's a really sexist comment'. They'd say 'oh, you've got no sense of humour. That was just a joke.' So, they do treat me differently than if I were a man. I think the City is changing in that there are more women coming in at the bottom but there's certainly a lot of the glass ceiling still about.

Employment in banking expanded rapidly after the 1986 Financial Deregulation Act. Indeed the financial services sector became a key part of the economic growth of London through the 1990s and into the new millennium, before the crisis of 2007–8. Despite the shift to screen-based trading and away from the frantic atmosphere of the floor or pit, women still found it particularly hard to find work as traders and the still-dominant masculinized, long hours culture of finance in general continued to make the workplace uncomfortable for many women.

'It's another country': European women in finance

Eidothea, who is Greek, came to London in 2006, aged 25, after graduating in Athens with a masters degree in economics and business.

My first job, my first job relevant to what I've been studying, proper job, was here in the UK. I did work at university but not full-time. Because my course was maths, I used to teach maths like a private tutor, for kids who were in high school and junior high school, along with maths and physics. So that was one kind of job that I did, more or less all the years that I've been through university, and through the masters as well. And then as well I was working in shops, part-time like in Christmas, in Easter, in the holidays, just like you know, staff in the retail shops, with clothes and things like that.

I came because the whole, I didn't come to do job hunting here, I just got offered this opportunity [in Athens] to come, so I thought it was a great idea to come over. For me it was very tempting to come and live in a different country. The job was very promising, in an industry I wanted to be, and it was booming here and, you know, it's the place to be in Europe compared to Greece, where the market's much more limited. And at the end of the day I had nothing else to lose since I had nothing else waiting, nothing else planned, so I just took my chances and came over.

This is how it happened. When I was leaving my masters, my professor that was in charge of my dissertation is a director in the fund, so while we were finishing the dissertation he just asked me if I would be interested to participate in a project for a hedge fund in London, to build up this proprietary trading model. It wasn't paid or anything, and he just said to me 'you know, it might develop into some kind of job that might be between here and London if you're interested'. And I was like yeah, you know, I was like besides myself. So I worked for it for three months or so in Athens, and then we came over too, and saw it in the fund, the guys, and they liked it and so I just went home with an offer, to come and work in London. It was something completely unexpected. So that's how it happened.

Now I work for a hedge fund as a research assistant, training in order to become a trainee analyst. The working hours were long, well, more than eight hours clearly, right? It's more than, towards ten, eleven hours, everyone was working like that and since I was junior I had to work more. . . . Hedge funds generally by nature usually are quite small, so when I first joined we were . . . one, two, three . . . we were five people, I was the sixth person to join. So it was quite like family kind of situation, small group of people, small team, mainly men. Only another girl who I was working with. I was single as well, more or less, so yeah, the climate was very nice, very friendly. For me it was very good environment as well, since I just came to a different country and everything and. It took me as well time, right, to get to know, to see how to operate in the new environment and everything. So from that aspect everything was absolutely fine and great.

My colleagues, age-wise first, as I told you they were like five males and one female. Age-wise the males were, I can give you a range, they were between 34, 35 to 40 max. They were mixed. There was one Italian guy, one French guy, two English guys and one half-Spanish half-Peruvian, whatever that. And the girl was English as well, so we were quite multicultural aspect, me being Greek as well. The males were all married, in the beginning of their families as well, some having some kids and some others not or expecting. The girl as I told you was single. Some of them had MBAs, some of them had just finished university, and some of them were just typical Essex boy who had just finished high school and went straight into the City and you know, type thing. They were like, they have already built up their careers and they moved and tried to do their own business. I was the one who was new.

So, I was gathering research; I was following analysts to their meetings. At the same time I was doing the part that I was employed for initially, which was to run a proprietary trading model, in terms of portfolio optimization, and suggest, advise basically the rest of the team with their results. The risk management and stress testing, do lots of programming and computing and build up all the models and everything for the fund, and for reporting regions, for day-to-day operations, attending some company conferences, writing notes, at meetings.

It was a bit hard work initially because it was very new for me, since I had parts that I already knew but there were many parts that I had no idea because I studied maths, and I had to study as well the side for the economic bit, in order to understand exactly what's going on. So at the same time I was taking courses and, you know, add up on the training. But I loved it. It was great. Gradually as time passed by and I accumulated experience and knowledge, at the same time, I got much more responsibility so I was more or less at the same level as the rest of the team in terms of things in day-to-day operations. Clearly I have to double-check things before, you know, I can have initiative but I have to double check with somebody more senior still, and get approval in order to go on with things that I need to do, that would impact on the profits and whatever, because your actions are completely linked to the profits of the company.

It's a small company so, whether you like it or not, you get involved with all sorts of things at the same time. I can say that every year I was getting more and more things to do and better paid. I still work long hours but now I think I just manage my time differently now, because initially I was just completely bombarded by information and I was trying to, you know, absorb everything that was going on around, and outside work the addition studying I had to do which I do still do because, you know, you, you always have a few days, you always have to study and learn more things, but I distribute my time better. So I have periods where I work very long hours, I can work like twelve hours, but there are periods when I can be more relaxed, be up to nine, eight, nine hours, something like that.

I haven't experienced any discrimination, not at all. I haven't felt, not because, neither because I'm female nor because I'm not English. Because the industry is very multicultural, by definition, it never occurred to me that people would approach or talk to me differently because I'm Greek or whatever, at a professional level. And neither because I'm female, even if it's a very male-dominated environment and stuff, no because I think, you know, how people tend to approach. Clearly, usually when they can see you might be like, oh you know an underdog, blah blah blah, but I'm sure that you can sit down and make sure that they approach you as equal and just put all the other stuff on the side.

Even though finance has an image of being quite macho and masculine, I don't suffer at all, from it at all, because let's say on my own I'm a little bit more aggressive. Personal level, well through university, you know, and masters, and everything that I've been doing, I'm used to being in a male environment which is much more . . . let's say I don't have the girly girl kind of attitude and I'm more, I like working with men because of that reason. It's more tough, and it's more straightforward, it's not too much flapping and doing around, it's very clean-cut and so I'm used to it and I adapt to it very well and it doesn't bother me at all.

I'm planning to move soon and go somewhere else and, you know, try to do even more and kind of climb up. Yes, and then when I feel much more established in what I'm doing and much more confident, then I'll be able to relocate this year and sell myself better. I'm looking to go somewhere else, because I've been with the same company for more or less three and a half years now. I'm a bit tired. It's been a quite tough year, let's say, couple of years, for the whole industry[3] so I'm exploring other opportunities right now, in order of changing job, trying to remain in the same sector, and remain in the hedge fund world, which I know, I know how it works, and I don't know yet. I'm currently, you know, searching around the place. Maybe here or maybe in Asia, I don't know.

Amalie also worked in finance. She was born in Paris in 1971 and moved to London in 1997, aged 26. Her father was a television journalist, and her mother initially an academic lawyer who then went into business for an advertising company.

I was a lawyer in Paris. I did a law degree and a business degree, kind of an MBA, and also I was a lawyer but for corporate law. So I was working at a law firm at the time, and I met now my husband, but he

FIGURE 6 *Women employees leaving Lehman Brothers after the crash, Canary Wharf, London, September 2008.*

wasn't then. And he was there for six months, there in Paris. He went back to the UK and I decided to join him. He's originally from Zimbabwe but he's been living in London forever. So I came partly for personal reasons, but it was also I wanted to have an experience abroad. I've always wanted that, and UK was quite good for me because, you know it's another country but not far from France, I didn't feel I was going, you know, very far.

I applied while I was in France. I applied to lots of law firms, couldn't find any job because at that point, in '97. Law wasn't very international in terms of, if you know French law, you just couldn't practise here. It didn't work out. So I applied to lots of law firms, couldn't find any job, and so I applied to banks at the end and I found a job in a bank. There's a kind of network of old people from my business school, they were some of them were working in that bank, and I sent a letter to them. It's much easier to start like that because they can just point you in the right direction. I mean I knew nothing about banking, so it was you know much easier that way. I just sent, I just sent letters to all the French people you know in banks in London, and one, he called me back and said 'you know you should come here for an interview'. I mean I didn't know him, only because he was in the network, but I didn't know him personally. We had a book every year published of you know everybody in the world working for, from the business school I went to.

The job was an analyst for a bank in the City, doing mergers and acquisitions. I was there about three years. It was very long hours. Quite hard. Very hard to have a life outside, but very good experience. They trained me really well. It's what I really liked about that job, they didn't expect me to know anything. They just knew they would train me. And it's very often the case when you start in this country, they don't expect you to know much. They want you to have a good background in terms of, you know, a good degree. They want you to be open-minded but they don't need you to know what to do straight away. They, they quite, you know, they don't mind training you, which is something that wouldn't happen in France at all. So that's for me, it was very new. They trained me for a long time, as everybody in my year, everybody you know hired that year was trained in the same way. Not just me. So it was a very good environment to work because they treated me really well. First of all we spent time in every department of the bank. There was always like senior people just being with you all the time and making sure you were, you know, you were in very different kind of jobs, to make sure you knew everyone, you started to learn about everything. It was maybe a year process.

So it was really hard and after three years, I just couldn't do it anymore, I had no life, I just was working too much. I was more or less started at about 9.00 am, but then I was working from 8.00 am to midnight, any time really. You know, in banking there's really no limits. When there's a deal, just you are expected to work any time, it's just the way it is. The pay was good at the time, it was exactly, you know, for that kind of job, a good pay for the hours we were working, you know, with the bonus.

I worked mainly with men. I was the only woman on the floor in our department. I was the only one. Because it was such a tough job, it's not always something that women want to do. So it was really men and it was quite young people as well, and very international, lots of Europeans. About 20 analysts. More women started to come at the end, when I left, more women were coming. But after a while you know, a woman wants to get married, have more of a normal life, and maybe have kids and, it doesn't suit with that kind of job.

After I left the bank, I went back to law for a year, in another law firm in the City. When I applied after I left the bank, it was a bit easier to find jobs in law firms, because they were slightly more open to foreigners. Banks were open to foreigners much before, but then, in 2000, it was easier with law firms. Suddenly they just opened more to foreigners. So I applied to one. I was a solicitor. Well, I wasn't a solicitor yet. I was a French lawyer but then I did a conversion course at the same time, to become a solicitor. The hours were slightly better than the bank, but still not you know, very, you had to be flexible very much, so it's still not perfect with kids obviously, so I left after a year, when I had my first son. Now I am back but on reduced hours for now.

'Work is where you are not yourself': an Indian in UK financial services

Posha is Indian. She was born and educated to masters level in Bhophal ('people know of that place because of the Bhopal gas tragedy[4] that happened') and spent several years as a highly paid and hard-working banker. Her experiences in India are included as they are interesting to compare with the long hours and culture of presentism that marks working lives in the City of London. After moving to the UK, Posha stayed in the banking sector but in a lower status job for a high street bank.

I did my Bachelors in Commerce and then I did my Masters in Marketing and Finance, MBA, everything in Bhopal. After my MBA, I got married, then moved to Bangalore and started working there in the banking sector. In investment advisory services. So I have been in the banking sector for the last ten years now, but five years of my working life I was in India and the rest in the UK.

I started with KPMG, which is one of the big five audit firms. I thought I'd go into accountancy and do my chartered accountancy course. So I did the intermediary, there are two levels, intermediary and finals, so I passed intermediary level and I was with KPMG doing audits and stuff and it was very, very high pressure job because I used to work until two o'clock in the morning, get up in the morning and get going at 7.00 am.

Working with KPMG there is a young crowd. They are all freshly out of colleges and they were like 20–22 years old and our group was very young. So we had people ranging from 21 to 29, there was nobody above that, everybody was in that. And then we had the boss who was 35. So we had this young crowd and so it was so easy to connect to everyone. Obviously I was from a smaller city so I had to adjust to their lifestyle and they're a bit modern and they're more westernized. But then I gelled in very quickly, I liked it and I kind of gelled with them.

But it was too hard, too long hours. So I left it basically midway, after doing my intermediary I said I can't do it anymore, so I left that and then I joined a small firm, an investment advisory firm, and we used to advise customers on investment products. So I took a bit of training with them and then I started off looking after a portfolio of customers. So banking or investment, that kind of started in 2001, I think. And so I worked with them for one year, then I moved to a bank in the private banking division as an investment manager.

We'd spent four years in Bangalore and then we moved back [to Bhopal]. When we moved back I joined ICIC bank which was a local bank, it's quite a large firm but then that was the one which had a branch in Bhopal so I applied as a relationship manager with them, and then I started working there. It was a culture shock in the sense that I'd never worked in a small city. I always worked in a bigger city so when I came back to a small city I was struggling. There is difference, there is a culture difference in work life. In work life there was a difference because people are not that broad-minded and they don't like women working still in Bhopal. So I had those work–life issues.

My job was to look after high net worth individuals, so basically look after their investments and savings. These clients were the rich guys of a place called Bhopal but the mentality was quite like, they would expect you go come to them rather than them come to you, because I'm giving you advice I would think that they would take me professionally but they would actually not treat you in a professional way and they would expect you to come to them and then they would not be there for appointments. You go there and are made to wait for 30 minutes before you see them, and it was just the culture difference, I think.

I think the men doing this job got on really because they were men talking to men usually, so they had this thing that you could talk and do business as well at the same time. For me I was more professional and I was like obviously I'm a woman and you've got to respect, from that angle. I didn't get that kind of respect from my clients so I didn't like it.

I was struggling there. Eight months I was in the job and I was not liking it at all because they would expect you to be there at eight o'clock in the morning and then be there until eight o'clock in the night, and the boss would leave at 10.00 pm so he would expect you to leave at 10.00 pm as well. And why would you, because you've done your three appointments? You've met your clients, you're meeting your targets, why should you stay until ten o'clock? So I would leave at 6.00pm and sometimes 7.00 pm and he didn't like that so obviously that was another thing that went against me. But I quit and I stayed at home. I also had my first child then.

So in I think six, eight months' time we decided we're going to go out and he [husband] said 'I want to study further.' So then he started exploring what he can do outside India. Some people suggested that he should do an MBA from outside, from UK, and because it was a one year course in UK, an MBA is a one year course in UK whereas in US it's two years. And with UK, what you get is the benefit that your wife is a dependent on you can work full-time, whereas in US, if you're a student and you go to US then the wife cannot work.

Her husband decided to do a doctorate rather than an MBA and so Posha had to find work to help support him financially.

When we came here my daughter was one year. I think she was 13 months when we came here. So the biggest thing for us was for me to find a job because it's so expensive to live in the UK. I started applying for job. So I came on the high street and started looking at the recruitment agencies. Went and had a chat with them, they said 'yes, we can look at certain possibilities'. I went to one which has got these part-time temporary jobs, you can do temping. So I applied there. They did a little test, I passed that and they said 'okay we're going to put you on to another project which is coming up, so we can do data processing and they'll pay you £9 an hour. Happy with that?' I said 'yes that's fantastic, that's great'. In the meanwhile we went shopping and my husband just picked up one of the local papers, and had put an advert which said HSBC premier relationship manager. My husband said, 'You're not going to get it, but let's try for it, what's the harm of putting the application through.'

But Posha did get the post.

In ten days from seeing the advert, I went through the application, the three assessment stages and then through the interview. And they said 'we're going to do the credit checks, that'll take four week time', and then I joined on 30 November. There was some restructuring that happened in November, they usually do the restructuring end of the year. So there was a restructuring that happened because the patch for which I was appointed for a relationship manager moved out of the area. I was very, very lucky that I found the job so quickly. I've done well in terms of my pay scales and everything so I started with £20,000 and I'm on £40,000 now, so literally doubled my income in four years. So I've moved up and done my qualifications, whatever was required and moved up, got a promotion and everything.

In the office as well we've got 40 people who working here, there are a few Asians, four or five of them and somehow the connect with Asians is automatically like that. So even if they are juniors, I talk to them more than my peers and somehow that social connect is there. Most of them were born and brought up here, but still I connect with them more easily and I can talk to them. I can share my feelings with them more openly than the people who are Britishers or from Western countries. But I never, ever had a problem at work where I felt that I was not being accepted as part of the team, which was the most fantastic thing. From the day one I got so much support from everyone, I never felt that I was out of place.

I never thought that they would promote me because, well, initially when I joined and obviously there is a different accent, you talk differently, and if you are meeting customers who are premier customers who have got £50,000 in savings, I deal with customers who have got £2 million in their account. Now, they are high net worth and they talk in a different language and you've got to be able to connect to them to sell to them, to do business with them. If I'm not able to connect to them in that way then they will never buy from me a product, they will never trust me for their banking. So initially to be honest when I joined and I was given this portfolio of 500 customers, I was struggling because I was not driving at that time and there were a couple of customers who said 'we would not want to deal with her because we can't understand what she says on the phone'. So there were problems like that. I've kind of overcome that very quickly because I'm very sales-driven and I'm very numbers-driven, achievement-driven, I make sure that that doesn't act as a barrier.

Some of the clients are very, very nice; they will accept you with open arms. Some of them will have inhibitions. They will not connect to you that quickly so you would struggle to overcome that barrier of actually being able to sell to them and build their trust because you're not talking the same language sometimes. To just give you an example, we've got premier banking and there is another level which is the next level which is private banking. In private banking you deal with people who have got more than £2 million, and it goes up to £50–£300 million, whatever, so it's private banking. To give you an idea of what the thinking pattern is, we've got in private banking they've got specialized desks. So there is an Asian desk, so there would be only Indian relationship managers who would be based in that desk to deal with the multi-millionaire Indian clients. Because HSBC already and any of the private bankers understood that if you don't talk the same language, you would not connect, if you don't connect, won't buy. . . . If you're talking to high net worth individuals you've got to be talking in their language. If they're talking about football you better know about football or soccer or whatever their interests are. And if you come from India you might not be able to talk about football because you're a cricket fan, so there is disconnect. So it's not only about the work but it's about the other bits that you actually become a family member to them if you are a relationship manager, talking about families, schools, this and that and everything.

I think I changed my accent a bit and tried to speak a bit slowly because there was a very good manager who told me that it was her observation that Indians talk very quickly and very fast, and that is probably one of the barriers because of which you can't put your point across. So I started talking slowly and when I would leave voice messages for customers I would actually leave a message and it gives you an option to listen to your message, so I would always, always press that button and listen to see whether I've communicated my message properly or not. If not, I would delete it and then do it again, just to make sure that I'm communicating in a proper way. So little things like that, things like understanding more about UK culture, weather, schools, things like that, so I kind of updated myself with that by just doing some research on systems and talking to colleagues, and asking questions really because they would use a slang and terminology which I can't understand, I'd say 'can you please explain what it means?' because I would want to learn so that I can use it next time. So things like that I picked up from my colleagues.

But to be honest, HSBC is one of the best employers to work for if you're coming from another country I think, they look after you really well and they encourage people from different countries to be a part of their team, really. There are lots of Polish customers now so strategically they will actually appoint a few of the counsellors who are Polish so that if there is somebody who is struggling with talking then they can actually go and find the Polish guy and then they can explain themselves. So I think they're very good actually that way. But socially again that barrier is still there, I think. I've been able to work on work-wise but not socially, I think. I think that will never happen because socially is where you are yourself more. Work is where you are not yourself, at least sometimes, you're professional; there are barriers around you because you have to behave in a certain way. So those are things you can learn more quickly than things you can learn socially.

'England seemed like really old-fashioned': web and software development

The boom in employment in the computing industry, ended by the dot-com crash early in the millennium, had some similar features to the banking boom. Interestingly, in an industry increasingly reliant on virtual means of communication, and what seem like cerebral tasks, the employment of migrant workers on contracts to write code became known as 'body shopping'.

Victoria is Singaporean Chinese by origin. She worked in the developing software industry in Singapore before moving to the UK in 2004, via New York.

I was born in 1975, so that's like I think really early days of independence in Singapore[5] I guess, and people were moving from the little villages to the urban environment. My father left us when I was young and my mother ended up working as a beautician. So it's quite hard for her because she wasn't, she didn't really know English and she was brought up in a time when it was okay to be Chinese-educated and then suddenly English became our national language. I feel quite sorry for her, like people of that generation. I had problems as well because my parents didn't speak English. Our parents are Mandarin speaking, and so I went to school until I think like about ten, before that I didn't really know what the teachers were saying in class. But I picked up on my English after a while.

After university I got a job as a web designer. I changed jobs quite a few times, but mostly it's web designer or like a, I don't know, what you consider that, like Flash. It's like, a bit like, design and programming, so it's mainly just computer jobs. I had like some friends from computer department and so I just talked to them and then they say, 'Oh, you can study by yourself and learn this thing and use this programme' or whatever. And so I tried and I think I was really lucky because that was the dot.com boom; so they just wanted to hire just anyone, and so I got the chance to do that as a job.

It was quite difficult at first. I remember I was told by someone where I submitted my profile and my portfolio for this job and I was told by that person that I was so bad that I should either give up or go and get training, and so I was quite insulted and saddened. But after that I thought she had a point, and then when I look at my work it was really not up to standard, and so I just tried and make it better. In the end it seemed to work, so it was really good advice actually.

The first real job was a web designer, in this like a set-up, there was maybe five people in the company and that wasn't really good because I didn't really know the job, whether as I was new and then I was the only person doing that job in that company. So it was a bit of a struggle and there was nobody to look up to or learn from and I wanted to learn how normal professional people are doing that. And so after that I quit that job and I was very lucky to find this other job in like a very famous big company in Singapore. It's Singapore Press Holdings, so they're like the main newspaper company, they were the only ones for a long time. So that was quite good because they were launching a new newspaper, and so I got the job, the news room, and it was really cool. So yeah that was my big break. I was there like about two years and then my department closed down because there was the end of the dot.com boom. Around 2002 I got, what do you call it, made redundant and I got a deal which is quite good as well and also the bonus I had the year before was really good, and so I was quite okay financially. And then after that I found out about this government scheme where if you are made redundant you get some incentive to retrain yourself and so there was this course in programming or something and so I went and trained. . . . I had to go through like four rounds of interviews and tests to get in and all that, but in the end I managed to get in which is really good. . . . It seems that self training is not enough, you need some paper qualification, so that course came in handy.

After the course I was doing like some freelancing job as well and meanwhile I was just actively looking for jobs abroad actually, and I didn't really want too much programming so I was just doing freelancing. And also that, just looking, and looking and looking, and after that I just got quite fed up with looking for a job abroad and I was, I did this really impossible, I just took the rest of my money and bought a ticket to New

York, and I thought, 'Oh just go looking for a job in New York, I thought'. That was really naïve. And so I got like a ticket and I can go there for like three months without a visa, so I just went over. I have a friend who was working there and then I knew some people from the internet and so I just went. One month I stayed with my friend in Michigan, which wasn't really looking for a job, it was a holiday, and for two months I was alone in New York. I just went to a place like a house-share and then, so just everyday going on the internet and try and find something and all that. Then I realized it was not as easy as I thought because of the visa requirement. I wasn't familiar with it, I would have needed something like a H1B or something in the States and it takes about a year to process.

And so I got one or two interviews, and there was this one that was quite promising. I went there and they interviewed me and they were quite positive, and then, but I guess getting the visa was too much for them or whatever, but it was quite, and it was nearing the end of my stay there, and so it was the last week of my stay actually. They were very hopeful but they didn't tell me. I wrote to them and whatever, and there was just no response, maybe that's the way they do things. And after that I just never heard from there again. I guess maybe they just tell all the applicants that or something, I don't know, it was just weird.

Also, I got a approached by this, like a really weird body; they call it 'body shopping' where they have this like a, some like, I think it might be like Indians or whatever, but like I had to go to this like dodgy place and then they sit like. They could send me up and whatever, but then I think it's those you read about where you keep, they just make you work like a slave or something and live in a house with like 20 other people and all that. For computing, but I think they send you out as a contractor or something, and then they only give you a fraction of pay or something. That's what I reckon later on, but when they were saying is that, I have to sign some contract with them and then I said, 'But actually I have, I don't really got that much experience in this field' which was true. They said something like I should fake my experience to get the visa or something like that, and so I thought, 'This is really dodgy' and so I'd rather be. . . . They're really just dodgy and it was also a bit weird. I don't know, I could feel like the place just felt weird, and then but at the time I didn't have like a bit of thinking like, 'I really, really, really want to work abroad' and maybe if I worked with them I could do it. But then I would have, like, this one room where I could forever, and he was like, 'You're naïve if you go with these people' and everything, and then so, in the end I thought 'Oh no, I don't think I could go through that' so I came back to Singapore, and try again.

I think it must have taken maybe about 1,000 applications at this point. It was online, so it's quite easy to apply, but it was like books and books and books and actually I can't really remember where I applied for this current job, and so it was like, 'Well this' and then suddenly –

occasionally I get some reply but most of the time when they hear about the visa they just, it's just too much trouble.

Then, so there was this growing company [in England] and so I think they probably really didn't realize how much trouble it would be. I applied and then they emailed me back and they said they wanted to interview me but obviously because being abroad and all that, it's quite difficult and so we arranged to meet on the internet and I had a camera, but they didn't have one set up or something. Anyway they could see on the webcam and then we talked on the, I think we might be talking on the phone or something or maybe through a microphone, I can't remember, but there was a bit of a lapse between the talking and the camera, and I couldn't see them as well, and it was weird, yeah. So there was the interview and after that, so it was quite positive and so, but I think there must have been like a very long time. I can't remember. It's at least a month between them saying yes and me coming over, or even me going there actually. It just kept dragging on because when I went to apply for the visa and all that, it's just everything took longer than expected.

In the end we found out, but there was like some complications and so I had to come on this, like a, it was a bit like cheating the system in a way because it's supposed to be a holiday visa or something like that. It's changed now but then it was a bit of a loophole, and so you could come here for like two years, and so I did. And then, so that was it. Tom, my employer, came to fetch me from the airport and there was quite a long wait because they had to do some X-ray and things, and then he fetched me from the airport to the house share that I arrange on the internet. They're all foreigners in the house: one of the guys in the house was from Malaysia, a guy from Australia and a girl from Spain.

I didn't really know very much about England, because most of our TV was like US and all that, and England seemed like really old fashioned. I didn't really think very much about England. It's quite nice here now. I think I came on Friday or the Saturday or something and start work on Monday with jet lag. I just really nervous and all that, and I think I was just, I just felt really weird and really nervous and shy because I went to the office and so everyone is a Caucasian and I remember I had to, we had this thing where we had to make sandwich orders and because we are out in the middle of nowhere. So we take turns to take each other's sandwich orders and call through the phone to the sandwich shop. And then I remember I was having a bit of a problem with tomatoes. I was thinking, 'is it tomatoes [English accent] or tomatoes [American accent]'.

It was quite small company. I think it was maybe 10–15 people around there, so yeah. The work was programming and things like that, yeah, quite basic, but I had problems at first. When I was first, when I first came here it was, I think maybe my employers . . . I think the trouble was here, or also my inexperience because I was still quite new in this field. And also I came over here and the work that I had to do is quite different from what I had done before, what I had studied, because computer is quite broad. Some of the time, the system you use here is a bit different, and we start working is different.

And also, it seems like, I don't know when I was in Singapore, I was always, I always felt that I was really competent in my company and among my friends I was, I didn't feel like I was the worst person there. And in fact, when I came over, it felt like everyone here was really smart and really good and so I was like underperforming. So there was a bit of problem with my employers I guess, but in the end they thought it would be quite bad to just send me back as well, and so we came out to this, like a compromise where I got like a pick up bonus and then started a junior position and all that, and continue on and then, that was maybe after, it was maybe the initial three months because like in the new job you get three months, like a review period, so it was within three months that I got like a pay cut, and then after that just continued as a junior position.

When the two years visa is over and I have to renew it, so I went back [to Singapore], like for, that was quite long actually, it was maybe two or three, two months or something because it took them quite a while to process and yeah, I had to, because it were papers. I had to like quit the job and then go back and then, yeah, I came back to the same job. And it's quite funny because it seems like I've become some kind of hero figure [back home]. I don't know why but like all my friends, they just thought it's just amazing that I'm abroad because I think lots of Singaporeans, maybe not so much now, but back then it was thought to be really difficult to find a job abroad, unless it's like say in China or some of these poorer countries, but it's hard to find a job in say England. And so, they were just all amazed. They thought I was some kind of extraordinary person, but I don't know. I think I was just maybe lucky.

'There's a lot of pressure in academia': university research and teaching

British universities expanded in both academic and student numbers in the post-war years, especially from the 1960s onwards. Women, including women born abroad, began to gain positions, although the ranks of the professoriat remained resolutely male-dominated.

Ani was born in 1968 in Romania where she did her first degree. She came to the UK initially on a scholarship at a university in the Midlands but later moved to Oxford.

I have a computer science engineering degree, a five year degree. Things have changed after the fall of the communist regime; it was equivalent

abroad to a MSc degree so I just did a five year degree but in terms of
the qualifications it's considered equivalent with an MSc degree. The fall
of the communist regime was in December '89 and I finished my degree
in '91 so it was more or less when things started to change. To start with
I got a job in a computer repair company which was very interesting.
They were shocked to see women, and especially women that went to
do the same work as well. They expected me to just move some papers
around. And I said 'actually I want to fix computers; I want to go to
customers too', and I did this for about, I think between six months
and a year.

What we had to do was there were some fairly unreliable Romanian
made manufactured computers which break very easily, and the idea was
with the customers called just either that they didn't know how to use
them properly or that they'd get our messages and we'd just have to go
and identify the problem and try to fix. But it's very interesting because at
that time we'd still try to fix the computer boards rather than just replace
them. So it's good fun intellectually. But they weren't very good quality so
they'd break very easily, they'd break if it was cold, they'd break if for
example I don't know, something with the computer, was, handled a bit.
So in terms of long term, it wasn't something which was worthwhile and
obviously the progress in technology, it wasn't really worth it but at that
time it just seemed natural and people were excited to have computers
and to start shifting from the big mainframe computers to personal
computers. It was a useful experience but I can't say I had any regrets
when I moved back to my university where I studied. A former professor
asked me if I'd like to start working there. I took an academic position
doing teaching and a bit of research to start with. Then that became full-
time. It involved running practical seminars, lectures, so this was between
presumably '92 and until '95.

And the way I arrived here [in the UK] was in '93 I had a one month
visiting scholarship at a university. He [husband] had one as well but we
came at different times. And then I worked with a very kind and very
helpful professor there at the computer science department. My husband
came to England to Oxbridge between '94 and '95, on a one year
scholarship, the Eastern European ones, and then he decided to apply for
a doctorate and then I said 'if he applies to be here for three years then I'll
try as well' and he got a place and within six months I got a place as well.
He got financial scholarship again, but in my case the way I funded my
studies was by working as a research assistant in the engineering science
department. And then I found out that there was a research project
starting and then I applied for the job.

I came for my interview for the job in March '96. I had to go back to
have a work permit issued, at that time you couldn't stay in the UK; I'm
not sure if things have changed. But if you had a work permit application
you had to leave the UK. So I went back to Romania and waited for the

work permit visa, and then I came back 24 April '96 and then I started my job. I just started doing the job and the thesis.

In terms of cultural change it was a major change after the fall of the communist regime because beforehand people weren't given passports. You wouldn't dream, at least with my family's financial situation, wouldn't dream of going abroad, travelling abroad. And it wasn't the tourist thing, it was I think the freedom which made a huge difference. And I even remember the first time I came to the UK, because I always thought that I might be asked things at the UK border, which I was. They would ask 'do you have sufficient money to live for a month and do you have a letter to prove the purpose of your visit?'

I think the freedom to, the freedom to go to conferences if you wanted to. Like a claustrophobic thing, before that there was no way; I didn't even think I'd travel abroad. And for example, the Romanian education is fairly thorough and structured, so throughout the school years we've learnt about places, geography, history, and I don't think I ever thought would I be able to go to Paris. It just seemed like it won't be a possibility. And it's not Paris as such but I think the choice, if I want to do it, will I be able to do it without being constrained by other people. So I think this, the fact that you do have a choice and also the visa concept, the fact that obviously you need to go and prove that you have the right to travel. So this was another major change [in 2007] when Romanian people didn't need a visa anymore.

The doctorate, it took a bit longer than usual. During my PhD I had my children so I did the job, my thesis and the children, which was quite exciting. My daughter was born in '99 and my son in 2002 so I started my PhD in '96, in April, although starting the job as well, it was sort of like doing the job. It was a project which had deadlines and it was two companies, so it involved visiting companies, getting to talk to people. I really enjoyed the work that I did as part of the project. It was slightly different than I expected in terms of the difference between theory and practice when you work with a computer-based environment. The human dimension I really enjoyed it, communicating with people and also getting the people to trust you.

So my son was born in May and I finished my maternity leave in October I suppose. I went to conferences in September. I finished my maternity leave six months, whatever, and I started this job as a departmental lecturer. In the meantime the project had finished and I started this job in July 2002 and I finished my thesis and submitted it in October. I think after I went back to work I had to finish the project in terms of deliverables, presentations, and also focused on finishing my thesis. So I've been in this job since July 2002. My job title hasn't changed but duties have increased significantly. We even had some issues in terms of how this job is perceived. To start with it was founded as someone who would pick up the pieces in a way, run the practicals, but not as a long-term career thing. At this stage, it's fine for me for family reasons and it started as a fixed term job and now it's a permanent job. And because it's a permanent job, I think the department also feels that we should have more responsibility. So to start with it was more like running practicals. At the moment, I'm doing projects supervision for undergraduates and graduate students. I have the examiner responsibilities. I'm lecturing, setting exam questions. So it's a significant increase in responsibilities.

I also have to do research which I do, but I don't think I'm doing as much as I should and I could. It's a very time consuming job during term time. It's managing everything, supervising students, organizing. It is good fun. Career-wise, it's probably not the best job because it has a heavy teaching load and there isn't as much time for research, but it's still all right, I think, just putting everything in terms of the fact it has flexibility so I can find someone if I have to go to school and I can work in the evening or the weekend I can do it. It works fine for me at this stage. When the children are older I might reconsider it.

Natasha, who is Russian, also worked for some years in an elite university. Her working life was varied: she had been a translator before taking the academic position and then moved into research for an international company. As she explains, her route to the UK was through marriage.

I was born in 1965 in Moscow into a family of two scientists, mum and dad, and my parents divorced when I was seven. There is not much to say about my childhood. It was a very happy actually childhood and it's very often painted in the West that people in the Soviet Union lead a very grey life. I wouldn't say it's true. In some ways obviously the economic side of it, we didn't have the huge variety of food that you have here or clothes or whatever, but it was compensated by intellectual lifestyle, my circles of friends. Cultural life was amazing, absolutely amazing I would say.

My mum was a lecturer at the university, and when I was 16 I went into study biology. When I went to the university, all university students used to have a stipend, like extra money, like a grant. In the Soviet Union you used to be given this money if you were any kind of student, but also if you have all stars, if you pass, certain kind of students with absolutely red, like red marks, they would get twice as much. I was a good student. My degree is Biology and Biological Sciences. But it's slightly different from the English system because it's a five year course and for the first two years you have to cover a lot of subjects, starting from higher maths, all the chemistry, so it's a kind of history and different aspects. I don't know how to describe it, and I had my first interview in the UK, job interview, and I put all of the things that I studied, they did not believe me. They thought I was fibbing because they said 'how can you do that, it's not possible'? I said, 'I had to do it', and again it was really tough. So for the first two years it was a lot of other subjects than what you specialize in and always when I put in my CV I would put Bachelor of Science and then Master of Science because the last two years you specialize in these particular subjects, so it's going to be more master's degree and your dissertation.

I graduated 1987, so I was 21, nearly 22. So when I graduated, I had already a place in a laboratory in an institution and I went to that place but I also wanted to do my PhD in Moscow University. I passed the exams to do a PhD in Moscow University, but I didn't finish. So I started it and I've done two years there. By then I was expecting my first child so I came to the UK.

I met John when I was 19, so 1984. At that time he graduated from university with a BA and Russian language was part of his course. But he chose also to do master's degree in Russian Art and Russian artists was a particular subject of his research. He had several British Council scholarships to Moscow so he was from Moscow University and I met him at one of the parties I went to. He was five years older than me so I was 19, he was 24 at the time. He was back two or three times and we got married in 1988. We lived in Moscow until 1990. We lived together with my mum. He didn't have a permanent job. He was training for journalist, BBC, some kind of English newspapers in Russia but he was irritating my mum. She said 'well look, he's not working properly, he should go back to England and get a proper job and try to understand that he should be responsible'.

Her husband went back without Natasha to start a translation business in the UK but that was unsuccessful and when Natasha arrived, her husband was living back home with his parents in a rural village in the north of England.

And when I came to England, people say it must have been a cultural shock to you. I say 'yes, it was a cultural shock but it was the opposite to what you expect'. To me I lived in Moscow. I always had an amazing circle of friends. It was very diverse and cultural so constantly every week there was something to do. We were being invited to parties and there were, artists, writers, photographers and musicians and you go to all these events. It was just absolutely vibrant. And then I come to a little village, with no money, with one street, and it was just awful. It was horrible.

At the time I have one year wife's visa but that year I was not allowed to claim any benefits, so I was trying desperately to find any jobs. I even was not allowed to work, I couldn't work for a year. I couldn't claim anything and I couldn't work officially. And I was trying to find things, obviously I was trying to do translations, it wasn't very easy, I must say.

Her husband then got a job in London and they moved there, just before her daughter was born, and moved again to a smaller town outside London six months later.

It was lucky, good circumstances. I was doing lots of translating by that time, got a computer and things like that so I was doing lots of work with others but I found my first job in the uni. I had an interview in '91, so she [the daughter] was just over a year. I went into Department of Biochemistry as a scientist and it was working in the research lab in the Department of Biochemistry part-time. That lasted for four years because it was slightly diverged, well it was completely diverged from what I was doing back in Moscow, my research, and during those four years I was trying desperately to do something I could finish my PhD that I started because I had all those experiments. And during that time I never earned a lot.

I got in touch with one of my previous colleagues from university. He was an English professor working in my field of research and I wrote to him a letter. He was in London at the research institute. He was my main contact so I became a member of that international group he was working in and I went to their meetings and met lots of people. And I was constantly enquiring for work in Oxford, that kind of research and unfortunately it was not possible. So for a time I was actually doing some voluntary work in his lab, while I was working part-time in Oxford, hoping that I might be able, if they get a vacancy or if they get a position for PhD so I can use that.

Then he put me in touch with a wonderful person at the Department of Applied Sciences, and said 'why don't you get in touch with her? She works at kind of the same interest that you might be interested in'. So because it was next door to biochemistry I just went across and met her and we immediately clicked like that and she was amazing, she was one of the amazing figures in my life as well because she was a kind of mentor for me. I was there for three years. Basically what happened is that she created the project for me. Oxford University funded for a year and it took off from there, and then you had different grants, but that allowed me to go into first full-time job, research position.

So I stayed there for three years and then I was moving more and more into medical side of that research that I started with her. I just knew that I wanted to move into completely medical field. That was building up to that move and I was just very, very lucky that I got that, again the network and again through another Russia friend and she was working in a lab and he was looking for a person to do one year grant and if it was successful there was the possibility to do a PhD. So I went into that job, I didn't have enough experience, so I don't know why she got me because obviously you had immediately to start producing results but she believed in me. So I started and I stayed there for seven years. And one of the things that I really enjoyed when I was in the lab was I used to supervise. I supervised several medical students on their projects, and also enjoy meeting people and doing things like that.

I was paid my salary as a researcher there but I was also doing a PhD. I started PhD in 2002 so I must have been 37. I finished it 2005 or 2006 and then in 2006 I was looking for another move. So I just looked into pharmaceutical world and got the job in pharma industry. This is a really exciting job because I spent all my life being a lab worm, doing my cookery in the lab and things like that. I'm now working field-based anyway so I can be at home sometimes. I can be very flexible. My company is based in Holland. My position, which is called clinical scientist, actually a lot of it was involved with physicians, educating them about the danger about the drug, I'm working with one particular drug, educating them about the data about the drug, and not just about the drug, about the disease. When I started I didn't know why? Did they need education, they're doctors, they should know? Well in fact they don't. I'm based in UK so I'm responsible for the UK and Ireland, also a little bit for Russia if they have a need for me to come and present there, but mostly UK now; so I just go and give presentations to the physicians and doctors. I enjoyed it very, very much, especially when I have excellent feedback.

My colleagues are a European team so we're a pan-European group and they were based in different countries, they support the same sort of functions. So that is one of the functions. Another function is also we try to identify what data is required to support the use of the drug in the future. And we shape new studies, clinical studies on a small scale but that is also very enjoyable because you sit with the doctors, you brainstorm and they come to crazy ideas and then you try to find a nice plan, how to do and then you put it on a table to the company and they decide or not it's feasible. So I do also a lot of interactions with people, I enjoy so, so much. I travel a lot, I go to all the conferences, I do a lot of work, and I'm not nine to five in the office, I work really hard and sometimes work until very late but it's my day, I can do whatever.

Unfortunately Natasha had just heard that her company was making her team redundant and she was looking for another job.

I'm currently doing lots of applications, but I might stay in the industry because I have already some people interested for me to stay, but again nothing is settled in stone, so I don't know. So we shall see how it will be. I don't know. But I think in the long run I just feel like maybe just doing something completely different. But not in Russia. When I go back to Russia I don't feel Russian but I found my job where I'm now via my Russian friends; I found my job in the university the last time, when I did my PhD via my Russian friends; so perhaps I am still Russian. I would say networking does a lot of things in your life. Thinking back, I probably escaped the most difficult decade back in Russia because I know '90 to '96 were really difficult for people who stayed there.

Simone is also an academic, whose route into employment in a university had been more straightforward than that of Ani and Natasha. Simone was

born and educated in Grenoble where she finished her PhD in 2008. She
then moved to the UK in August of that year to join her husband who had
been in the UK since early in 2007. Simone's first position was as a researcher
at Cambridge, where she worked for five months funded by a French
postdoctoral award, before moving to a lectureship in a midlands university.

The PhD in France, how it works when you have a scholarship for your
PhD you have also on top of this a contract to be a temporary lecturer.
Essentially you are paid when I was doing my PhD but I was teaching at
the exactly the same kind of teaching load as now in England. So I was
teaching a lot and doing my research. So essentially I'd been a lecturer for
four years in the same place when I was doing my PhD. That's why then
I came to the UK I had already a long list of teaching skills etc. I was
accepted as a postdoc researcher in Cambridge that is where I went with
the idea initially of going back to France.

Once I was in the UK the key thing, I think, was that Pierre [her
husband] wasn't keen to come back because for him job opportunities
were much better in England. So I said 'OK, why not?' and essentially I
started to look for teaching jobs. I think I applied probably two weeks
after my arrival. I applied to first job in London but it was far too early
so I wasn't shortlisted and two months afterwards I applied for the job I
have now. I had previously worked with some of the people because here
we were doing sort of students exchange between this university and
Grenoble. So they knew my work; they knew my publications and I also
knew what they were doing. I say 'OK, why not have a try' and actually
I applied in I think I applied in November and was shortlisted in December
and I was offered the job in January and I left Cambridge in February and
I started the position early March. So, everything is good, everything
went quickly. I wouldn't say I went here from career perspective it was
more personal reasons which made me stay.

In Cambridge it wasn't hard. The work as such wasn't hard. I think I
kind of struggle with Cambridge because I thought it was too Harry
Potter. Probably also as regards to my personal background, I felt a bit
awkward with all these posh kids who could think that everything was
basically coming from the sky, so you don't have to think about, I mean
students were so. . . . It was not hard as such but I think because it was
only research and because I am so used to teaching, being in contact with
students. It was actually not difficult but I think I'd rather be in a position
where I have more contact with people, because I was kind of on my own.
I was working a lot in the library which is good from a research perspective
but I think I like to have a job where I have different features of my job.
It's not only research.

I think at beginning too, because I arrived there, was a problem of
confidence of me talking in English all the time. I think it was probably
more about me feeling not as much in my ease as I could be because of

the sort of not language barrier but still it was not my own language. Obviously you are a foreigner. Okay, so you don't speak English perfectly and you are in academia. Why are you supposed to write perfectly? It's very, very difficult. A lot of people would feel that they can may be write in a way sometime and comment about your English. Colleagues can comment about your English. Students here in the UK will comment on your English accent a lot. And it makes you feel bad about it. You can also take it as advantage I am also an international member of the staff teaching. I think I find the foreign aspect, but there is also some positive because I am French I could actually bring relationship from France, teach students in French.

I love my job now but it is difficult. I think there is a lot of pressure in academia to perform – in teaching, in research, in publications, in administration, whatever. You are supposed to be good at everything. Initially there were not many young women. It's actually increased over the time and it was nice to be able to chat with a young woman in the same position and I've discovered that there is much more also women community. And there is a really nice atmosphere.

'All I am good for is academic stuff': challenging traditional stereotypes

*Three decades before Simone, **Shami** found her career as an academic gave her the courage to leave an unhappy marriage and make a life as a single mother. Born in 1951, she defied convention in India, as well as challenging academic conventions in Oxford where she started a doctorate in 1988.*

My childhood was very secure. I was brought up in a good family; my parents were together for nearly 50 years. My mother didn't work but she was very well educated for that time. So, she sort of ingrained into us the whole question of education and I didn't have to do any work in the house. She never needed me to do anything as long as I studied. As long as I did well academically they were happy. Now I say 'I wish she'd taught me housework'. I look around and wonder where I should start cleaning, because all I'm good for is reading, writing reports and doing things like that, academic stuff. So all that was smooth sailing.

My mother was keen that I should go to an all-women, all-girls college and I was admitted to one of the well-known women's colleges but in Delhi University and known to be good. I did Philosophy for my first degree and for my MA, which wasn't the normal thing because everybody was doing more vocational stuff like Economics or Science. I did really well academically, was top of the university and all that, so there was no problem. I just walked into a job. I just went into the first job and started lecturing, I was a college lecturer. It was an out of town, campus college, all-women college, which again my parents were very happy about. I continued to live at home, that was what really caused a lot of problems for me because, well not problems because I wasn't doing anything, but I was just expected to go to work and come back and I found it very frustrating and very stagnating. I didn't do anything apart from I was lecturing, I was teaching and I was enjoying the teaching bit. I was doing Plato's *Republic* and I could. I was doing the same thing year after year, and I could get up in the middle of the night and spout Plato to you, that sort of thing. It still gave me a buzz. Teaching was very good; I enjoyed the teaching. But I used to tell my mother, the way you've brought me up, the sort of education I've had, you can't expect me to be content with this sort of thing. And she used to think that I was very wayward and wanting to live on my own and things, and there was no way.

Marriage seemed to offer an escape.

Of course it was an arranged marriage that I had and I was very happy. I was 26 when I got married, which according to Indian standards is pretty old and the thing was that you have a child straightaway and I wanted one and so did he. So I got pregnant straightaway but my marriage didn't work. So within six months I was back home. I was pregnant and I was back home with my parents and that's where I feel I was lucky that my parents were the sort of parents they were. There was no pressure on me, in fact my father said to me 'Life's too short to be unhappy' and he even said 'There are as many fish in the sea as ever came out of it.' I remember him saying that.

   It wasn't easy. It was very, very difficult, especially having the child on your own but mine was a good job, a university lecturer's job. At least I had that to fall back on. The status of a divorced woman is so low; people don't treat you properly and they take a lot for granted. Living alone is so difficult, paying your telephone bill, paying your utility bill and things like that. So I just wanted to get out and the one skill I had was academic, so academia was something that could help me. I know a lot of women in India wouldn't be able to leave a marriage; a lot of women would stay on. I remember my mother telling me once that 'In my time we wouldn't have been able to walk out so easily. It's only because you had a good job and you were financially independent that you were able to stand up for yourself.'

Shami continued to stand up for herself. She left her family home to live independently and started a relationship with a man of African heritage that she met through her work, despite the disapproval of her parents, especially her mother.

She'd be really nasty about it, she'd say 'You're divorced and you've got a son and you've still got all these men sniffing around' and she would say if I have a black grandchild I'm not going to look after and all that sort of thing. It's all racism in many ways and I used to tell my parents that if educated people like you can talk in this way what hope is there? They were very, very against it [the relationship], but he was the one, that was the one relationship that really supported me and was very valuable. He lived with me for five years there [in Delhi]. I mean, people still ask me 'how did you get away with it?' I said I just held my head high and I don't care. He was living with me and that's it. I just didn't bother.

In 1988 when her son was nine, despite her relationship and a promotion, Shami left to pursue a doctorate at Oxford University. Her partner was encouraging.

He was the one who sort of persuaded me, he said 'With your academic qualifications you'd easily . . .' and I really wanted to get out because it's stultifying in many ways because you teach about 20 hours a week when you're a lecturer and you're in charge of the department and there's no time then for any other thing. You can't do research, there's no time for research; there's no time for individual development.

In Oxford Shami also found herself challenging conventions.

The day before I left Delhi I got a telegram from the college saying no place here for a child and they knew in all my letters there was no way I was going to leave him. So I came here and they said 'we can't establish a precedent, we can't have the child on campus' and I had this lovely big room and I just felt, I said 'he's a very quiet child' and they said 'no, and don't try to smuggle him in because there's no way we can allow a child on campus'. And then the Women's Group really came up and they said they've never had a mature student with a child, how can they behave like this? And the Women's Officer took it up and they give me student accommodation outside the college where I could keep my son and they even came up with money for my son, which I hadn't expected. So that was really good.

Her second struggle with the university came when she was about to be awarded her degree and it was expected that she wear academic dress, including a skirt, for the ceremony.

They told me that I would have to wear a black skirt. I never wear skirts, you know. I wear trousers yes, but I don't wear, and for something as special as that, so I said 'no, how can it be and why can't I wear a sari?' And then a new administrator said 'Well, you can see why there should be rules and everyone wears black and white and you wear a multi-coloured sari'. I said, 'I'm hardly likely to wear a multi-coloured sari because in India when you get your degree you wear a black sari and a white blouse' and then the Women's Officer again, she would have to go back again and I said 'no, I'm going to take it in absentia; I'm not going to go and receive it because I don't want to wear a skirt' and I even said 'I'm sure Indira Ghandi wouldn't have worn a skirt when she went up to receive her doctorate.' And the day before the ceremony, I got a call from the Vice Chancellor's office. They said 'you can wear a sari provided you wear a black sari with a white blouse'.

While studying, Shami did some teaching at the university as well as stretching her scholarship funding by baking.

On my student visa, I couldn't start working full-time until I got the work permit but I could work up to 20 hours while I was a student. I worked as a research associate for six months and I taught too. And also I used to bake cookies and muffins and brownies for a cafe. So before my son left for school I'd wake up at five, bake for three hours, go and give all the stuff in and then go to the department. I used to take a few lessons in, what was it, research methods, so it was very enjoyable. The interesting thing there was that there was no racism there. You can't, there was no, I never felt that the fact that I was Indian made any difference really, it wasn't. It may have been more subtle and maybe there is a glass ceiling and things and people do talk about that but because I didn't go into academia I never experienced that.

After finishing her doctorate, Shami began a career as a community educator, starting as an outreach worker with new migrants.

I got a job. The job was for outreach worker and that's again something I keep telling my learners here, especially the ones who come as migrants, people who come from Sudan for instance, they have very good academic qualifications but they come here they're not able to translate those into jobs and they don't want to take up low status jobs. And I keep giving them my example and saying that if I had said that I was a Reader in Delhi University and I'm not going to do that job, I would still be looking around for something. But that gave me the first step on the ladder and I've made of it what I wanted to. But my mother didn't approve of it at all. She said 'You don't even have someone to wash your cups and make you a cup of tea. Have you come all the way from India to do this sort of a job?' But it didn't matter to me at all. Twenty years on I'm still making my own tea because I don't expect anything different.

One of the first things I did was to move into training because unemployment was so high. So I said give them vocational training to help them into the labour market, in employment and not self-employment. So that's what I started off by doing. At first I was just one woman in a room and at that time the first course we had 12 people and eight computers or something and they had to share. Today we have last year I think it was 1,500 people who studied and I have 20 members of staff now. So it's really, really grown.

Funding is coming from the Skills Funding Agency still, the LSC [Learning and Skills Council] and the European Union, we get funding from all these and that's the major difference because when I started the bulk of our funding was just from the LSC and that was our bread and butter, but that meant it was one audit stream and now we've got about eight to nine strands of funding and each of them needs to have its audit trail kept separate so we're working far more for less money, but I feel that we are serving a need, we are meeting a need because we've got hordes of people on our waiting list, people that want to come and study with us, learn English, and we don't have the funding.

My job now is just overseeing. Again, like when I started I used to do everything, that's what I tell all of them, I've done all of this. I've been at reception, I've looked after all the paperwork, I've done the recruitment, everything, but now I just run the whole thing and look at ways of growing. Making the bids, you make about 10 bids and you get about four or five, so you put in so many and each of them takes so much effort to do, there's a lot of work involved in that but some of it, I've got used to it now because I've been doing it for so many years. It's very satisfying. I still get a buzz and just the fact that I've done all of this and it's grown and I keep thinking that even if I were to leave, I'd like it to continue as an institution because it is playing a part in the local economy.

Despite this success and fulfilment, Shami found she sometimes had to struggle against patronizing attitudes and racist assumptions.

I could feel the racism amongst people here [in the UK], I still feel it. I always feel if someone like me with my education and my position should be spoken to like that and looked at like that, what hope do the others have when they don't have? Not knowing English doesn't mean that you're not intelligent or that you don't have skills. Because the people I work with the local authorities, the job centre, what was the Learning and Skills Council, it's now the Skills Funding Agency, all these people whom I go to for funds and there's always this thing that they just think of me as another ethnic minority woman and I have to justify myself and I still feel that when I meet someone new it's like a hit or miss situation. Like there was this guy from Business Link and he just said to me 'So do you want the grant or not, do you want the money or not?' because he's arguing about something. I said, 'no thank you' and I said 'I don't like being patronized. Just because you're giving me money I'm not going to . . .' And he went back and told them 'She told me I was patronizing!' Then later he became a friend but, you know, you have to stand up for yourself and that's not something that I needed to do back home.

After thirty years in the UK, Shami finally decided to become a citizen, albeit rather reluctantly.

I didn't do it for all these years but last year both my son and I answered the Citizenship Test and we got the British passports. And when we went for the Citizenship ceremony, that was another trauma because we knew what it was – swearing allegiance to the UK. I admire the place and I feel I've done well here and I've contributed a lot. That's what I always think that the politicians need to be aware. What about what the migrants? Suppose these people were to leave? I went into hospital recently and all the nurses were, there was no English nurse, they were all foreigners of some kind or the other, immigrants. So if they were to leave the whole infrastructure would collapse. And someone like me is paying high taxes and paying taxes since day one and has contributed considerably and helped. This should be recognized more, and should not be overlooked.

The women in this chapter were in professional occupations, in the main earning good salaries. Their narratives reveal fascinating details of their backgrounds and journeys to the UK, as well as the tasks involved in their daily working lives and the social relations established at work. They show the ways in which many of them faced various sorts of discrimination in the workplace, on the basis of their sex, their ethnicity, or their skin colour and the way they spoke. As Posha noted, it is often easier to 'connect' with people from similar backgrounds, even though she herself made sterling efforts to fit in by learning about British culture and mores. Natasha was shocked by the cultural change involved in moving to a village, after a rich and varied social life in Moscow. Shami, like Posha, was Indian, but she was prepared to challenge British assumptions and the practices of one of the ancient universities rather than to adapt to their rules and practices. The narratives of all these women, however, are inflected with enthusiasm for their career choices and for the opportunities that moving to the UK had opened up, despite initial difficulties and the very evident need to work extremely hard. And although these women may have earned more than many of the migrant women in earlier chapters, they too faced the challenges of combining waged work with other demands, of building a career while establishing a family and caring for their children.

7

Serving the Public:

Offices, Hotels, Shops, Salons and Buses

Among the consequences of the transformation of the UK labour market into one in which service sector jobs are numerically dominant has been both the growth of feminized jobs and the increased significance of interactive forms of work: those exchanges where both the provider and purchaser or consumer of the service on offer are present. Even in the knowledge work discussed in the previous chapter, clients, students, research subjects and interviewees, are often present and part of the interactive performance that constitutes providing an acceptable service.

Bankers' clients are sometimes, although not always, active participants in the exchange of advice. They may also expect to be entertained by their advisors, sometimes in the sorts of venues where women may feel uncomfortable or out of place. The stories in the previous chapter illustrated some of the behaviour that women working in the financial sector are subjected to and, right into the new millennium, behaviours that verge on harassment remain evident. A campaigning organization, the Fawcett Society (2010), has documented the continuing sexualization of many exchanges in the City of London. University teachers also provide a work-based performance for an audience, giving lectures and running seminars, and hoping to hold the attention and enthuse the young people who listen to them. In universities, new forms of assessment that typically involve students commenting on their lecturers' performance have been introduced. Here too inappropriate comments or behaviour are not unknown. But as earlier chapters also revealed, dealing with the public when engaged in various forms of body work and domestic work in homes, institutions and hotels is not easy.

In this chapter, the focus is explicitly on the general public in arenas that are less specialized or enclosed than the more private spaces of an individual's home, a bank, a hospital ward or a lecture theatre. Here migrant women are employed in spaces that are accessible to the general public – in shops, offices, hotels, salons and on public transport – where the only condition of entry typically is having the purchase price. In these interactive exchanges, migrant women may find themselves disadvantaged by limited fluency in English or by stereotypical assumptions about 'foreigners' held by the public. Too often, they are also subjected to aggressive attitudes and behaviour that make their working lives unpleasant. As the narratives show, women in these sorts of 'servicing' work often frequently change jobs, and may move between sectors as well as types of employment. This sort of work has become more precarious in the twenty-first century, often constructed to be part-time or contract based, but as the stories reveal, insecurity has long been a common feature of waged work at the bottom end of the service sector.

'I was another pen pusher': office work after the war

Dagnija, born in Latvia in 1919, worked as a teller in a bank in Riga during the occupation. After leaving Latvia, she was employed in offices, in the DP camp and in the UK, dealing with a semi-public – other displaced people.

I was in the bank [in Riga]. I was a counter clerk, as I failed the university examination at 18. It wasn't the right moment and I wasn't very serious about it so I didn't get into the university. I was single then; well, occasionally engaged. I was young then.

And I was lucky enough [later in a camp in the British zone], I don't know why. My parents both spoke English, so well somehow or other, the English language I was familiar with it, you know, so I got into the UNRRA, United Nations Relief, what does the A stand for? I don't know.[1] It was one of the big relief organizations in Germany. So I just worked there, again just a semi-secretary. From there I was sent to the HQ of the British zone, and my parents were still in the other camp. And I was asked to go to England, about 12 of us as a reception party. I was to go to Hull where they sent agricultural workers and miners. We arrived there, I remember, first we arrived in Tilbury and then London. I remember the barrow boys, all the oranges, everything there. That was March 1947 and then we were sent to Hull on Humberside and I remember I was allocated to sit at the switchboard; never seen one in my life but I soon learnt it. We were a very nice sort of a crowd, girls and men too. Perhaps ten girls of different nationalities, a Lithuanian, an Estonian and two Latvians. But we knew we couldn't go back. But we were all young; we tried to do something. We all worked together, we went on excursions. We lived in a little bungalow with small rooms for each and one big sitting room and a couple of bathrooms and we didn't have to cook. The meals were provided. The men lived in big barracks and we registered them. The Ministry of Labour was there and we were acting as interpreters, telling people where they had to go and work.

When we arrived the WVS [Women's Voluntary Service] meet us and we were given 10 shillings spending money. In Hull we had £4 a week, it was very fine. We worked and worked, but it was very interesting. Then it closed down and we were transferred to Bottisham, near Cambridge, at another camp. There we had another crowd, Estonians etc., a British Latvian – an English woman who had married a Latvian.

I was another pen-pusher there, just in an office, mostly to translate and sort people out. In Bottisham it was under the National Coal Board and the prospective coal miners had English lessons and they had to learn certain commands for down in the mine. I think I was there til 1948. Then I was transferred in 1949 to London and that was National Service Hostels Corporation and they ran those hostels. No choice, no; I was just sent there but what could we choose? Only I went there and the others went somewhere else.

'We opened a shop': self-employment in the grocery trade

Marta, also a Baltic Cygnet, had been a live-in help in her first years in the UK. By the mid-1950s, she was married and had moved to Corby, a new town in Northamptonshire, where there was a reasonably sizeable Latvian community.

My husband had this idea he wanted to open a shop of some kind so we found premises in Corby and we opened a sort of grocery and continental foods sort of shop. My second child was born there. So we left Wolverhampton in December 1954 and opened the shop the next summer. We moved there because my husband knew people there. There were lots and lots of Latvians in Corby then,[2] not now. I worked in the shop and we had baby sitters, Latvian women, but later on I worked part-time and I got people working in the shop instead of me, part-time so I could spend more time with the children. But to begin with I had to be there myself. It was quite difficult really.

The shop was successful up to a point. It was the time before supermarkets started and when they did, the business went down because the shop was sort of right on the one side of the town, really on one side on the edge of the town. Had it been in the centre it might have been different but . . . and we also had a van for delivering and also selling from the van. It was all right but nothing fantastic and so on. It was hard work those years.

'She'd pile me up with plates': working as a waitress

Moira was born in Ireland in 1937. She came to England in 1954, encouraged by her brothers who had emigrated a few years earlier. Her first job in the UK was in a hotel. Before then, she'd worked for a doctor, helping in the household. Like many women with little education she did a range of jobs, often doing work well above what might be expected and doing a really good job.

I was born in Tipperary in '37, 1937. I went to a national school in County Tipperary at the age of four. I left school at 14. My parents were very poor really, they were very poor and my father worked on a farm. There were eleven of us in our family, eleven children, but four died young, back in those days, they died young, yes. One was two, and one was about a year I think. I was the last, the youngest. They were very poor my family. In those days people were poor anyway in Ireland and hence the reason for coming to England.

It was fairly tough really. We didn't go hungry or anything like that, and we were very happy, but there was this thing that, when I was fourteen, I went out to work and I was looking after six children with the mother [as a live-in help]. I wasn't really looking after her; I think she was looking after me, I do. Then I had to leave there because I developed TB in those days and that was a very dangerous thing to get in those days. And then my family doctor, he would come and treat me at my home, and I had to stay in bed for six months. And then at the end of all that, when I was cured by the doctor, my family doctor, he asked if I would go and work for him.

I wasn't actually classed as a nanny with the six children, no, no I wasn't. It was like you were classed as a maid with the six children or whatever, but when I went for the doctor, the doctor's house, it was different because his wife did all the housework and all I had to do was answer the door when he had private patients and look after his four children. It really was a case of looking after the children, making sure they were safe, get their meals, eat with them. Actually, the doctor's wife even did the cooking and the shopping; she was great.

I stayed there then for nearly a year and then my brothers arrived home from England and they hadn't seen me, so they asked 'Where was I? What I was doing? Was I in a prison or something that they hadn't seen me?' as I was only six miles away. I was living in and I was getting no time off, only a half day. I'd get up on a Friday afternoon and I'd go home. Sometimes I'd catch a bus, then later I had a bike, but I would ride that bike in, back in on a Saturday morning, the six miles on that Saturday morning to start work on the week again. Yes, it was very hard; it wasn't hard work, but I was in all the time for a very young person, and I thought that was it. I used to give my mother, when I got the 30 shillings [her weekly pay from the doctor], I used to give my mother the pound and I would keep the 10 shillings, because I wasn't going no place anyway, and I was supplied with uniform in the doctor's house. Yeah, my job there was quite good.

I was, by then, by then I was coming up for, I was nearly 16 when I went for the doctor, I was then nearly 17 and then I left for England with my brothers. My mother and father didn't want me to leave because they'd seen all their family leave for what and they were very upset that I would leave, and they wanted me to stay at home, yeah. But my brother said, 'You come to England, it's great over there' he said, 'And, you'll get lots of good money' so that's why I'm here. And I came over then in the '50s, about '54 I think it was.

My sister-in-law she took me straight to the Queen's Hotel and I was in there working straightaway. She took me into the Queen's Hotel [in Abingdon, a small town near Oxford] then and I'd never been in a hotel before. But anyway, I didn't mind and they put me into the still room, where I was washing up, making tea and coffee and the toast, and that was no problem. I lived in. Then after a few months their manageress came to me and she said, 'You're not staying in here any longer, we want you in the dining room' so they trained me into silver service then. Then they said, 'In the afternoon go in the office. If there was some kind of vacancies, go in the office; they might want to rest'. I had to do the office, not a lot, but just see if there was vacancies if someone phoned, and the afternoon tea sometimes. So I was doing general work in the hotel, but mainly the dining room, mainly waitress work, which I loved in the end. I loved that. I got to know a lot of people, so that was lovely.

I was being paid £4 10 shillings[3] in those days. And then I would get my tips, a week, with all my food. So, I went from 30 shillings to £4 10 shillings and then I would get my tips, that would be vary, tips always vary, I sent £1 back to Ireland. I wish I had sent more then, but a £1 wasn't a lot looking back, I said it to my friend I said, 'I wish I had sent more money' but she said, 'Really, we had to try and buy clothes and do things ourselves' she said.

Then I got married in '59, 1959. I met him in the hotel. But we were very young. I was a little, two years older than him, so as I was 17 or 18 was I, 17, 18? Yeah, he'd be about 20 – no he'd be 16, I was only, he was only 16 as I was 18 we'd say roughly then, which was ridiculous really. So, then my family were against it, they felt he was too young. I took him over to Ireland and they said, 'No, no, no, he's too young, he really is'. Anyway, we did split for a little while, then we met up again, then we went back together, and then we got married when I was 22, in '59. But then I stayed married for many years, for 25 years, and then it broke up, it broke up; the marriage broke up completely, a complete breakdown.

I worked at the hotel about five years before I got married. But in between, I left that hotel and I went to work at the Pied Piper [a cafe] for a few months. The Pied Piper no, no, it was a great, great business going on, three course meal, 5 shillings and they'd be queuing up to come in. And we worked really hard there again, we worked hard, running round. . . . She'd pile me up with plates, about six plates, and the plates were bigger than myself. Then, in '59, I lost my little temper, because they give me a lot of glasses to wash and they shouldn't have done. I was getting a bit big for my boots and some of them were saying things, and I listened to what they were saying, and I was the one that said it, 'And I'm not staying and I'm going' and I went and I had nowhere to go; I had no home, no nothing. I was out on the road. I went, I just went. I just went, out in the world, no job, no home, no nothing. It was frightening actually, it was frightening. You were very young, and it's frightening actually leaving your homeland also, that's frightening. I just did come to England, but it was frightening for quite a long time. And anyway, I found a place to stay and then they liked me a lot at the hotel, so then I had to apologise to the manageress that I was sorry, and she said she'd have me a back in again so they had me back. I only stayed out for about three months I suppose really.

I went back to them [the hotel]. My ex-manageress said that I was silly, that I shouldn't have done. I was young and they realized I was young and I had this, you know when you're young, you do things sometimes that you wouldn't do normally and it's just that – I didn't even . . . that's what I did, yeah, yeah. But the funny thing, I will have to tell you this little bit, the funny thing was on a Sunday morning when I was at the Queen's Hotel, when I arrived first, and I was in the still room, the washing up, I was just doing it all, making the toast and everything and then I looked at the clock. Half past ten, I thought, 'It's time to go to Mass' so I went off to Mass. And the next thing is, they thought, 'Where's she gone, where is she? She's gone' and that was it. So the manager had me in the office and he said, 'I'm sorry, Moira, but' he said, 'I know you have to go to Mass, but you must do the washing up first'. But he was very good, he was very considerate because his wife was Irish and she understood I think. But I never said, I didn't say anything to anyone, I just went.

Moira left the hotel on her marriage and then moved to a cleaning job at a training centre for workers at a government research centre, Harwell, where she worked for many years on a casual basis. In the 1980s, cleaning was outsourced by the Thatcher government and Moira found her conditions worsened.

I know I worked there for about 40 years altogether, but I did cleaning elsewhere in between. And then later, contractors took over from the government. They took over and they cut the hours that I'd been, they cut my hours in half, the contractors, so you were given five minutes to do that, 10 minutes to do that. That was hard work.

In between, before I went back, I worked at a school. I had adopted Deborah [her daughter] I think then, around that time. Then I took a school job, a part-time school job, just part-time. It was on my doorstep and that was so hard. That was the hardest I'd ever done in my life. And the reason I went to that school was because Debbie was there, and I wanted to be home with her and I'd do anything just to be at home with her, and so I stuck it, for I don't know, so long, a few months I think really, but I couldn't, it was too much for me. It was killing me.

Then I went on to work at the convent for another bit. That was easier actually, the convent weren't such, they weren't such slave drivers, but it wasn't really, really hard, no the convent wasn't. So, I left there and then I went working again for Rush Common [the hostel], and I went on supervising, like Dining Room Assistant cum supervisor. If the supervisor was off I had to take over, and our job was to get all the men off to work in the morning. So I'd be up about five in the morning, in the kitchen for about quarter to six, get all the place ready for the people coming in for breakfast, any staff, make sure all the staff are on, make sure if anyone wasn't on, get somebody in, in place. That was quite a responsibility, but that was my job, and that was supervising on the day off of the supervisor, and then took over for three months when the supervisor's husband was very ill. So that was quite an experience.

And then I asked if I could do part-time. And the only part-time I could get was part-time in the labs at Harwell. But they were red labs, the labs that had to have special training. They wouldn't have contractors in them and then I went in to help the staff. I cleaned in those labs, but then I also went on to help like sterilizing glasses, making up mixtures, weighing stuff, doing everything for the scientists. And gradually I became part of the support group and that was my last job, Harwell. They trained me into it and they loved me in that area, yeah the top man said I was a little diamond there, he did, yeah. And so that was my favourite place really, Harwell, it was my favourite. Yeah, but that wasn't hard, I should have been doing, helping those, doing that work all the time, but Peter [her second husband] gave me the confidence, he said, 'Come on, you can do it'. It was easy actually, it was easy. Just helping them and doing advice really, because some of the, you had to do things right, because if you did something wrong, you'd ruined their experiment, yeah. They were doing cell culture and microbiologist area, so it had to be done right. Yeah it was lovely.

As she grew older and lived longer in England, Moira came to regret her Irish accent which, she believed, had a direct and negative impact on her relationships with co-workers and the public.

The only thing I found hard was when they had the Birmingham bombing.[4] I really, really would have given the world to have lost my Irish accent. And my neighbours were lovely. I was living next door to a teacher in a lovely area. That's where I was living and she was lovely, and I felt, I thought, 'This is horrendous, we are here in this country and they are looking after us so well' and I really, really was feeling upset about that: that upset me the most.

I didn't want to open my mouth at all that day because I didn't want anyone to know I was Irish that day. I was so ashamed that they were doing this, and every year I used to think, 'I wish for peace in Ireland, I wish for peace, I just wish for peace.' And then there was Mountbatten,[5] all those people I was thinking, and my sister, my foster sister, I had a foster sister she said to me, 'If this happened in Ireland' she said, 'They'd kill every Englishman around.' We were all disgusted, the good Irish, you see. And this is why now I feel with the Muslims now. I can sympathize with good Muslims. I wouldn't discuss anything with them, of course I wouldn't, but at the same time I can think, 'I bet there are a lot, a lot of good Muslims' and the bad ones can make them look . . .

But we never ever had any trouble, no we never had no trouble at all, never. I think it's because they knew me, they knew me, I think. Oh, we did have one little incident at Harwell, because they thought there was a bomb scare, right inside. Well, it's highly unlikely because the police are paid, but anyway, we all had to go out into the yard and they were searching the offices and things like that. And I said this to one of the bosses, I said, 'I feel awful' I said, 'I really do feel awful'. 'Don't worry my dear' he said, 'half my ancestors are Irish' and that's what he was like.

On the till: working for Tesco

Amrita was born in India in 1957. Aged 22, she married an Indian man who lived in the UK in the February before she completed her BA. She then moved to England to join her husband. She held various jobs, including working at Heathrow. In 2005, like Jasbir and Saran in Chapter 3, she started looking for work again after being involved in the dispute that summer.

I began applying for jobs here and there. Then I filled out the form for seasonal vacancy at Royal Mail at Langley and at Hounslow. I got the job at both places. But Hounslow was closer to home, so I took that one. So I started there, but later, those who went to Langley were made permanent, while those at Hounslow were kept only for four weeks. Then I went for computer classes – at Hounslow – for people who did not work. I had wanted to learn about computers for a while. So I asked at the job centre about it, but they said there was nothing available. But I went there by myself and enrolled. Then there was this other training – on how to write CVs, on how to do interviews and things like that. It was two week's training. So I told them about it at the job centre. I told them there that I may not be able to come and sign on time. He said, if I went on the training I could not sign on. I argued with him, but they said they will have to arrange it else I will not be allowed to sign on for two weeks. I then decided to not tell them anything and went directly to the course for two weeks.

It was good. They told us how to present ourselves at an interview, how to talk. Then at Tesco when I applied for the job, I had attached the certificate that I had got from the training. It said, 'customer service' on it. The Tesco manager later told me that she had given the job on the basis of that. So it did turn out handy, didn't it?

On 28 September 2006. I started part-time there at the till. I worked 4.00 pm to 10.00 pm for three days a week – it was a total of 16 hours a week. Then there was a vacancy there for a job in the price inventory. It was a full-time day job, and was permanent. All of that suited me. So I asked my manager if I should apply for the job. She said, 'Why not?' So I got it, temporary for three months, and then got made permanent. Four people had applied for the job. There was this man who often used to be late. I was never late during the four months that I worked there. If anything, I would arrive a few minutes early. My attendance was 100 per cent, and I had that letter from my manager at Tesco after three months into the first job. So I showed it at the interview, also that I always used to come back from by break on time, and all that. So they gave me the job. I felt good. I was not sure that I would get it. No one knew me there, and there were lots of people there who had worked at Tesco for a lot longer. But I was the one who got the job.

You know, there were a lot of white people who worked there. So I had thought, you know, that there will be some, you know, but there was nothing like that. Everyone helped. It was easy-going here. Where there are more Asian people working in a place, you have to work harder. The management puts pressure on you, and our people also work harder, so they expect more out of you. The pressure is on. Where white people work, where one goes to smoke, others go off too. In places where our people work, if you go to the loo twice within a short time, they will point out, 'She just went a while back, and there she goes again.' That's what they say to us. That's how it was at my previous workplace. The management used to keep a close eye on how we worked, kept the pressure up and encouraged the staff to grass on each other. Here at Tesco, everyone does their work in peace. No-one is keeping an eye on you. You go for your break, come back peacefully. You also have to help out customers when they can't find something. And many times we have these customers – these old people, and we know who they are – who come there and ask. Not because they can't find something, but because they are lonely and want someone to talk to. So we understand that and spend a few minutes talking to them. Those that are in wheelchair need help getting things down from shelves. I am happy working here.

'Just laughing at us': working in a family business

Ellen was born in Hong Kong in 1962 and came to the UK at the end of the 1970s. She was not sure of the exact date, although she thought her father arrived in 1964. She was involved in homework, in her case as a school girl in Hong Kong, helping her mother but once in England she was employed in the family fast food business, working first for her father and then with her husband.

I come from Hong Kong, and my parents, we immigrate, the whole family coming to England over about 30 years now. Yes, my father, first he worked in a restaurant, I think, yeah, doing restaurant and helping the kitchen. And then learning to do some cooking. Then he owned a business, a Chinese takeaway. He came here early before us to immigrate. He came here first and then after ten years we come. I came here about 17. Before in Hong Kong, my two older sisters, they started working. Doing sewing in Hong Kong. They're sewing the shoes, sewing the bra, something like that. They do it in a factory but sometimes they can take it back home. They can take back home to do some little bit of work there. And my mother bring some things back home to do it, doing the house thing, like the plastic flower. Stick the plastic flower together. I did it when I was little as well, I helped. Seven or eight I think, yeah; do it at home, helping my mum do some little bit of work. We take it from the factory and then how much we've done and then we take it back so how much they charge for a hundred flowers or something like that.

I came here with my mum and my three sisters, coming together. And my other eldest sister, she already marry, so she went two months before me, before us. She went with her family and her husband.

Once in the UK, Ellen worked in the family business, initially with her father and mother.

We helped him [father]. Helped a little bit, and then we started helping as well. We started helping doing some easy one. In the morning I learn English, in afternoon just helping in my father's shop and in the evening helping as well. I went to lessons half a year to nine months, I think but I find it a bit difficult, yeah, so I give up and also I was so tired because in the evening I was helping in the shop as well. So I find I haven't got much time to learn, too tired, stay helping my father's shop and after my father half retire, I was working full-time, so yes, with a lot . . . most of the things I need to do it, so I haven't got time as well so I haven't gone back to school anymore.

When not open time, the afternoon, we need to order things for the evening, already ordered, that we cut. We chop the meat and vegetables ready for the time open. After when we finish we need to wash up, clean up everything so at least we need to finish about 12.30 pm. Yeah, so a bit too late. Customers, my other sister, yeah my sister did it. She understand the order, understand the customers, and now she married an English people. We came here, we didn't understand so we just have all the friends Chinese. We just go out with their friends is all the Chinese so we haven't got much time to learn English as well. If you go out with people that speak English, you can learn a lot. But we find some, the young English kids, they're a bit . . . always speak . . . just laughing at us because before that they, like that, 'chinky', something like that. We don't like it. Yeah, they're horrible and then we go to the shop, get the newspaper and that lady serving called out 'that chinky wants some'. The lady, she's over 40, she can speak like that. It's not very nice. So we just find before we're quite difficult to understand in here. We just thought they will . . . doesn't like our Chinese so they already find speaking a different . . . laughing at Chinese people. If you bully . . . I think it's bully people isn't it?

Some were very nice but still got some people, they . . . I think when they came here not very nice ones should be . . . they've got a little bit drunk, too much drink. Yeah, too much drink they feel . . . yeah. We find sometimes they're still swearing and they are talking not very nice things like 'chinky', something like that. But they just say you are from different country, they just thought you don't understand what they said and they're saying a lot of not very nice things. We find that before we always got trouble in the shop, yeah, they're teenage. They want a lot of trouble when they come to the shop.

We call the police. Sometimes they really can't. . . . Oh yeah, my brother, my other brother, they've been fighting with a customer because they haven't paid the money and they take something and go out, they've gone, they run out. My brother chasing them and he'd been beaten. The other man, he got a broken leg and went to hospital for a month. So I think I heard my father say that when he came here about 30 years, when he first came, most Chinese shops, takeaway or restaurant, it always happened. The customer, yeah, they won't pay the money and they make trouble and they're fighting with the customer. A lot of change now, I think. I find most English people, they're most polite.

Ellen married a Chinese national who had lived in England since he was five. He owned a takeaway that sold both Chinese food and fish and chips. Ellen had two daughters and began to work fewer hours.

At the moment I'm working part-time but that chip shop. I help in the evening time, only two days. Yeah only two nights, so I have more time. I've got few English friends, not many because I don't know how to make a friend. Yeah, I got one English friend, she's my daughter's, the friend's mum. We went shopping once a week about two years ago but this year I find not much things to do, so I didn't call her to go out for shopping because my girl doesn't need me to shop for her. They can choose her thing. When they are little I can buy something for them and the woman, I can help do her shopping for her.

But I have a lot of Chinese friends. We meet a friend in here, every Monday. We've got a lot of friends come here every Monday. Sometimes we just go out shopping, we just arrange if we've got time to go. We go in together. I still am Chinese, I think. Chinese, yeah, but I won't go back to my country when I retire. I won't, no, because I settled down here. I know everything in here. In Hong Kong they change a lot. Everything. I don't understand what they're going to do. Everywhere is sort of change, so I can't settle down in Hong Kong. I think I will be dying here.

'Tiring of the public': working as a hotel receptionist

Mari from Brazil was 28 when she moved to London eight years previously. She had a degree in hotel management and had planned to move to the USA but found both her lack of money and her poor spoken English were barriers. She was able, however, to obtain a post in a London hotel.

America was never a possibility because we have to get visa in Brazil to go to America. To get the visa you have to prove that you have a lot of money so it was not the case, I could not possibly. I came to London because my friends were here. So I thought I could stay with them for some time, which I did and they were there. I had people I knew before for quite a long time. My plan initially was to stay here just for one year and a half and I'm here for eight now. It's quite a long time. After one year I had decided, 'I'm enjoying. I have learned so much in this one year and a half. I don't want to go back now'. But I didn't intend to stay that long.

Before emigrating Mari had worked for several years in Brazil.

It was all in hotels but in different hotels. The first one I went there doing the same job as I was doing before in my holidays – on the telephone. Then after the summer I started working on reception, reservations. I was just learning more as the years passing by. I think I had three jobs in three different hotels.

For the first few years in London, Mari worked in a factory making pasta in the morning, looked after a friend's children in the afternoon and went to night school in the evening so that she could improve her English and apply for a job in a hotel. As well as learning English, Mari took a course in hotel management and as part of the course she started a placement as a receptionist.

It was terrifying. The first three months was terrible. People come to me and I could not understand their English, thinking I can understand but all the different accents and stuff like this. So people literally come across to me and ask me something, I'm like 'what did they say?' 'Just a moment' and I'd find someone else. Yeah, it was tough. I thought I could not make it. So I went back to school and asked them if I could get out but because the school funded the work placement for you, you have to pay for them to do that. And I said 'can you change, can I get another job where I don't have to speak to many people?' 'No, no, you have to pay for it; there is conditions, we have an agreement with the hotel' so I have to stay. If I have to stay, I have to make it work and I think it was the first time I was in an environment I was used to, but all the terms was all different.

I stayed three months in the main reception. Then, after three months, I said 'I want to be moved.' The hotel has, like most hotels, they have executive lounge with a receptionist. I asked them to transfer me to the executive lounge after this three months. I could manage myself, because the lounge was more private. It was less amount of people and people had more time to . . . they are more calm than to have a queue of 50 people in front of you. I did like much better the executive lounge and I stayed there. I didn't want to move. They didn't move me for almost a year or more than a year. Then I asked transfer to reservations, so I moved to reservations. It's in the office. Because the hotel has central reservation, the people in-house do just the paperwork, just checking if they have the correct rate and all the requests are there. So I was doing four, five months, then they move me into reservations in the same department for group reservations, which just deal with more than ten rooms.

I wanted to move because I was tiring of public. It's quite strange. My friends say I'm like a person, a vet, who doesn't like animals. I was at a stage that I didn't like guests anymore. I like the hotel environment but I like the paperwork, I like office and more organization than face-to-face. People keep asking you the same question, different people but you're the same person being asked the same question like 15 times a day. I think I felt in some way some people could be quite unrespectful. It's like 'okay, I'm the guest, you're here to serve me' and I didn't like that. It made me really, really angry.

'Sorry for the queue, my colleague is in lunchtime.' 'In lunchtime you have all this queue?' It's like 'yes, we need food as well'. These kind of thing make me really, really angry so sometimes I was really quite rude. Also because usually the people in the lounge were more repeat clients, and so I made quite good friends. I had a good relationship with people in this private club. But I know, and I have seen, never happened to me but I have seen some guests come to one of us and say 'can you call someone who speaks proper English?' And then we are in a position that we can't say what we think. I don't know how to deal with people who are rude. I wish I knew. That's something I'm still trying to work. I know I work in a hotel and I know I have to be nice, but my face shows and I can be really sharp; I can give a really sharp answer and that won't do.

Reflecting on why she found 'the public' difficult, Mari summarized the characteristics of guests from different parts of the world.

Japanese people always really nice and very, very correct. I had one guest which I had made some money change. He gave me 2,000 yen and I gave the exchange for 20,000 yen, so I gave out ten times the amount in pounds and for a mistake like this you have to pay in the hotel, in some case you have to pay. And the next day he come back and he gave me the money back. The Japanese are very patient and they are very . . . they respect you as a person.

I think the Americans, they are the worst. They are very demanding. They don't come to England expecting to see England, to adapt themselves to what we have, how the way things are here. They want to be here with everything they have back in America, so they complain about the size of the rooms because they have massive rooms there. All our rooms are never going to be as big as theirs, never. I think they are very, the Americans, they really look down on you. But it's not generally. There are some very nice people. It's quite hard to explain, to stereotype but we are just saying major things. The Arabic countries, they don't give a shit. You're not a person.

Even though Mari had moved from the front desk to an office job, she had to conform to the hotel dress code in an industry where first impressions are important, even when some employees are in back-office jobs that are largely invisible to the guests.

Appearance, appearance all this counts. We can use our own clothes so it has to be dark suit, plain top. It has to be smart. You have like a specific things; you can have just one bracelet, you can have just two rings but if you have an engagement ring and a wedding ring, you can use three: you can use them together. Earrings have to be small, make-up can't be flash make-up. Room attendants, they have to have skin colour tights, can't be any other colour. Men, if they have shave, they have beard or moustache, they have to be clean cut and stuff like this. Perfume cannot be strong; socks have to be black for men, stuff like this. It's important because they want a standard of things and also because I think some people don't have the criteria, some people is going to turn up with loads of rings and jewellery. They don't look professional if they do and if they're working in the kitchen, it's a health and safety issue. But also it's just to keep the things, people more equal, everybody equal, treat everybody equal. There is a few exceptions, like if it's religion-related then they have to go to HR and explain that it's religion related, they will be allowed.

I want to stay in London but sometimes I have my doubts about staying in the company, about the whole hotel environment because I think in general it's low pay. It had crossed my mind to change to do something else, something completely different which perhaps it was more rewarding. Hotel can be quite frustrating, you do quite a lot but is never good enough for everybody so it had crossed my mind to change career completely. To be a florist, to work in a nursery, something like this.

'It's difficult to find a job, especially if you are good looking': model, secretary, receptionist

Almost sixty years after the Baltic Cygnets began to arrive in the UK, the expansion of the EU in 2004 opened the way for young women from the now-independent Baltic States to come to Britain to work.

Jenny, born in 1980 in a seaside town near Riga, in Latvia, had moved to London in 2002, on a student visa, to take a course in spoken English at a college. After two years, once she had the right to seek employment, she stopped studying and looked for a full-time job with the encouragement, or perhaps the insistence, of her family in Latvia.

My family, they was okay [financially]. I mean they send me to England to study, and I studied first. I used to spend money but after they said to me 'okay, you are not that young anymore. You can, if you want to, stay in England, so you have to be doing by yourself something. Go and work, make yourself money and income and think about your life.'

So, I look for work. Oh, first job . . . first job . . . oh my God, when was that? Yeah, I used to work for, for some beauty salon. Yeah, I used to work there for maybe half a year, I don't remember how long. It was quite difficult you know actually too, I mean the hours was quite long as well, and I remember there I was paid like £4.50 per hour. Maybe low because I had no national insurance number.[6]

Then after, I used to be receptionist there. After, I was doing some gynaecologist's clinic, as a secretary, but it wasn't so long because you know there is involved men, it's very difficult to work . . . to find like . . . because it's very difficult to find job, especially if you are good looking, you know, in this country, because at the end they want something else, they doesn't want your job, work what you do for them. And there I was maybe for two months. Then I used to do, because back home, I used to do some modelling as well, and here I did as well. Modelling, yeah. I did it in Latvia as well, but was more about photo-modelling; it wasn't catwalk you know because I'm not that tall, you know? Yeah I used to do Miss Bikini Latvia 2007, I think. And I was the winner. And in London as well, Asian Woman I did for *Cosmopolitan*. I did some catwalk as well, for some small fashion shows, you know? In Café de Paris, I remember.

The clinic, the gynaecological clinic: he didn't pay me at all. Because I worked there for one month, and he was saying to me 'Okay, next month I want you to come with me to Spain, I want to decorate some another clinic', something, I don't know, I said 'Spain? Just me and you?' and he said 'yes'. And it was like for me strange because I applied for receptionist secretary in London, for gynaecologist's clinic, I was surprised. I remember it was based in Bayswater. And I just said to him 'Okay, can you pay me my wages?' He said 'I'm going to pay you in Spain' and I just didn't go and just left the job because I understand there is this bullshit.

Then I used to go and look for job everywhere, and when I used to bring my CVs as well, you know . . . especially where it was working some beauty salons, you know. I tried some offices for receptionist, because I did study as well economy,[7] you know? But if there is a man it's very difficult, because you can straight away see the way how he looks at you, and there's no point to come even he will say 'Okay, come and try on Monday, then we will see.' There's no point because you can see what he wants from you, you know? So I had that experience but even I didn't come to work. I mean I used to come, err, I don't remember. Maybe there was some places I came for maybe one week, you know? But that's it really, yeah.

I used to work for some building company as a secretary, but I didn't work there for long time because that was my friend and he really needed someone to help him, for one month, and I just worked there for one month because he asked me to do some paperwork, to help him and this is what I did. He used to pay me I think £6 per hour, and I used to work like eight hours per day only. Yeah, he used to pay me £50 per day, so I was eight hours from 10.00 am til, I don't remember, 5.00 pm. He paid cash. Then after, I used to do the properties as well. We used to have, as well as for my friend, I used to work for him. I still work there, helping him to rent the flats and taking the rents. As well, if there is any problems, I call to try and sort out, you know. I still work there. I still help him. Just part-time. I don't have to be there all the time, you know, because there is already like, everyone is, like the flats is full, there is 18 flats.

And now I'm here, a dry cleaner's, like maybe, I think, two or three years already. And I work legally here, as a receptionist, you know. I'm working here like part-time, all the time, I'm not full-time here. Like two or three days a week I'm here, from eight o'clock til 6.00 pm. It's ten hours. There is another girls as well, two of them. They are from Eastern European as well. Different times, different times we work. It's quite boring but there's nothing to do, you're just sitting you know. But people [the customers] are fine, they are fine. I mean now people became very stressed because of the business crashes[8] and they doesn't have money, and they're quite moody and negative, you know, you can hear a lot of things. They try to cheat you as well. But I mean like we have a lot of clients. I mean they are for a long time all customers, and we're trying to be very nice to them, and we understand that they have bad times. We have bad times, everyone has bad times, you know? But otherwise everything, I mean, is fine.

However, Jenny ended on a different note.

I became very strong in this country because you have to go through so much here, you know. I mean all the time there is problems with job, you have to look for job then, you know, in the job somebody's try to, you know, to cut you in the job or something, you know? I mean it's very difficult. Really I was thinking to go away from this country because, you know, it's very difficult. I mean I get used to it. It's good to make money in this country but for living and all this, I mean, it's really shit, this country.

'Customers, they can be aggressive': driving buses

Nadia, a Polish woman in her early thirties, came to the UK in 2005 and by 2007 she was working as a bus driver. Like Jenny, she too had a negative view of Britain, although of members of the public rather than the country as a whole.

I always, if you ask me about the reason why I decided to apply for being a bus driver, I was always dreaming about having a job which I would like and I never wanted to have a job just for money. I always wanted to find that kind of job which would give me a lot of pleasure as well. And when I was working in the photographic shop which I was really enjoying, I actually didn't think about change. But because of financial reasons – we bought a house and I thought it would be better to earn better. Then I thought what else I could do that would give me more money but also a lot of pleasure. I thought I always wanted to be a train driver and I always wanted to be, to work in motion, to meet people, to be in constant movements. I thought what it might be. And then I see so many women here are bus drivers and that idea came to my mind. And I just thought I would be a bus driver then. So I just applied. They advertise the job; there was a position opened. I had some friend whose husband was a bus driver. And she was telling me 'oh, it's such a good money; it's so easy and you know just go and get the job'. I thought well, why not to try.

I applied. I had to pass all these tests. I had to go through all these procedures, you know, to pass all these steps, just to be employed. It took me something like two weeks of reading the books *Highway* as it is called in English, which I could not understand in the beginning. But I wanted to get this job so much so I just prepared myself perfectly. And I remember I was so scared of that test and I passed 100 per cent. I didn't even make one mistake. I was so shocked, surprised. And later they employed me and they offered me the course to get a driving licence. Then I had to learn how to drive. I was actually employed in the company but I still had to continue learning and then at the end I had to pass the test again – theory test and driving test, which was like, you know, very stressful for me because I never drove the bus before. It seems to be difficult but when you actually sit in a car, you set your mirrors, you find out that it's not so difficult. It's quite easy actually because you can see the whole length of the bus. It's very often that passengers do not realize that. And also driving a bigger vehicle is easier because everybody makes a way for you. So driving itself as driving, it's really pleasant, a really easy thing. I didn't have any accidents during all these five years. The other aspects are more difficult but I think I'll tell you in a minute.

I started as a bus driver and I am still a bus driver. However, when I started to work there some lady from the office asked me if I have some kind aspiration to go for some higher positions. Basically, she told me that with my kind of education[9] I could apply for a managers' course. After completing this course I could become either a manager or supervisor or, you know, controller job or let's say an operation manager job, this kind of stuff. But I wasn't interested because of two reasons. First of all I believe that if you start to rise too fast, you can fall down quickly. And I just wanted to know the company from the very bottom, you know. Eventually, step by step you know. Let's say it's a career ladder. But later I changed my mind because the more I knew the company the less I wanted to work, you know, higher, because my company is quite strict. Basically, there are a few reasons to complain about it. But I am happy there. I've just decided that as long as it would be possible, I will just do this driving job.

And the other reason, except what I've just told you, I just can't imagine the work in the office with papers. If I had to be like a manager or supervisor or someone else, I would have my office but I would be very unhappy because I wouldn't meet people. I wouldn't observe the world around. So that's actually the main reason. Of course money is much better but, you know, life is not only about money. There is a different wage in week days and weekends and in bank holidays. Average I would say, if I don't do any overtime, average I have per week something like £380 [in 2012], that's what I have in my pocket, so that's after tax already, which is not bad because in total in a month it's something like £1,600 without any overtime. But overtimes are also available. I can do as much as I want because they always struggle with the drivers. If I wish, I could earn more. Sometimes there were some months when I was doing six days a week and my average was like £450 per week. So that's really not bad.

Physical driving is easy. However, customers' service, you know customers, sometimes they can be aggressive. Sometimes, yes, they can be aggressive because you know it's too expensive for them. That's the reason. Or let's say they shout at me that the previous bus driver didn't stop. So I open the door, I am on time, I stop at the bus stop, and they suddenly start shouting 'vow, vow, vow, the previous driver didn't stop', and I say 'don't shout at me. I am not the previous driver and I've stopped here for you. Come and take a seat.' And sometimes people react like 'call the company, call your manager'. But I say 'no, if you want to call, call the customer services'. You know it's not my job to call about that the driver didn't stop. So, sometimes people don't want to understand very simple things, very simple. Sometimes they speak to me in slang. I don't understand too much of slang. So I always ask them politely 'could you please repeat that?' And then they start laughing at me like 'vow, vow, vow'. I was called very often 'go back to your fucking country'. I've been called 'fucking Polish bitch' many times, many times. That's this kind of incidents, it happens, I would say, two or three times a month. So many times I was called bitch. I was called stupid Polish or bloody foreigner or that stuff that is not pleasant. It's quite sad when you try to do your job properly and you do everything correct and suddenly they just come and attack you without any reason. So these things I think is quite stressful.

Another additional stress is the fact that I cannot reply in the same language as they do. Because if only I reply in their language, if they swear on me, if I swear on them I can be sacked. I need to balance, I need to calm down, I need to always keep control on my emotions. Whatever I do I cannot swear, whatever I do I cannot be rude. Because it's always that additional thing. Okay, if they complain, the company will see CCTV and they will find out that if somebody told me 'fuck off' and I replied 'fuck off' and then I am in trouble. That person is gone, that person left my bus, but I am in trouble. These things I find sometimes are very, very hard. But fortunately, it doesn't happen very often. So, I just manage. I just get used to it, I just get used to it and it's this kind of stuff when you think 'oh well, life, people'.

The other thing, it happens very often then people have a bad day and a bus driver is actually the only person and the first person who can be attacked. So they come to the bus, they are upset already about something else what happened. And you are the first person who they speak with and they just treat us as a boxing bag, you know. This is sometimes, you know, quite stressful. I try to understand that, but sometimes I just can't, I just can't because you know. I try to explain the reasons. I try to think why they do it. But for them it's like, you know, you are just a servant, you are just a servant. You are there for them; they treat you like a dog, sometimes, they speak to you like you are a dog. They call you bitch, they call you fucking foreigner. Excuse me but that's what. So these aspects are very stressful.

I would say the most problems I've got with people who, in my opinion, who are just taking benefits, who are unemployed or they have problems with alcohol or drugs. That's the biggest group of these trouble-makers. However, I am quite surprised that very often I hear the same stuff from people who look absolutely normally. They have suits, they have the bags, they have a very nice posh accent, they have these kind of rings on a little finger. They come to the bus, I say 'ticket is £1.90' and they say 'oh, fucking bloody expensive'. I say 'well, that's the price, you either take the bus or you can walk'. It's not me who sets the price, but it's me who is taking the blame for it. You know it's kind of, like, these kind of comments, sometimes it happens that you hear it from people from whom you absolutely don't expect.

I didn't expect discrimination about being a woman, however discrimination about being a foreigner, yes, definitely yes. Very often I could hear very abusive comments about my accent, because that is the thing which, you know, is the first sign that we are not from here. And very often people were just they were laughing. They just start to laugh especially when they go for a party and a little bit drunk. They want to take a beer to the bus and I say 'you can't take the beer to the bus which is opened. If it's closed, it's okay'. I don't mind because it can be shopping but when I tried to stop them bringing alcohol, they are abusive. They like 'oh, this is England, this is an English bus and you are a Polish driver. You cannot tell me what I can do in my country or what I cannot do in my country'. That's what I've heard. That's the honest truth. I just said 'yeah, but this is the English rule that you cannot bring the alcohol, it's not my rule, you know. I just the person in charge of the vehicle and as far as I am concerned I will follow the rules.' It's like you are not from here you'd better shut up and do your job. That kind of responses I've heard a few times and this is not very nice.

We have a roster and they allocate you somewhere, week by week. It's just on my route. So today I did that from 6.40 am to 3.50 pm. Next week I would originally do that but I swapped with somebody because we can swap. As you see, sometime it's 8.45 am sometime it's 9.25 am, sometime it's 7.12 pm. Shifts are different but the average 40–46 hours per week and sometimes in the week there is like 37 hours, sometimes it's 42 hours, sometimes it's even 47 somewhere. It changes but you can also swap with other drivers. Let's say I don't like to do night shifts so I swap with those people who don't like to do early shifts, to wake up at three o'clock in the morning. So they do my lates, I do their earlies. It's very flexible.

Promoting Chinese culture: teaching the public in a museum

Li Jing also works with people. For twelve years she has been a community worker in London, but before that she had a diverse set of jobs, including working illegally. She is the Hong Kong Chinese woman who came to UK in the early 1990s when she was 26 to, as she explained in Chapter 2, make 'my dreams come true'. She gained a degree in fashion at a London college but then found it impossible to stay in the UK.

When I finished studies, I couldn't get a work permit. I got a job from Wallis and Company, you know the fashion company. I got a job. But I didn't have a work permit so I couldn't work. It's not easy to get that job; it's a very good job I can tell you, with Wallis. You know they don't take just anyone, because I was pretty good in my degree, and I knew the people there, and I was lucky. But unfortunately because of the work permit, I couldn't get a job. The company didn't want to apply for me because they never have. They don't need to. There are so many people they can employ to be honest. They do me a favour, but they didn't want extra. When you have a work permit, you have a specialist. Why you need the work permit to employ these people, when at the same time you can employ any student in England? They do fashion design, so many good students.

So, I didn't stay. I had to go back to Hong Kong, to work about ten months or one year, I can't remember, earned money and gave it back to the government, because I borrowed a loan from them to do my studies here. I was go back to my old job. I was trying to get a fashion design job, however, when I graduate about 29. It's very old for like fashion designer there. And also, I think people they starting to employ the overseas people to become fashion designers in Hong Kong, because their Western look, when you employ them in your company. They think they're more like different. So it was quite difficult for me to get a job, I think especially because of my age. If I was about 22 maybe I could because I got a first class degree, in one of the top colleges in England. Just because I think my age, and because they started changing to employ the Western designers, the Chinese look. And the other reason, I don't have serious working experience as a fashion designer. You know I was working as soft toy engineer, when I went back there. First I picked up a job in retail, with an Italian fashion company, retail as a sales lady, because they will train you up to be a merchandising, in that direction, but still the money was low.

So I was like I need the money. So I went back to my old job, to the soft toy job like as a manager, for about ten months, I think ten months and then I decided to come back [to London] and try again, yeah to try again.

Li Jing had met a British Chinese-heritage man when she was a student and they decided to re-establish the relationship.

So I came back to the UK but I couldn't get a job. It was a terrible period for me, because like coming back for my boyfriend, I couldn't get a job because I didn't have a work permit. I worked as a waitress, and I had another job working in a garment factory in Bethnal Green, as a quality controller. It quite upset me, with a degree, because you know, because I can't stay at home not doing anything, so I went to work for about £2.70 an hour [in 1995]. It was okay, just better than staying at home all the time, but it was quite upsetting. I did try applying for some jobs, but I didn't have any luck. I still didn't have a work permit, so I worked like waitress and like quality control. They just like illegal jobs; obviously I couldn't work as a visitor, it was illegal.

The quality control job was in a small factory in the East End of London owned by a family friend.

The quality controller for example, it's a full-time job, I think standing for nine hours. We had lunch, but I had to cook for the boss. They took me out for an hour before the lunchtime, to help them with the cooking. So cooking for like ten people within an hour. The boss is someone I knew, they gave me a job. It's a Chinese person, you know, a family business. I know them through friends. The other workers [were] some Chinese, some Africans, African-Caribbean community. Those two communities, I would say.

I was a few months there, I can't remember how long, and then I moved on as a waitress, because I was used to it. When I was studying in England, I did a part-time job waitress, and, the hostess, so I had experience working as a waitress. And then I decided to get married. And after I got married, trying to find job, then I found myself got pregnant, so I just not really bother.

Before her daughter was born, Li Jing worked for some weeks as a tutor in fashion design in a casual position.

So I worked, after marry, I worked for the Victoria and Albert Museum as a fashion design, fashion tutor, it's a technical course. So, like teaching Chinese women to make Chinese and Western clothes. It's a course for making Chinese dress and Western dress, a course for 20 weeks. The women they had to come for the whole course. Most of them they wanted to learn the Chinese dress, but they have to learn Western dress as well. So we had the tutor for the Chinese dress and the tutor for the Western dress. The people [students], they're local, I can understand a bit more, and it's very good for me to get a job. I think with the course the year before, the tutor wasn't able to communicate with the women because she was young and had no experience with the local British Chinese. They're not local British, they're Hong Kong Chinese, but they're different mentality. That young lady maybe difficult to communicate with the older mature women. So I was working with them well and we enjoyed it, both of us. So we became friends later on.

The Educational Department [of the V and A], they wanted to promote the Chinese community culture, like Chinese New Year, the Autumn festival, they do activities in the Victoria and Albert Museum. This was a clothes-making course, and it ended with a fashion show. So the students make their clothes, they were able to present their clothes in the show at the end of the course. The students all Chinese women. So the course actually brought a lot of Chinese women more confidence, in communication as well as education. The course is very, very good, and they have induction for the women to teach them, when they become a student now again. For a long time they haven't been in learning, they know the rule, respect the teacher, respect your attendance, things like that, before they start the course. And then they had ten week course from me, and it's quite tough. Although they most women, they know how to sew, we had to help them to make their own pattern and design their own dress, so they have to present it at the end. Although I'm not a very good teacher, I was happy with that job, although I'd hate to become a teacher. It's one of the things I wouldn't do in my life – doctor, nurse and teacher. I'd say to myself I don't want to do these three.

Then I had my daughter and then about when my daughter was about a month old, I saw the advertisement for this post I'm working in, so I go for this interview and I start working for this job since my daughter five months old, for 12 years now. The job title is called Community Lay Health Worker. We start as a team of four of us, the Chinese community worker, Bangladeshi community worker, and African-Caribbean community worker, and British-born, we call white community worker, as a team. The aim of the project is it employs some casual workers, promoting health activities in the local community. It's quite a casual thing, so they called lay health worker. The job includes training and youth and development course, and then bringing in more cooperation into the community work. We have a large Chinese community living locally, and the Chinese group, they started 26 years, been gathering in this organization for 26 years. I would say the group have been recognized as one of the oldest groups in London and maybe even in England.

I like this job, although working with humans is very different atmosphere from working with a piece of work, and when you working with community you have to do it one-to-one and one-to-whole group.

Although I'm capable of doing that, my personality and character are quite open-minded and talkative. I mean I can talk to all different levels of people. That is actually my strong point as a community worker.

Li Jing was happy in the job that she found, despite experiencing the impact of stereotypical assumptions about her skills and attributes as a Chinese woman – subservience to a boss who expected her to cook for him, and an assumption that as a Chinese woman she 'naturally' would be adept at making Chinese-style clothes. Her interactions in the job at the museum that she describes near the end of her narrative were students, Chinese women in the main, who were happy to be in the class. As the other narratives make clear, jobs that involve interaction with the public are not always easy. For Ellen, for example, orientalist assumptions were expressed in far more unpleasant ways, from racist terminology to violence. And as Nadia made clear, her interactions with the bus passengers she encountered everyday were often far from pleasant. Many of these women seemed resigned to the often low wages and difficult exchanges with the public rather than finding pleasure in their work, although their determination and their perseverance and commitment to hard work shines through the narratives. As Jenny noted, 'it is really shit, this country' but nevertheless, most of these women seemed resigned to staying. Ellen wearily concluded that she would probably die in the UK. In the next chapter, as well as talking about their family life, the older women begin to think about retirement and perhaps returning 'home', sometimes to a country that they had not seen for many decades. Throughout all the narratives so far, 'work' and 'life' are clearly connected, as well as details about migration and moving jobs and home within the UK. As I argued in the introduction, the boundaries between home and the workplace and between different types of employment are often blurred for women, as their circumstances change over their lifetime. Bearing and raising children, for example, continues to have a far more significant impact on the working lives of women than men, despite the wider availability of childcare to purchase in the market and men's growing involvement in the lives of their children in recent years.

8

Home Life:

Housework, Family, Community and Retirement

The workplace is not the only location where money is earned, nor the only place where work is undertaken. Several of the earlier narratives have demonstrated the significance of home as a site of waged work: making toys, helping parents (usually with mothers) to assemble, among other things, plastic flowers, looking after children, perhaps as a nanny or au pair, cleaning other women's houses while they are 'out' at work, and, more recently, checking work emails and finishing reports while in some senses not 'at work'. All these tasks and jobs that have been described in earlier chapters blur the boundaries between home and waged work.

The home is not only a place of employment for some women. All sorts of unwaged jobs are done at home by women on a regular basis to keep family life on an even keel. Clothes need washing and ironing, shopping has to be done and put away, meals made and floors cleaned: all those repetitive tasks that no sooner done, need doing again. In the 1940s and 1950s when some of the older women here first arrived in the UK, housework was often dreary, as well as heavy and demanding, without many of the 'mod cons' that make it lighter work now. The introduction of smokeless zones in towns from the mid-1950s[1] had a significant impact on housework, for example, and later the widespread expansion of central heating and double glazing made it easier to keep houses clean, although more expensive to maintain. And the growth of the 'white goods' industries over the decades resulted in the expansion of ownership of washing machines, tumble dryers, and microwaves, as well as other consumer goods, including, of course, a television and a car (see Table 4 in Appendix 1). More recently many households possess what may seem, to older women, an astonishing array of electronics. Whether maintaining and using all these belongings makes work or reduces it is an open question.

As well as the daily and often monotonous side of work in the home, women (and it is still women in the main) provide love, care and support for others in their households: what in the labour market is termed 'affective labour' but in the home is termed love and caring for others. Women look after the emotional and material needs of other household members – their children and partners, but also often, in the multigenerational families common among some migrant groups, grandparents and grandchildren too, who may have arrived in the UK later than their own children or their parents. Love and care is, of course, not a one-way street and support in households is often, if not always, a reciprocal relationship and family support, especially with childcare, is often essential in facilitating women's waged work.

Migration, however, sometimes destabilizes traditional ties of affection and belonging and may challenge pre-existing bonds and patterns of responsibility. Some men, for example, may resent the growing freedoms open to women in UK society or the relative financial independence a job may bestow on women. However, in many cases women's incomes are an essential element of family survival and most men recognize this and support their partners' decisions. Most of the husbands of women strikers, for example, whether at Ford, Grunwick or Gate Gourmet, were supportive of their wives' decisions, albeit perhaps reluctantly in some cases, and they helped their wives and partners in various ways through the involvement in struggles with employers. Sahdev, for example, who was involved in the dispute at Gate Gourmet in 2005, recalled that her family were supportive.

> My family were okay about it. 'You have to give others the support; you have to stand together.' What else could they say? True, the fact that I could no longer bring the money home caused a lot of problems for us. I won't deny that. But we did not have any arguments. I was not given a hard time for participating in it. There were fights in other houses; I have heard such things. But not in my house. My husband understood that there was nothing I could do about it.

Sometimes, as Sai reported, during the Grunwick strike in the mid-1970s, it was the older generation who were worried about their daughters' reputations.

> Many [women] stopped attending the pickets because their families said it was not appropriate that our women should be standing on the picket line. 'What will people say?' The parents used to put pressure.

In general, however, for many migrant women, multigenerational families were crucial in enabling mothers to earn when their children were small. As Faheema, of Pakistani heritage, explains, 'my mother-in-law, their grandmother, looked after them'.

Family reunification was perhaps particularly important to families who had been torn apart by war and exile. Diana, one of the Baltic Cygnets, recalls her struggle to recreate family life.

My sister and parents hadn't come [to the UK] yet. There in Germany they found her husband. He was a soldier and he came with us as well but he was working on a farm in agriculture and then in two year's time he got his wife and little boy. And then there was a big struggle to get our parents because when we were in Germany we had been through all these things. And we said 'we were not going to part' and so with a big struggle and help we had our parents here. When my parents came, for some time my father lived with me and my mother with another sister because there was not room together.

As the earlier generations of migrant women age, they too may face growing dependence on others, finding it harder to manage everyday tasks, as well as eventually having to face the death of their husbands and partners, and, eventually, their own demise. A number of the women displaced by the Second World War have died since they told me their stories and most of the women from the Caribbean who arrived in the 1960s and 1970s have now retired, although some are still active in community and voluntary work.

In this chapter housework and childcare are the main foci, but stories of first finding or owning a house, often a struggle, are also included, as well as stories about involvement in communal life. These latter activities typically take place beyond the physical boundaries of the home but are often based on continuing connections with women from the same national background and so the 'homeland' becomes an important metaphor as well as the social glue of connection. In the home and in the community, memories are cherished and retold, often by older women, and children are initiated into some of the customs of their mothers' homeland.

Establishing a home and a family

Diana worked in a shoe factory in the 1960s, once her children were at secondary school. She and her husband scraped and saved to buy a house in the late 1960s.

All my money went to buying the house, that's how it was. I stayed at the factory until I was 60. It suited me. There was the shops at dinner time where I could do my shopping. On Saturdays I cleaned the house and everything and then on Sundays we sometimes went out.

When I got my first washing machine? That was very late, very late, I think it was '70s or something and then it was second hand because we had to pay for the house and the children's clothes, they cost quite a lot of money. But we didn't have television for ages; the first colour television was when my husband retired in 1979. And we never had a car, we couldn't afford that but, do you know, we were very happy together. That was the main thing.

Letting rooms to compatriots was one way in which some of the early post-war migrants managed to save in order to buy a house, rather than to rent or continue to live in tied accommodation provided, for example, by hospitals.

Illona, working as a hospital domestic in the late 1940s, yearned for greater independence than 'living-in' permitted.

So after a year, I think, I asked if I could live out. My mother had a friend and she lived with her in one room and I lived in another room with an English family, you know in digs. I suppose it was all right. They were ordinary people; we got on with them. I had that little thin bedroom over the hall. Only my bed, and orange cases was my bookshelves, you know. I think we lived there for a year and then my friends parents' bought a house and they lived in the attic and let the other rooms and, I lived in one room, my mother with her friend in another and my future husband lived in the smallest room. That's how I met him.

Marta also came to the UK in the late 1940s as an EVW. She worked at Courtaulds in the 1950s, and she and her husband were able to buy a house relatively early in the decade by letting rooms. Like many of the women across the decades, Marta and her husband coped with childcare by working opposite shifts.

It wasn't unusual for people like us to buy a house. I think the psychology of it, because if you have a house you have a sort of a foot, a room in the place. You are not in somebody's way, you have a house. And also we had to take in lodgers to help with payments and so on so. Every room in the house was let. We only had one room to ourselves. That is how everybody did and also some other women sort of cooked for the lodgers, which I didn't. Well, I did for one, but I don't like cooked for other people but I did for one man. He sort of insisted. But some women did for a whole crowd of people, did cooking and what not but I didn't. So, yes, I mean, yes, people wanted their own place. That is how you can explain it. You don't want to be sort of underfoot or in the way of other people all the time. You want to have your own little corner sort of thing. All the lodgers were Latvian too. Word was sort of passed round. There were a lot of single men looking for rooms then.

We were very busy then. Then the first child came along and for a period I didn't work and things were quite hard. So, by that time he was doing two shifts, so for a while we did like the opposite shifts so we could look after the child. The factory was quite close and we could change over very easily and the child would sleep at midday and so we did opposite shifts. Looking back I shouldn't have done it but that is what we did.

Brigita came to the UK to work in the textile industry in 1948 but was working with her EVW husband on a farm in 1952 when she had her first child and so had no problems with childcare.

When my son was born I was still working on the farm, you know where he [husband] was sent there, and he [son] was put in a pram and I could take him with me. I was feeding turkeys, well 3,000 hens and turkeys at only at Christmas. I didn't have to keep to certain hours as long as the hens were fed in the evening and morning.

*Sometimes, women were lucky enough to make casual arrangements with British women, who worked for them and their children, as *Elvira* found in the early 1950s.*

We lived with the old lady [as tenants] and a lady across the road had a daughter of the same age and she took mine in the day. It worked well and I was happy.

Sharing housework and childcare with husbands by working opposite shifts was common among these migrant women, across the seven decades.

Parvani, of Indian heritage, and her husband both worked for Ford at Dagenham in the 1970s and 1980s.

My husband was working the shift work. You know, and to be very honest, you know what, Indian husbands, now they have been changed a lot because in England they are, but at that time, Indian husband think that housework is not their work, that is ladies' work, you know? It's the custom, but he was on the shift work. Whenever he had time, he just help me. He was a very good husband.

*And in the twenty-first century, these arrangements for sharing domestic tasks by working different shifts were still common. *Catherine*, a refugee from Kenya, was working the night shift packing mobile phones when her children were born in 2001 and 2003.*

Their dad, he used to work at night too but we used to have a difference [in shift patterns] of two days. So we had to look for somebody to come over to our children and we pay her, but it was only for a few days. On

most days I used to come in the morning at around 7.00 am. Have a nap
before they wake up and all this. When they wake up, I wake with them
and the good thing is that my sleep is not very sound.

*Maria, Indonesian by birth, and her husband also managed by doing shifts,
in their case at BMW in Oxford.*

I'm on the blue shift, my husband in the red shift. For example, he's
working the night shift, he's finished working he have to drop me, I'm
working the morning shift and then he'll look after my son and then
when he's start working but I'm not finished he have to drop my son to
nursery because nobody looking. My sister-in-law she have to work and
she have to look after their child as well.

Questions of language

Before trying to find acceptable ways to combine waged work and childcare,
migrant women had to face pregnancy and childbirth in a new country and
often found that they were dealing with doctors, nurses and midwives in a
language in which they were not confident. For some women too male
doctors were not what they were used to nor preferred.

*For **Bashira**, who migrated from Pakistan in 1979, feeling unconfident in
spoken English caused her acute embarrassment when she needed to go for
antenatal appointments.*

Because English, I know English, I can read properly but I can't speak. So
that was very upsetting because I can't speak any at all. And when I was
pregnant after my marriage, I have to see doctors, go to doctors, go to
nurse, everything and then I missed . . . 'oh, I don't know anything'. So I
take somebody with me all the time, some family, even anything I can
share, I can't, sometimes your privacy you can't share with your elders or
youngers and that. And my sister-in-law go with me and she's young and
I feel ashamed with the doctor; and if I go with my father-in-law sometimes
that, well, that's, oh my god, too much.

*Taslima, who was 19 and eight months pregnant when she arrived in the
UK from Bangladesh, faced similar problems.*

My daughter, she was born in '97. And I did the, you know, A level, in our
country but English is our, you know, second language. We know how to
write, read but when you want to speak, this is hard to speak the English.
I understand everything and I feel you know embarrassed when I came in
this country, because everywhere is English. I can't communicate with

anyone and I, you know, when I went to the doctor and my husband he was busy, I need to go with someone else, like neighbour. I need to tell them 'I want to go to the doctor', and I feel really embarrassed. And then I decided I need to learn English, because every time I can't involve anyone, because you know our ladies, we've got some things we can't tell in front of other people, when I went to the doctor and I need to you know discuss everything in front of other man. So then I decided I need to learn English.

*Fifty years before Taslima, in 1947, **Erica** had a son. She was not embarrassed by her lack of English but instead she was shocked by the poor health of some of the other expectant women, illustrated by the assumption by the nurses on the delivery ward that all the mothers would have lost their teeth.*

I came to the UK in 1947, already married and I was pregnant straight away. I had John (well we called him Janis but he changed it later) I had him in hospital in Newcastle. 'Can you see I still have my own teeth?' And they said in the hospital 'can you take your dentures out?' I had such good looking teeth. And I couldn't understand and the sister looked in my mouth and said 'you have your own teeth'. My English was very little then.

*While learning English was important for all the women migrants across the decades, continuing to speak in their native language was also important for many women, although it sometimes caused problems, as **Elvira** explained.*

Our social life was mainly with Latvians. And we speak Latvian all the time at home. First of all when we only had one girl [daughter], she did not know any English at all when she started school at four. So I sent her to the nursery school at four before proper school at five but she was very quiet for months and never talked. And I realized then, poor kid, and I thought 'no, it's wrong in a way'. So with the other two we spoke English too and they had their elder sister to talk to too. But we still speak Latvian and they answer in English, although they speak Latvian too. When they were younger, they went to weekend school [to learn Latvian], and all the wars and the tears and they complained, 'what do we want Latvian for? We will never go.' But now they have all been and they said 'good job we learned'.

Erica had not realized that her son must start school when he was five.

I didn't know that at five years they must go to school and the doctor said to me 'have you registered your son for school?' and I said 'why? He is only five years old'. Because in Latvia they start at seven. He went there and he spoke only Latvian and the teacher asked 'why you don't teach your son to speak English?' and I said 'because I don't speak good English'.

Diana's children, however, had learned some English as toddlers.

We spoke Latvian at home but they played with neighbours and so they spoke a bit of English when they went to school.

Finding childcare

For women who remain in the labour market when their children are babies or toddlers finding adequate care is a long-standing problem. Although childcare in the UK is expensive, the provision of childcare places by institutions and firms eventually became more common. Some of the women who had higher paid jobs with better terms and conditions were not only able to take periods of paid maternity leave but also found that their university or firm provided childcare. In the 1980s and early 1990s, however, many women in highly paid jobs employed nannies in their own homes, as well as women to do the cleaning, ironing and other domestic tasks.

Caro, a Canadian, had worked in London for a decade as an executive in the sales division of an investment bank. She was six months pregnant at the time of this conversation, and explained:

I have never really done much at home. I have the fine art of cooking dinner down to twenty minutes flat from start to finish. I have a cleaning lady and she does the ironing. When I have the baby, I plan to go back after two months and look for a nanny share. Time off for having children is a bit of a dilemma [in banking].

Asked about her husband, she said:

He's a money broker. He's a gorilla actually. He's been let out of the zoo, but actually he is terribly good around the house. He does washing up; he does loads of washing up.

Isobel, from New Zealand, a more senior executive on the corporate side of banking, married to a diplomat, had two children in the late 1980s.

We have a day nanny and someone who comes in at night. We both travel a great deal and just could not manage any other way. The children will go to boarding school when they are a little older.

Ten years later, Ani, from Romania, a university researcher when she had her children, benefitted from a workplace nursery, although as she explained, initially it was not easy to access institutional provision. Women in highly-paid, 'masculinized' jobs such as banking and academia became more willing to talk at length about maternity and childcare as the decades passed, perhaps as the numbers of women in employment slowly grew and it became more usual to combine a career and child-rearing.

I had my daughter in '99 in August and my son in May 2001. I had two maternity leave periods and after each of them I went back to work. I had six months regular, what counts as a full-time maternity leave. With my daughter, I worked until the very last day she was born, which was fine. And she was late actually. So people would ask me, when is your baby due? Two weeks ago! But I think I really enjoyed the work that I did. When she was born, my husband's parents came and stayed with us for about three months, also they stayed with Maria [daughter] as well. They came slightly earlier, just to get used. It was their first grandchild as well. So they stayed for a few months and then my sister came and stayed with us for a few months and we had a summer holiday and then Maria started going to a childminder.

To start with, it was difficult. So this was for about three months and then there was a family, childminders actually. There are these mixed feelings in terms of should I go for a childminder, should I go for a nursery? And I had spoken with the lady from the university, the nursery, and she said 'my children went to a childminders'. And actually she gave me a list of nice people. So it was just wondering what is best. So we started with a childminder and it was alright and they were very nice but one day when Maria had quite a big bump on her head and I didn't say anything but just my heart sank. So my husband said 'why don't you phone the university waiting list, because you have been on the waiting list?'

I phoned the university nursery and it was really funny because of course I started crying because people start crying in this position, and I said 'we were given two week's notice by our childminders, and I'm pregnant' and the lady said 'and are you single parent?' I started laughing, she didn't hear, I'm sure she didn't. It was like she had a tick list: what conditions do I fulfil? And I said 'fortunately not'. I put the phone down and then I phoned my husband. And then they phoned back and they gave us a place. So this is how nursery experience started and Maria was happy.

She was one and about five months and they were very, very good, I must say. They allowed us to take her for a couple of weeks gradually beforehand and she was such a bubbly, happy child and I think in a way it was harder for us than for her. But she was happy and I think she enjoyed other children's company and I was from a certain perspective. I was happier there because I felt if there is a problem I can talk to someone, whereas with a childminder, they are just them and the children. So when I had my second child then I had no doubt and the only way was if we would get a place. And we did get a place.

By the time her children were school-age, Ani's husband was commuting and so she had to take her children to school as well as do most of the housework.

He's commuting. But the children are older now, they understand things better. But it is harder, different . . . when he was working here, it would be easier whereas now when he leaves at 6.00 am and comes back at 8.30–9.00 pm in the evening. The children, they ask 'when is daddy coming?' I take them to school unless I have something. And we have some very good friends, Romanian ones, that we've met here and their children go to the same school and sometimes we take turns. If they have a problem then I help, or my husband helps and the other way around. And there are obviously after school clubs as well.

And I am lucky, my job, it has flexibility so I can find someone if I have to go to [events at the children's] school and I can work in the evening, or the weekend I can do it.

But as Ani explained, the choice of childcare is always a difficult one for most women and not everyone found care outside their homes suitable. Posha from India arrived in the UK when her only daughter was 13 months old. As her husband was a student, they were eligible for help from the university.

Childcare was such a big issue because we had registered her. If you're at the university you're on the waiting list. You can get Kids Unlimited [a local nursery provider], you get subsidized rates on that if you are through university. So we went there. We put her there but because it was a new country, obviously she was used to having her grandparents around all the time, she was in a house where everybody was looking after her, I was not working, and suddenly from that we pull her from that and move her into a new country, new atmosphere, new people who are talking in a different language and also putting her in a nursery. And she just did not adjust. Because I had four weeks until that time, the credit checks were going on, I had this time to settle her into nursery. The first day I put her in, because she was bottle-fed, she did not have a single bottle of milk all day and at four o'clock when I went to pick her up she was like, she did not eat anything. And I was like I can't handle her. Obviously I was in tears and I said 'I don't know how I'm going to work and at the same time look after her and she's not adjusting'. So two days we tried and then we pulled her out.

Luckily in the flat we were living there were a lot of students and one of the student's wives was not working. So she said 'I'm looking for some extra money than I can actually get, so I don't mind looking after your daughter'. So we actually appointed her as a childminder. She was not very experienced, but she was very, very nice. So the good thing was that my daughter stayed at home. She was from Chile, so she talked in Spanish and she taught my daughter Spanish language as well. She would tell, 'where are your eyes?' and she would tell you in Spanish, eyes, nose and everything. So she was one year, like 13–14 months and started, but she adjusted well because we were not taking her out of the house and putting her in a new environment. It was somebody coming to the house, so she as comfortable with that. As long as I'm in the house, it's fine. So she had her toys and everything and the childminder used to look after her.

So that carried on for a year and after that we found another childminder because this lady was moving out because she had finished her Master's, so they were moving out. We found another one who was from Germany, and she had a same age son so they would play together. We would leave her and then pick her up at a certain time. Because my husband's obviously term time is limited, so when he used to get off, he used to look after her and during the time he had term on, then we used to have childminders looking after her. So that went on until she was three and then we put her in a nursery after that, three, three and a half, then she was comfortable when she was more socially, you know, she knew how to interact and all that. And three and a half is when she started going to full-time nursery and then after that she'd been in school.

Housework

Most of the women in this book worked for the majority of their adult lives, always by necessity when they first came to the UK but often also by choice or inclination. Some of them found that they were bored at home and disliked housework.

Phyllida, born in Ireland, was a mother of two. She moved to the UK in the late 1950s when her children were small and initially was not employed.

I had always worked and I missed that part of life and I missed the adult company and being able to go and do something, because housework is housework. You do it and ten minutes later it's back to the same thing again, whereas I got so much more enjoyment out of my working life.

For many of the women of Indian heritage, marriage entailed living in a joint household with their husband's family, typically before and often after migration. For some young women, perhaps less submissive than common stereotypes suggest, the adjustment was not always easy, as Sai, who was married in India but who lived in Tanzania before moving to London, explains.

I used to think that if I did not find anyone who I liked, I would not get married. My health used to be frail in those days, so I used to think that if I got married and had too many [domestic] responsibilities, I would not be able to take it. But his family was very small. He just had a brother, a sister and only mother – his father had passed away earlier. When there is a small family, the responsibilities are less. And also when the family is outside [India], it's easier. Their mindset is different and the workload is less for a new bride. And my mother-in-law was also different from others. If I was sitting down, she would not make me get up to do a task. But I was very diligent and would perform all the tasks. I never thought I was a 'daughter-in-law' and she never behaved like a 'mother-in-law'. My husband had said that when we got married, that we have to live together and make it work, run the house together. There should be no mother-in-law – daughter-in-law business. My mother-in-law was good, but my husband also had his head in the right place, and he had power in the house, so he could support me. He could see that I was doing my best. I said to my mother-in-law, 'If you follow me around saying "do this", "why have you not done this?" I will not be able to manage and things will slip. If you let me be, I will do my best. I'll stay awake all night if need be and will not complain to anyone that my mother-in-law makes me work hard. But you must never "force" me to do anything.' And that's what she did.

Then after a while, when things were a bit difficult, my husband decided to set up a separate home. Not a separate house, but separate floors of the same house. We split everything. We had separate kitchens. Ate, cooked separately. There was still some difficulty for me, living in the same building, but I put up with that because my husband was good natured.

*When **Sai** and her husband came to England in 1968, she found herself isolated and lonely.*

I would say that I did not mix with anyone because I did not know the language and I stayed at home all the time. But I used to get bored at home – I did not want to stay at home all day. I wanted to work. I wanted to work, so I did. My first job after two months at home was in laundry but I did not find it bad. And my work helped us save. In 1972, four years after we came here, we bought a house. We bought the place for £8,000 of which we had a deposit of £2,000 and took out a mortgage for £6,000. And we paid it off over 25 years. We had to pay a lot, but we raised the children here. They grew up, went to college, got married. We are free now, we have paid it off.

*Some women did leave the labour market when their children were young but often returned quite quickly. **Milda**, one of the Cygnets, was one of the* *exceptions. She married a business man who liked her to be at home to entertain his colleagues and clients and for many years she was a housewife and mother.*

We bought a house and my husband was so fussy. You had to have all the cooking and the entertaining and so on. I didn't work. I looked after children and then the house but then later when they were older, I started again as a nurse, part-time, only three hours a week, at a little local hospital.

'I don't need him to live': difficulties in marriage

*If Milda alluded to pressure from her husband, **Georgina** was more open about some of the difficulties in her marriage. He husband, a Jamaican, came to the UK in 1950. His first job was as a crane driver but he studied part-time and became a lawyer. Now retired, Georgina has an active social life as well as spending a few weeks each year on her own in Trinidad, where she was born.*

Looking back, I was very young and naïve in my life, in my marriage, very innocent. My husband was very worldwide, a lot of things I didn't understand and I didn't know. I was a late developer. All I wanted was an educated husband, educate my children and a professional who can live a decent and fair life and to be married and live the rest of my life as a family, and to hold this family together as I was brought up. It would have killed my mother if my marriage had broken up. I think I suffered a lot in my marriage because of my husband. I knew he loved me. He wanted me as his wife but he was the big flirt. I could never say 'yes, I've caught you with this woman', because I was very naïve but I could always feel a difference. It was very hard. When I look at my life, I look at my life as difficult as Princess Diana and being through what she has been through.

But then I look at myself, I'm a proud woman. I've held my head high. I have worked; I have educated my family, I have made a man of my husband; I have fought through the wars; I've got a wonderful daughter. I am so proud of her. She has made me feel that my life has been . . . all the suffering I have been through, she has made me feel that way. After my husband was qualified, our marriage was very difficult because being Trinidadian and Jamaican, I had that clash of 'now he's a lawyer, he should not still be married to someone not from his country' and I fought to hold my marriage together. I have achieved it and I feel he has made me into a self-sufficient woman. I love my husband, I want him for his companionship but I don't need him to live. I think every woman can do that for themselves, I encourage young women to do it for them.

Moira, who was born in Ireland in 1937 and had lived in England since 1954, left her marriage after years of unhappiness. Reflecting on her decision she talked more generally about how her own divorce and scandals in the Catholic Church had affected her attitudes, for the better she believed.

The church was my life, it was my life. I was very staunch Catholic, very staunch and very happy. When things went wrong in my marriage it took a lot away; it took a lot away. And things happening with priests and everything; it took a lot of away, paedophile priests and all those people. I didn't experience anything from a priest, I didn't, but listening to what they've done and all that, that affected me. I just thought, I used to look on them as gods, and I've realized as I've gone on through life they're not. They're human like any, but they're not, they're even worse than that, the things they've done. So you get wiser as you go through life. But, I don't have the same feeling as my family in Ireland have for priests; they're great friends with the priest. I don't feel the same about them as I used to, because I always feel of what I've read about them and seen about them and it's all out in the open, and it's been very bad, so that has changed me quite a bit. Like going into confessions I think, 'Why should I go in there and tell them anything, I'll just tell God myself.' You see so I have changed, and I don't feel guilty about any of it.

I would never have thought when I left Ireland I'd ever be divorced. I never would have thought that. But England has been good for me, because it's broadened my mind, and it's good, and travelling around the world [in retirement] has been good; it's all been good, it's an experience going through life. I love England and I would never go back to Ireland, so you see life changes you, things change.

'The circle has come round': community groups, hometown associations and volunteering

One of the key issues for migrant women is keeping former customs and language alive while they are living in the UK and bringing up their children there. Although most of the migrant women who have told their stories in the preceding chapters never went 'home', they try to keep memories of their heritage and country of birth alive for their children and for their friends. In their own homes, telling stories, speaking in the family's original language and, for some, making annual trips back 'home' are all important ways of keeping memories alive. Some women are also involved in voluntary groups based on language or ethnicity, sometimes raising money to support friends or families elsewhere, at other times cooking food, making or dyeing cloth and knitting to unite women from similar backgrounds.

Fida was born in northern Uganda in 1950 and fled with her family to Kenya during internal disorder in Uganda. She had seven children and her husband, a business man, 'turned to what he loved best – evangelism – so he spend most of the time travelling and preaching in different places both nationally and internationally from time-to-time, leaving me to do most of the work on my own'.

At the end of '76 we fled our country. When we were in exile in Kenya for the first time and Idi Amin[2] bombed part of Tanzania and the Tanzanians came to defend and pushed him out, we decided what are we going to do when we go back home. I thought about my childhood dreams and desires. Because I spent most of my time working in the field with my parents, I needed farming. I needed a farm of my own and I needed it to be just as I learnt in my geography. The American prairie land farming with combine harvesters and things like that. That's what I wanted to do and I really, really wanted. . . . My parents used oxen for ploughing and we were digging with our hands and I thought 'hmmm, when I have a chance and educated I want to have a tractor and a combine harvester for my farm', and so I told him [her husband] 'I want a farm.'

Fida never got her farm, but continued to live between Uganda and Kenya, although her husband was badly treated not only during Amin's rule but also by the successor government.

The new government which is in power today destroy my home on 7 April '86 and that day I lost my son, I lost my husband, who fled into Sudan. My husband never kept quiet. As an evangelist, it was 'blah blah blah'. The present government were not happy when he say 'what you're doing is wrong'. He came back from Sudan, and he was arrested, brutally beaten. The next thing we heard on the news was he was killed. That was what was happening, but if it ended with him we would still be in Uganda but they came home and attacked us and they beat me so bad. I was kicked so many times on the head and they hit me with a gun here, so I was semi-paralysed for a long time. That was November '87.

Eventually we had to flee. Money was raised by Christians from Uganda and there was a lot of communication between my in-laws [already in the UK] and the people in Uganda, so money was raised. I can't even point a finger to how it all happened, but I was being treated like luggage really. I didn't know who was doing what. I move here and I move there, that was all I could do. So I ended up in Britain. I managed to flee into UK on 18 January 1989, a traumatized woman.

Fida was unfit for work but rebuilt a life in the UK with her seven children and eventually became a significant part of a community group for Ugandans born in the north of that country.

I started to volunteer with Asylum Welcome which was a new resource talking with other refugees and I came to volunteer with them, and one of the community worker ask me 'is there something you want us to help you for your own community?' 'What do you mean?' 'Do you want to do anything for your community?' I say 'yes, of course I want'. In 1999 I call my community – northern Ugandan only – to ask them what do we do, because I was very worried about our children and our grandchildren. Because our children were no longer speaking our language, our culture was not being passed on because it is always passed on by seeing, doing, hearing and saying it. 'What are we going to do?' And our grandchildren were not speaking our language at all, so what can we do? Why can't we write our stories down, tell it, record it, have it transcribed and then translate it in English so that our grandchildren would be able to know some of these things.

The people were willing to help, so we started to meet, discussing what we want to do, and many people were coming with different ideas. They wanted to do textile also, learn how to do things that they will one day go and use them back home, maintain whatever skills and then learn new skills. That was something that I was doing it, I would say, over the remote control by telephoning other people to help. So I left some of the women already doing a few things like storytelling, tie and dye, and different things. But that went just for a little while and there was too much work for me, I couldn't coordinate it from a distance, so the women just disintegrated but then 2003 when I return [from a visit to Uganda] then we started it again.

Fida was involved in applying for a grant, to support community workshop activities.

We got the funding and we bought most of the equipment that we had asked for. As a result other people started to donate things to us like machines, material and things like that. So we have run different workshops here, knitting, sewing. We managed to do one thing that we talked about in '99, to have our cultural dance here, and this time it wasn't us the mothers, it was our children, the ones that we came with when they were young, who actually organized these events. And we called it Acholi Day[3] and we had lots of people including the Mayor here. To me that was the climax, the top, that was the stamp of approval when the younger people came up and did what they did in fulfilling what we had all written. They all written down, they hadn't read it, they just did what we had wanted doing. So now the circle has come round and as a result now I can take time off and rest without worry, because as it is our culture when the younger people take it forward now. It was a refugee initiative and we have two days of the week which is open to the entire community, whoever wants to can come and learn how to sew, knit, discuss, passing skills, so the people are coming to pass their skills to different people. I am so happy to see some people who had never done knitting before are now knitting; some people are now sewing, enough to sell, and other people are beginning to who cannot speak English, because other people are taking their time to help others with English.

Although it's not a paid job I've found this to be more fulfilling than anything else, because I tried to get a paid job and I couldn't.

*Several of the older women became more involved with their community on retirement. **Vieda**, for example, began to do voluntary work after her husband died.*

For the last fourteen years, I am now working for the Latvian welfare fund, and I am the London treasurer for five years or so and I am reading in for the blind people the cassette. A big magazine they send in from Canada. It takes some time and it's something to do.

Grieta *too, the oldest woman among the EVWs, was also involved in charity work.*

My friends now are still Latvians. We do a lot of charity work. There is what you call it for the old people and for the children. We sell for the Christmas bazaar and money goes to Latvia.

Ruta, *however, had worked on a voluntary basis among the Latvian community over her entire married life, despite marrying an Englishman. Among other activities, she taught for many years at the Saturday schools that were central in teaching the second generation the language and customs of the parent's or mother's homeland.*

There was a Latvian community in Leicester [where she lived at the time of the interview]: about 200 Latvians. There was a Latvian parson and there is another Ruta there on the other side of the hill. And when I was in London when we kept in touch with the Latvian community, like going to celebrate Midsummer's night and New Year's Eve and so on. I dragged my husband with me into the Latvian community and in London I was teaching at a weekend school. I took a little class of the little children on a weekends. And Leicester City Council gave us a school for the Latvian children and I was doing Sunday school. My children attended the

Latvian Sunday school and did the folk dancing when they were small. In 1970 I think or something like that, I started with the Latvian community and they elected me on a committee. I am now on a committee and I do the information work. I am officially the information officer for the Latvian Welfare Foundation in Great Britain.

Retirement and going 'home'

The women who came to the UK in the early post-war decades were retired by the time of the interviews – some of them reluctantly and others gladly. Among the retirees were some of the nurses from the Caribbean, Ireland and elsewhere and, like Vieda, all the other EVWs, who by the end of the twentieth century were already in their late seventies and eighties. As these women, who were not born in Britain, began to age and to take retirement from waged work, they often started to reassess their lives and their attachment to the UK. For many, however, return to their country of birth is impractical and their ties to the UK, especially family ties developed over many years, are strong.

As Georgina explained, 'I have a six months old grandson. He's my joy; I couldn't leave him.'

Tracey, born in South Africa in 1945, worked in the NHS for almost 40 years in the UK and took slightly early retirement to spend more time with her husband.

He retired first, and it's one of the reasons I retired. Because doing shift work and when the children are home and they're all having supper and argy bargy, it was all right, but I hated going to work and knowing he was at home by himself and he was having supper and things, all these things.

And Vieda, who came to the UK in the 1940s as an EVW, was adamant about not returning to her homeland.

I wouldn't go back [to Latvia] to live. I am too old now, and anyway all my things are here now. And so even though you are born [elsewhere], you belong to two places. I think all displaced people, one sort of part you are Latvian in an emotional sense but in a practical sense and for other things I am British and I feel that here I have to play my part and I am very much interested what is going on here, with the politics and everything because I live here and England has been good to me, even if it was hard time. But you forget those hard times and England is my home and I could not go back.

Vieda did make a number of visits to Latvia after it became an independent state again in 1991 but found she was not only ambivalent but felt guilty.

I regularly visit to Latvia every year. First year when I went back I felt like a traitor. I felt very bad, because it was so bad there, everything. I remember as a child the big fields, barley or flax, all beautiful, growing and clean because Latvia came up from 1918 to 1940, for twenty years I think her status was just behind Sweden. And it was good. Those years were good and I remember it like that. Those years were good but when I went back it was such a contrast. It was dreadful, dreadful. All the old houses, half broken down and everything.

And you know I felt guilty, why I should have stayed you know and done, lived all what they lived. It's a bit of patriotism I think and when I go I still feel, many people who lived in a way, many people who live here in England or in America, Australia and so go back and brag but I could not do that. I think I will never be able to do it for I always feel I should have been there when the times were bad.

Ruta *also visited but would not return permanently.*

I first went back in 1992. In 1991 my cousin came here. We parted as schoolgirls and we meet as old ladies. I went in 1993 and 1994 and then just last year. I went back to my home village. When I first went back it was tears, tears, tears, one big cry. Even last year I felt I was walking back into the past. Nothing is changed. I went where I used to walk to school and looked at the houses and they are all drab, nobody around. People peering through the curtains as you walk by. And do you know, I couldn't remember a thing and I arrived by the school and I asked myself 'what are you looking for, because you don't really belong there anymore?' I was in my teens, 18 [when I left] and I go back as a 70-year-old.

Janice, *a nurse all her life, was born in New Zealand and moved to the UK in 1970, only nine months after qualifying as a nurse in New Zealand. At the time of the interview, she had retired from full-time employment but still undertook a small amount of paid work, as well as some volunteer work.*

I'm going to continue belonging to the nurse bank so I can do one to two shifts a week if I wish, and so I'll just give my availability the week before. And also I do one day a week for the British Red Cross. I do skin camouflage with them and I've been doing that now for three years, because I wanted to do that so that I had something for when I did retire, that I enjoyed doing. It's voluntary work, yes, I work there one day a week, and that has been really, really rewarding, so that's a couple of days. And then my husband works from home so I'll be helping him as well from home, and hopefully having a bit of leisure time as well.

I would like to go back to New Zealand eventually but my husband is an only son and his mother doesn't keep all that well, so I would never leave her, because I'm one of four children. So really my priority is here. My daughter is independent now obviously, but once my husband retires perhaps. I mean, he's English but he gets on very well in New Zealand. He likes the lifestyle; he gets on well with the family and he would adapt very well to the New Zealand way of life, but I think I'd just have to see how it goes when the time comes, yeah. Because a friend of mine emigrated back to New Zealand about four years ago and she was miserable, absolutely miserable, found it very hard to adapt, so I've taken that on board. She'd been looking forward to going back to New Zealand all her life over here and it didn't quite work out as she had hoped.

I have dual nationality now. You can have duality, kept my New Zealand, you can have two nationalities, so I've got dual nationality with my New Zealand passport as well. I did it about ten years ago, that's all. I'd been here for a long time, but once I got married, you see, I didn't have all the problems with my passport. I was automatically domiciled because I was married to a British citizen, so I actually had free entry. So of course I never really worried. But then when we were travelling to the continent, I always used to have to go through a different sort of, you know immigration hall, to everybody else and I used to be holding up everyone. So I thought it would be more convenient if I had a British passport, so I got one. I've had a British passport now for about the last ten years.

Papla, *of Indian heritage but a migrant from Kenya in the early 1970s, found that as a widow she lacked the confidence to go to India alone.*

To be very honest my husband has left money for me in India. I have to go to India but I am not going because I am very scared now over there, because if I get ill nobody is there to look after me. So I am very scared to go to there, to get ill. And Kenya, I was not interested to go because my two brothers, my two sisters in America. So I go to America to see them instead of going to Kenya. They are very educated; he has PhD and he is very, very well settled there. My sister is there, my sisters are here, so I am not interested to go to Kenya definitely and to India, I want to go for my money, so perhaps I will.

But as she continued she no longer felt much attachment to India, appreciating the welfare provision for older people in the UK.

Actually I think that, yeah, been living in England now for a long time so we are just like you. We have the Indian, we eat Indian food but there is still so many things we like that is English and British. But to be very honest, if anybody asks me, I like British, I like London, I like English people because they are very honest, they are very good. And another thing I like here is when you're old and when nobody is for you, the government give you help and in no country you will get this help. That's what it is like in this country and I am very grateful for this England, that they help the people who are suffering. No other country will help you. If you haven't got money in India, your children won't look after you.

Taslima, younger than either Vieda or Papla, had moved from Bangladesh to London in the 1990s, and had no desire ever to return permanently. Indeed even to return for a holiday was a daunting prospect for her.

I won't go back, not permanently, because I can't live in Bangladesh now. Because now, I've got different lifestyle, because Bangladesh is different lifestyle, and these countries is completely different. It's time, you know, everything we follow the time [in England]. In Bangladesh we don't, you know. You don't have to, because Bangladesh, my sister, my sister-in-law, they don't work; they think only husband can work and earn money. They like to eat and look after the house and like housewife. The summer holidays, I don't like, every time I'm thinking, you know, 'how I will stay six weeks in the home, without work, without go outside?' So you know, I'm not decided to go back to Bangladesh. I prefer life here.

Migration, for whatever reasons, whether forced by circumstances or carefully planned, changes lives forever and inevitably brings with it significant changes in the lives that these women might have expected to live. Over the years in which they have been in the UK, they have had to cope with loss and regret: the loss perhaps of family, out of reach because of distance, cost or changing political alliances, as well as by death, the loss of friends who remained behind, sometimes the loss of language, of common customs. They have also, with courage and resilience, faced up to and seized new opportunities and, sometimes, overcome struggles to find employment, establish family life, make new friends and rebuild communal links. Common themes in many narratives of migration tend to emphasize rootlessness, a sense of not belonging, and the trauma of leaving home, especially when movement is not freely chosen. While many of these emotions are evident in the stories told here, especially those in Chapter 2, as this chapter shows, the responses to migration are often complex and, inevitably change over time, as migrants establish lives in the UK, and build links across and within diasporic communities as well as with the British population. For many women, having children who were born in the UK is a key tie to the new country. Taslima is not alone deciding not to return 'home', nor in explaining her preference for a life in the UK.

These women, born in numerous different places across the world, have lived in British towns and cities, many of them for many decades, and they have been part of the British labour market for most of their lives. What their narratives, in this chapter and in the previous ones, reveal is their resilience and determination, sometimes in the face of considerable hardship and discriminatory treatment – the nurses who were never promoted for example, the owner of a fast food takeaway subject to racist labelling, the bus driver persistently sworn at by passengers. But these women are also fierce and determined and have constructed lives also full of joy and pleasures, despite the determination of some of the British public to see them always as strangers or 'the Other'. This British imaginary construction of otherness and its changing outlines over time, as well as prospects of a new, more optimistic version of a cosmopolitan British society, is the subject of the final chapter, changing the focus from women migrants to the reactions to them by the host population.

9

Afterword:

British Identity and 'the Other'

A nation is a story that a people chose to tell about itself . . . at its heart is a deep-felt need for those people to be connected to the place where they live and to each other.

Kingsnorth 2015: 3

This final chapter differs in its aim and focus from the rest of the book. Its aim is to explore the dominant story of belonging to Britain and the ways in which is excludes newcomers who are seen as 'the Other'. As the earlier chapters have shown through women's individual stories, migrants to Britain often had to face hostility from the British and sometimes from migrants who arrived before them. Fear of strangers, worries about competition, assumptions about whiteness as the unmarked norm and racist attitudes combined to construct new migrants as Other, as different from and inferior to the 'locals' who belonged there. The East European and Irish women who came to the UK in the 1940s may have been white but their spoken English and their accents differentiated them from the people who they lived among and with whom they worked.

Migrants from the Caribbean and later from East Africa and South Asia were instantly differentiated on the basis of skin colour and in their early years in Britain suffered hostility and discrimination because of this. They were, as sociologist Sheila Patterson (1963) noted in the title of her book, *Dark Strangers*: a title itself that today seems discriminatory. The 1960s and 1970s were difficult years when post-colonial migrants faced signs in house windows when looking for somewhere to rent that captured the spirit of the times – 'no Irish, no blacks, no dogs' – as well as struggling against unequal treatment in the workplace and violence in the streets of some of Britain's major cities. Five decades later, Britain is a different country – more diverse, perhaps more at ease with its multicultural and cosmopolitan society – and yet there remains fear and unease, as well as discriminatory attitudes and behaviour that continue to construct recent in-migrants as outsiders. This chapter flips the coin, as it were, to look at notions of British identity and changing attitudes to migrants across the second half of the twentieth century.

So far the emphasis has been on migrant women, rather than on the white British population, and on the ways in which these women often found themselves restricted to the lowest rungs of some of the poorest jobs in the country across the entire post-war decades. The aim has been to document the ways in which migrant women were constructed as 'less eligible' than 'native' women for different types of employment, as well as to counter or complicate conventional accounts of post-war social and economic change. As I argued in the introductory chapter, typical stories about labour market change in the UK, like narratives of migration, tend to emphasize loss and regret, in this case not for attachments to the homeland described in Chapter 2 and in Chapter 8 about community but for the loss of the sorts of heroic employment undertaken by men in the manufacturing sector. These nostalgic narratives or stories of loss typically have ignored the growth in female employment over the second half of the twentieth century and into the new millennium, as well as the evident continuities in the sorts of tasks undertaken by women workers. Although the narratives about employment in Chapters 2 to 7 have illustrated many of the major changes in the British labour market over time as women's employment became more significant, they have also documented significant continuities in both the sorts of task involved in 'women's work' and in the often discriminatory and unequal treatment of many women in waged work. Even in the sorts of well-paid employment that became more accessible to many women over the post-war era, as they gained educational credentials, for example, and more labour market experience, gendered patterns of recruitment and promotion persisted. Women are still in a minority in many professional occupations and typically are still trapped on the bottom rungs of the hierarchies, often subject to differential treatment on the basis of their gender. Among women in full-time employment in 2015, there remains a gender wage gap of 16 per cent – for every £1 a man in full-time work earns, a woman earns 84 pence. And for women in part-time employment, the gap is much larger.

In the less prestigious and lower paid parts of the labour market, where employment is now growing fastest, women dominate numerically. Here in caring, catering, cleaning and clerical work, many women born abroad, as well as British women, find themselves doing traditionally feminized tasks. As the stories in earlier chapters have shown, for migrant women, the combination of their gender and their nationality, constructs them both as ideally suited for these forms of work and less eligible for other, better paid positions, and continuities are evident as women now do for wages many of the tasks they traditionally undertook for love in their own homes. In recent years, these sorts of jobs, often casualized and underpaid, as well as feminized, are growing rapidly, as poor conditions, low pay and insecure contracts, including the pernicious zero-hour contracts offered to, for example, employees of large supermarket chains, have become more common.

Although the number of workers in the UK labour market has increased over time, and unemployment rates have fallen, including since the 2007–8 recession, there is now a real problem of what the journalist and social critic, Polly Toynbee (2003), more than ten years ago presciently termed 'poor work' – that is employment that pays too little to ensure a decent standard of living. In the early 2000s Toynbee took a series of low paid and casual jobs, one of them in the House of Commons' nursery and although she is a renowned political journalist whom many MPs know by sight if not personally, like the women in this book she found her job made her invisible. Women who mop, clean or serve meals are seldom noticed as individuals. Many women who clean literally are unseen, changing sheets in hotel rooms when guests are out or cleaning board rooms and offices in the City during the late evening or early morning before well-paid workers arrive at their desks. Nevertheless, as Beatta, who worked as a chamber maid, explained in Chapter 4: 'even if they don't see us, we still have to look nice'.

Too many workers in these bottom end jobs are now insecure, as are the growing number of workers in professional positions who are on short-term contracts. Indeed the labour economist Guy Standing (2011) has identified a newly emergent social class in the UK, termed the precariat: all those people in casual and insecure employment, who despite their different family and educational backgrounds and different jobs have interests in common because of the temporary and insecure nature of their waged work. But it is at the bottom end of the labour where conditions are most exploitative, and where extremely low pay is rife. Too many workers are paid below the living wage, and even, illegally, below the minimum wage, and many of them are women who were not born in the UK. Without the labours of these migrant women, however, many of the essential parts of serving the public would be neglected or done less well. Beds would remain unmade in care homes, hospitals struggle to recruit nurses, the foreign clients of banks would be less well served by bankers unfamiliar with their languages and customs, and university departments would be less interesting and less diverse places than they now are with a growing number of staff, and students, not born in the UK. Standing perhaps under-estimates divisions in the labour market that on the basis of gender and ethnicity, as well as class position, continue to divide the migrant from the local population and so reduce the possibilities of a politics based on precarity. He also ignores the continuing power of the dominant story of belonging that constructs people born elsewhere as the Other in the UK.

The extraordinary lives of the redoubtable women who populate the pages of this book are a remarkable testament to the significance of migrants in the economic and social life of the UK, but over the years, as I indicated at the start of this chapter, their lives have not been easy nor has their reception and treatment in the UK always been fair and equitable. As Paul Gilroy vividly captured in the title of his book, published two and a half decades after Patterson's, *There ain't no Black in the Union Jack* (2002 [1987]), the population not born in Britain, as well as the people of colour who were, are still too often excluded from the British imaginary, from an idealized notion of Britishness that takes as the norm customs, values, behaviours and an ethnicity that continues to see 'strangers' as 'Others', subject to unwritten, and increasingly written, tests of belonging before they are accepted as equals, whether as acceptable workers for different types of jobs or as British citizens. Over the seventy years seen here through the voices of migrant women, new entrants to the UK have been subjected to increasingly restrictive immigration regulations (see Appendix 3) and expected to conform to notions of belonging, constructed through changing policies ranging from belonging on the basis of assimilating to a British norm, through multiculturalism under which 'traditional' values and beliefs are still seen as important (a sort of different but equal ideology) and back, more recently, to a version of social cohesion that emphasizes the significance of certain 'British' values including democracy and gender equality.

Over the post-war decades, however, skin colour, language and religion variously or in combination, have been the basis of a politics of difference that constructs incomers as less eligible members of society than the settled population, or what Robert Winder (2004) bluntly termed in his book title *Bloody Foreigners*. As an afterword, I briefly explore here the history of the changing meaning of belonging to the UK and ideas about the place of migrants within the nation. There are numerous excellent studies of belonging, of British identity and the ways in which the migrant population are constructed as different and so excluded from the national imaginary, despite the growth of transnational migration and the globalization of technologies and cultures, some of them the source for the argument here. As the events of the twenty-first century have illustrated, xenophobia and exclusionary politics on the basis of religion and Islamophobia have deepened in Western Europe in the wake of the events of 9/11 in the USA (2001), 7/7 in the UK (2005), the attack on *Charlie Hebdo* in France (2015) and Western interventions in the Near and Middle East.

In early decades, moral panics about cleanliness or about sexuality, about fertility, about fears of urban unrest, or about competition for jobs and for housing, were more significant, as well as visceral notions of difference – people who look or sound different, whose ways are unfamiliar, whose food was unusual – were also the basis of differentiation and discrimination. It took many years before chicken tikka masala – a hybrid version of a South Asian dish tailored to 'British' tastes – topped a poll of the nation's favourite food in 2002, only to be replaced ten years later, according to the Food Network, by a simple 'Chinese' stir fry.

The cultural critic Stuart Hall (1990), himself a migrant from the Caribbean in the late 1950s, has argued that reactions to immigrant populations take several forms. They include a retreat by the host population into notions of Britishness that emphasize difference, mirrored by versions of diaspora identities among incomers that emphasize older traditions and customs of the homeland. Both versions of identity may lead to a nasty politics of exclusion, including the rise of proto-fascist organizations such as the National Front and its replacements – the British National Party and the English Defence League (Eatwell and Goodwin 2010; Goodwin 2011). Another consequence of this politics of difference, identified by some, is what has been termed the development of 'parallel lives', where, based on research on residential segregation in some British cities, a predominantly South Asian heritage population, for example, is found to live in different areas from the numerically dominant white group. Recent analysis by the Centre on Dynamics of Ethnicity (2012), however, found that residential mixing between groups had actually increased between the 2001 and 2011 Censuses, rather than exhibiting greater separation. As well as the two responses based on exclusion, Hall identified a more optimistic version of social inter-connections and change, that he termed 'translation'. In this third response, both the locals and the incomers are changed in positive ways by migration, producing new hybrid notions of identity. However, in a YouGov poll in 2012, 64 per cent of those questioned agreed with the statement that 'Britain is losing its traditional culture'. It is to this notion that there is such a thing as a traditional culture that I turn to next.

Invented traditions and national identity: no place like home

The question of what defines a homeland and its association with territory is and has been one of the most pressing questions in modern times as ideas about the connection between nationalism and geographical place lie behind political unrest, wars and religion, as nation states rise and fall. Assumptions about ethnic or racial purity lie behind the terrible differences that have been claimed to exist between, for example Aryan, Jew or Slav, between Hutu and Tutsi peoples, behind other tribal wars, behind the apartheid Republic of South Africa or 'ethnic cleansing' in parts of the former Yugoslavia, as well as the rise of states based on sets of less disastrous traditions. These traditions and customs are often, as Hobsbawm and Ranger (2012) argued, ones that are invented, including in Britain the 'traditional' Christmas with its decorated tree, introduced by Prince Albert in the nineteenth century. Indeed many of the ideas of Englishness (and I use this term deliberately as Scottish and Welsh nationalism challenges the union) date from that century, based on a mythological construction of

England that itself is based on sets of cultural assumptions that were a significant part of Victorian intellectual thought. The passage below sets out these assumptions.

> In its neo-gothic architecture, Pre-Raphaelite paintings, chivalric poetry, socialist utopias, and its insistence on the earlier harmonies of rural life and artistic production, Victorian intellectuals of the most varied political persuasion sealed a pact between a timeless and mythical vision of the nation and their selection and installation of an acceptable cultural heritage.
>
> Chambers 1989: 89

This vision excluded not only migrants from outside the nation but its own urban industrial working class. The poet, T. S. Eliot, born in the US but an adoptive English man, in his notes on English culture, an essay written in the 1950s but published as a paperback years later (Eliot 1973), had a somewhat wider vision of the nation in a less idealized rural utopia. His imaginary England included the northern working class, but nevertheless was one that still excluded the foreigner. Here he is defining national culture in the Britain of the 1950s:

> It includes all the characteristic activities and interests of a people. Derby Day, Henley Regatta, Cowes, the twelfth of August, a cup final, the dog races, the pin table, the dart board, Wensleydale cheese, boiled cabbage cut into sections, beetroot in vinegar, nineteenth century Gothic churches, and the music of Elgar.
>
> Eliot 1973: 31

Almost a century on the list may be different, a point I shall return to in a moment. This singular vision of a notion and a people united by common customs into an 'imagined community' (Anderson 1991) was what permitted the anti-immigration politician Enoch Powell to say this in a speech in April 1976, as Britain, or perhaps England, was being altered by in-migration:

> The nation has been, and still is being, eroded, and hollowed out from within by implantation of unassimilated and unassimilable populations . . . alien wedges in the heartland of the state.
>
> Powell 1976

The European Volunteer Workers who came to Britain from displaced persons camps in the 1940s were termed, in official discourse 'aliens' and migrants from Ireland had only de facto rights of citizenship but migrants from the former Empire often held British passports. Powell, however, although he recognized these rights, in a speech in Eastbourne in 1968, drew a distinction between formal membership of the nation and visceral belonging based on language, sentiment, custom and ethnic identity. 'The

West Indian' he asserted 'does not by being born in England become an Englishman (sic). In law he becomes a United Kingdom citizen by birth; in fact he is a West Indian or Asian still' (quoted in Gilroy 1987: 46). National myths, as well as the close association between the Church of England and the state, allowed Powell to foster the assumption that English identity is white, ethnically homogeneous, even Anglo-Saxon, despite a long history of invasion and settlement.

Powell's racist views were challenged in Parliament and by new legislation against racism but also by the actions, attitudes and behaviour of the new population in Britain, which changed common perceptions of cultural norms and practices, not always quickly and often painfully, but gradually. As I noted earlier the roast beef of old England has been replaced by chicken tikka masala and a stir fry as the nation's favourite dishes, a rather trivial but nevertheless significant indication of cultural change.

Hybridity or not?

The movement of people from different parts of the world, captured in the earlier chapters through personal stories of displacement and change, has had a profound impact, not only on Britain, but on the rest of Europe. Stuart Hall (1990) reversed the older phase 'the West and the rest' to 'the rest in the West' to capture the changes in Britain over the second half of the twentieth century. That old version of the modern world established during the nineteenth century has been transformed by global movement and transnationalism, as new versions of citizenship emerge to capture multiple senses of belonging, or perhaps 'unbelonging', as homelessness becomes a literal and metaphorical condition for growing numbers of people in the world. It is almost as if, as the anthropologist Marc Augé (1995) suggested, the world is now a gigantic travel terminus in which people are reduced to passengers, a faceless population, differentiated only by a number.

There is, however, a more optimistic set of terms and debates, connected to Hall's notion of translation that I introduced earlier. These terms, including creolization, mettisage and hybridity, capture the changes connected to migration, changes in both the people who move and the people who do not. The 'new' hybrid Britain includes not only increasing numbers of dual and multi-heritage partnerships and children but also changes in cultural customs, in language, music, food, and ways of living. It is worth asking students, your children and their friends to replace T. S. Eliot's version of common cultural symbols and acts with their own as an example of the changes since he was writing in the 1950s about cabbage and dog races. The idea of melding and mixing that lies behind terms such as creolization should produce new identities and new places, sometimes termed a third space, in which the negotiation between sameness and difference, between continuity and rupture in beliefs and traditions might produce a new consciousness, and new cosmopolitan identities among the hybrid populations of some of Britain's towns and cities. As I suggest in the section that follows, attitudes towards the Other are more positive in places in the UK with a significant 'minority' population. And since the 1990s, there has also a growing literature that examines the meanings of whiteness, previously an unmarked and taken for granted category, somehow innocent of ethnicity (Dyer 1997). As Roediger (1991) showed for the USA in the nineteenth century, and as I have demonstrated in this book, certain groups continue to benefit from 'the wages of whiteness' as people of colour and other 'strangers' are defined as less suitable employees for many positions in the labour market.

The optimism captured in terms and claims about hybridity and cosmopolitanism has, however, a challenge in ideas about diaspora and multiculturalism, about the continuing salience of 'homeland' traditions among in-migrant communities, and about fears of the Other (Amin 2012). Multiculturalism is a complex term, combining both difference and a common identity, and defined in political and policy terms as 'the recognition of group difference within the public sphere of laws, policies, democratic discourses and the terms of a shared citizenship and national identity' (Madood 2007: 2). While assimilation was expected by policymakers in the earlier post-war decades, from the 1970s onwards the British state became more sympathetic to the claims of marginalized groups for the recognition of their customs, practices and beliefs. The distinct claims of multiculturalism were controversial from the start. As many critics, from both the left and right of the political spectrum, argued, it was an agenda for increasing separation between communities. As the 'new left' governments of Prime Minister Blair were replaced by more conservative governments and as migration became more differentiated and diverse in the twenty-first century, the notion of 'cohesion' replaced multiculturalism in official discourses, placing an onus on both locals and migrants to develop joint customs and practices. The tolerant celebration of difference that lay behind multiculturalism was challenged, as I have already suggested, by political events in the new millennium. However in a powerful and positive argument for multiculturalism as a new form of political philosophy, Tariq Madood has suggested that the 'new ethno-religious mix' (his term; 2007: 8) in many of the larger West European cities, including London, especially the growing Muslim presence, is a new challenge to the state that should not be ignored but which demands a positive response. However, issues such as sexual repression, political violence, banning the head scarf in France and sexual exploitation of children in British towns have resulted in a colder climate and a difficult reception for Madood's arguments. Nevertheless, they do not invalidate the urgent need to reconsider the political recognition of the Other and new forms of political and institutional measures to ensure greater acceptance of difference.

In the final section, I explore the changing attitudes by the British public towards its changing population as expressed in opinion polls, to assess how far attitudes have changed in recent decades.

Public attitudes to the Other

Immigration was identified as one of the key issues during the election campaign of 2015, as competing candidates argued about numbers, about the possibility of capping in-migration and about the effects of foreign workers in the labour market. Although there are numerous studies of immigration, of its causes and consequences, of policies and regulatory mechanisms, and perhaps even more of different groups of in-migrants, there have been surprisingly few analyses of changing public attitudes over time. In 2014, however, the public opinion organization, Ipsos MORI, published a survey entitled *Perceptions and Reality* (Duffy and Frere-Smith 2014). This study assessed changing attitudes among the general public since 1974 and is the basis for the discussion here. The authors of the study emphasis the complexity and the importance of geographical variation, noting that it is hard to generalize across the entire country. In towns and cities where the size of the foreign-born population is larger than average, attitudes tend to be less fearful or suspicious. People living in super-diverse areas, such as inner London, are the least likely to express negative attitudes, whereas white and ageing communities in northern manufacturing towns and areas that currently have low numbers of migrants in their population are most likely to express concerns. In the broad-brush summary that follows this complexity is ignored but should not be forgotten.

Ipsos MORI has been asking a question about the most important issues facing Britain since the 1970s. Opinion polls since 1974 exhibited an initial peak in concern about migration in August 1978, when 27 per cent of the population said it was one of the key issues facing the country. This was the year when the strike of South Asian women at Grunwick, discussed in Chapter 3, came to an end and although there may have been no direct connection, the mass picketing in the streets of north London across the summers of 1977 and 1978 received significant media attention (McDowell et al. 2014). As Duffy and Frere-Smith (2014) suggested, without a direct reference to the Grunwick strike, images of struggles between 'migrants' and the police often increase public anxiety. Public concerns receded after 1978 until a second peak in October 1985, but at a lower level, that was related to race riots that summer in a number of UK cities. Concern about immigration and race issues then remained low, until a much more significant rise from the start of the new millennium, which as I suggested earlier is connected to the emergence of so-called Islamic fundamentalism, radicalization and fear of terrorism but also to higher numbers of in-migrants. In the early years of the new century, concern about the economy had replaced immigration as the key issue that the British public worried about until 2012–13 when the economic situation began to improve, and immigration again become the most significant issue of concern.

There is perhaps little that is surprising in the types of worries expressed by the public. Over the decades, the most common fears include a belief that there are too many in-migrants and the host population is in danger of 'being swamped' – a common image, used in speeches by Margaret Thatcher in the 1980s when she was Prime Minister – that Britain is overcrowded, and that migration is more of a problem than an opportunity. Since 1995, the annual British Social Attitudes Survey has included a question about whether immigration totals should be lower. The percentage who answered yes increased steadily from that date, but even in the mid-1990s when net in-migration was around 60,000 (the tens of thousands that British Prime Minister David Cameron wants to return to) rather than almost 300,000 as in 2014, 63 per cent of the general public suggested stronger controls on numbers.

The surveys also identified an age-specific or life stage effect, as older generations are more insistent on control. Even the views of the baby boomers, relatively liberal when asked the question about immigration numbers in the 1990s, were more negative when they were questioned again in 2013. Attitudes vary by class too, as people in working class jobs are more likely to fear competition from foreign workers. Interestingly, although 37 per cent of those surveyed in a parallel study, *Small Island* (Ashcroft 2013), thought immigrants took jobs from the British population, 67 per cent recognized that they often undertook the sort of work British people refused to do. It is in exactly these sorts of jobs – in catering, cleaning, caring, the retail and hospitality sector, as well as in what remains of the manufacturing sector, and the hard monotonous work in agricultural industries – that many of the women who came to the UK to live and work across the decades since 1945 found employment. Their participation freed British women for other tasks and other sorts of work, although many British-born women have also found employment in these jobs over the years since the end of the Second World War. The complexity of attitudes towards in-migrants and changing ideas about British identity, about belonging to the nation (itself now a more contested notion as the UK may disappear in the future), and about new forms of cosmopolitan citizenship increase the necessity of an urgent debate about migration and the place of people born outside the UK in its labour market. Even in a world marked by movement and globalization, the need to belong to a community and a place remains a central part of communal and self-identity.

Last words

I hope that the stories told here will prove to be both a useful and an inspiring source of information about migrant women's lives, as well as about the changing nature of work and employment. The intention is that they provide a stimulus for the general reader, students and their teachers to learn more about the events of the relatively recent past. Through the vivid words of the 74 women who, in earlier chapters, spoke directly to the reader from across seven decades, it is possible to glimpse not only the ways in which working lives have changed since the end of the Second World War, but also to capture some of the major events since then through the eyes of women who were there. Some of these women walked half way across Europe; others struggled in independence movements, seeing their fathers or husbands assassinated for their beliefs. Famine, wars, escape from sexual violence, as well as the search for employment, were reasons for leaving home and, as the narratives document, many women came from backgrounds of unremitting toil and family poverty, hoping to escape economic hardship though emigration. Their lives in the UK have not always been easy. Even for the well-qualified and most affluent among them, discriminatory attitudes have marked their workplace experiences. In the narratives, there are many examples of the ways in which women born outside the UK were made to feel out of place, treated as the Other, not white or not white enough, not British, not from 'here', called racist names, treated unfairly in the workplace, and denied promotions. And yet, these are also stories of quiet heroism, of hard work, and pleasures found at home and in the workplace.

As economic integration in the European Community increases, (assuming the UK remains a member), as global businesses seek labour across ever wider spaces and as wars, unrest, climate change and food shortages continue to affect population movements, transnational migration seems likely to continue to increase. In summer 2015, the large scale movement of people seeking asylum in Western Europe led to a crisis in EU solidarity, as several member states refused to cooperate in a plan to allocate refugees across the Union. According to United Nations (2013), 232 million people in the world lived outside the borders of the state in which they were born, up from 175 million in 2000, and in recent decades women have been an increasing proportion of total number. Their contribution to the economies of what are often termed host countries and the quiet heroism of their everyday lives deserve far greater recognition.

Appendix 1

Half a Century of Change:

UK 1951–2001

In the following tables some of the major changes in the UK over the second half of the twentieth century are summarized, including the number and origins of in-migrants, women's labour market participation, housing conditions and the possession of consumer durables. One of the key sources for statistical information is the national census of population, taken in every post-war decade since 1951. Other data produced by the Office for National Statistics (ONS), including the annual report *Social Trends*, as well as the Labour Force Survey and the Family Expenditure Survey (conducted between 1957 and 2001), are also important sources of statistical information about social and economic change. The Research Paper 99/111 *A Century of Change* (Hicks and Allen 1999) produced for the House of Commons is also a useful source of information about social and economic changes across the entire twentieth century, although it does not include any information on gender differences.

Migration

The UK was a net exporter of population from the 1950s to the 1980s, as families migrated under arranged passages to Australia, New Zealand and South Africa and emigration continued in later decades. In the 1990s, however, the trend was reversed. In 1997, for example, 96,600 more people migrated to the UK than left it.

By 2001 the origins of the foreign-born population in Britain were diverse, with more than 50,000 people from one of 24 countries recorded as living in the UK and almost that number from the 25th country (see Table 2). The distribution reflects close ties with Ireland as a country of emigration, Britain's imperial history as well as migration within Europe, and there is also perhaps a surprisingly large number of Americans in the total. These 25 countries accounted for 74 per cent of the total non-British-born population living in the UK in 2001.

TABLE 1 *Total population and foreign-born population in the UK* (thousands)

Year	All	Foreign-born	% of total
1951	50,290	2,119	4.2
1961	52,807	2,574	4.9
1971	53,928	3,190	5.8
1981	56,352	3,429	6.2
1991	57,808	3,835	6.7
2001	59,009	4,897	8.3

Source: National Census of Population, various dates.

TABLE 2 *Birthplace of foreign-born population – 25 largest groups, UK, 2001*

Rank	Nationality	Number in the UK	Rank	Nationality	Number
1	Ireland	533,901	14	Nigeria	88,378
2	India	467,634	15	Cyprus	77,673
3	Pakistan	321,167	16	Canada	72,518
4	Germany	266,136	17	Sri Lanka	67,938
5	USA	158,434	18	Poland	60,711
6	Bangladesh	154,362	19	New Zealand	58,286
7	Jamaica	146,401	20	Ghana	56,112
8	South Africa	141,405	21	Uganda	55,213
9	Kenya	129,633	22	Spain	54,482
10	Australia	107,244	23	Turkey	54,079
11	Italy	107,244	24	China, PR	51,078
12	Hong Kong	96,445	25	Malaysia	49,886
13	France	96,281		Total	3,032,834

Source: National Census of Population 2001.

One of the effects of EU expansion in 2004 and 2007 was to increase the rate of growth of the foreign-born population in the UK. By 2011, the total had risen to almost 7,500,000, just under 13 per cent of the total population

TABLE 3 *Employment of women, millions, UK*

Year	Number	% of working age
1951	6.3	40
1961	7.0	47
1971	8.5	55
1981	9.9	59
1991	11.6	66
2001	12.7	73

Source: National Census of Population.

of the country. The rank order of countries also changed after the accession to the EU of a further 13 countries, including Poland, the country that exported the largest number of people. The 2011 census recorded 521,000 migrants born in Poland, a nine-fold increase since 2001 and moving it up to second in the rank of countries. India headed the list.

Although women's employment rose significantly over the post-war period, their pattern of work differed from that of men. Almost all men until the end of the century worked on a full-time basis whereas women were almost as likely to work part-time as full-time.

The employment participation rates for women in-migrants are complex and variable. Non-British white immigrants have similar employment rates to the white British born population. Indeed they were slightly higher between 1979 (when labour force figures for in-migrants were first collected) and 1986 and then similar or just lower until the end of the century. For some non-white in-migrant women, however, employment participation has been significantly lower than for other groups. They include women from Pakistan and Bangladesh, although Indian, Chinese and Caribbean women had very similar rates of participation as the British-born female population over the 1980s and early 1990s, falling slightly lower by 2001 as these women aged (Dustmann et al. 2003). Caribbean in-migrants, for example, are noticeably older than the rest of the population.

Social class

Of the employed workforce, the key change has been the decline of unskilled and semi-skilled jobs (classes 4 and 5) and the growth of professional, managerial and technical (classes 1 and 2) occupations. The proportion of skilled jobs (class 3) remained largely constant. These changes reflect the decline of manufacturing, and the rise of services and women's employment. The percentage of employees in classes 4 and 5 has declined from just under 50 per cent in 1951 to about 28 per cent in 1991, whereas the proportion in classes 1 and 2 has increased from under 20 per cent to almost 40 per cent in the same years. Seventy-five per cent of all workers, and 92 per cent of women employees, are now working in the service sector.

Sex segregation in the labour market remains marked. In 2013, 82 per cent of all employees in caring, leisure and other services, 77 per cent in administrative and secretarial jobs and 63 per cent in sales and customer services were women. In skilled trades, however, women were only 10 per cent of all employees, 11 per cent of process, plant and machine operatives and 33 per cent of managers and senior officials.

Unemployment

The highest rate of unemployment over the second half of the century was in 1986 when just over three million people were unemployed, about 10 per cent of the workforce. By the end of the century, the rate was slightly over 4 per cent.

Employment among non-British born populations

Migrants tend to be young when they arrive in the UK, with a concentration in the age group 25 to 45 and so they are of working age. In 2001, the foreign-born population comprised 10 per cent of the working age population in the UK as a whole, but 30 per cent in Greater London, reflecting their propensity to live in the capital. In 2000, 9 per cent of British-born whites of working age lived in London, compared with 40 per cent of the foreign-born, and 45 per cent of British-born ethnic minorities.

Employment rates among the foreign-born population varied depending on the relationships between age, gender, family status, and religious beliefs, as well as educational and skill levels. The average employment rate among migrants in 2001 was about 64 per cent, compared with 75 per cent for the UK-born population, but rates varied from 81 per cent for migrants from Australasia, to 52 per cent for people from the Indian subcontinent.

In 2001, the foreign-born population was concentrated at both the low and high end of the skills distribution. The foreign-born were more likely to be highly qualified, with 19 per cent of working age people holding degrees, compared to 15 per cent among the UK-born population. However, a greater proportion among the foreign-born population also had no qualifications (19 per cent compared with 16 per cent).

White in-migrants have similar employment participation rates as UK-born whites. Minority immigrants have on average lower rates, with Pakistanis, Black Africans, and people from the Caribbean being the most disadvantaged. This is true for both men and women. Pakistanis and Bangladeshis are among those with lowest participation rates.

Overall people from other industrialized countries tend to do better in the UK labour market than those from poorer countries, but an employment disadvantage, or ethnic penalty, for migrants exists consistently at all skill/qualification levels. Both highly-skilled and low-skilled migrants have difficulty competing for jobs with their UK-born counterparts, though the gap is generally larger at the lower-skill levels (Haque 2002).

Strikes

Trade union membership fell across the five decades, although among women rates actually increased. The number of days lost to industrial action also fell from the end of the 1980s to the lowest across the entire century by 2000. In the 1970s and 1980s, however, 200 million working days were lost, in the main by strikes by male workers, although women were significant actors in the strikes at Ford, Grunwick and Gate Gourmet mentioned in the oral histories, as well as in strikes by council workers. The key strikes in the late 1970s and 1980s were by the engineering workers in 1979, the miners in 1984 and 1985, telecommunications workers in 1987, postal workers in 1988 and by council employees in 1989, 1991 and 1992.

Leisure and sport

Trends in leisure activities have changed significantly since the end of the war. In 1946, 80 per cent of the population went to the cinema at least once a year, and often more frequently. Some of the Baltic Cygnets mentioned how important going to the cinema was for them, helping them to learn to speak English. By 1960, audience numbers had fallen to 501 million from 1,640 million in 1946 and by 1984 to just 60 million, as television displaced the cinema. However, as multiplex cinemas and arts cinemas were introduced (the first multiplex opened in Milton Keynes in 1985) audiences began to rise again.

Participation in sports has increased, although more leisure time is spent watching sport. Men are more likely to be active as players or coaches than women. About 12 per cent of women and 20 per cent of men participated in at least 30 minutes of moderate activity three times a week in the mid-2000s, rising to 41 per cent for women and 60 per cent for men just once a week. The rates decline with age. For women the most significant activity is going to keep fit classes (Women's Sport and Fitness Foundation 2013).

Housing, domestic appliances and consumer durables

There were enormous changes in the pattern of housing occupation and in the possession of appliances and consumer goods over the second half of the twentieth century, although the number of households continued to be larger than the stock of dwellings over the entire period. In 1945 as the war ended most households lived in private rented accommodation (55 per cent) often in poor conditions. A third (32 per cent) of households, not all of them affluent or middle class, owned or were buying their own home, as the narratives of the EVWs made clear. By 2000, owner occupation had risen to 70 per cent, and private renting had fallen to 10 per cent, with 20 per cent of all households living in social housing. This tenure had been more significant in the 1970s and early 1980s until the Conservative government under Margaret Thatcher introduced the right to buy their house for tenants of local authorities.

A mass market for consumer durables and household appliances was established in the 1950s, as more affluent working class households began to purchase the sorts of goods previously only found in middle class homes. Average real earnings of industrial workers rose by more than 20 per cent between 1951 and 1958; and that by the spring of 1959 the average working-class household income was about £850 per year (gross), with nearly half of all employed working-class families having an annual income of over £1,000. National surveys showed that by 1959 among the more prosperous half of the working class 85 per cent of all households had a television set, 44 per cent a washing machine, 44 per cent a lawnmower, 32 per cent a car and 16 per cent a refrigerator. In addition 35 per cent of the families in question owned, or were buying, their own house (Beynon et al. 2003).

By the 1980s, most households in the UK had a wide array of domestic appliances. While there were still class differences (see Table 4), almost all households had a fridge and a washing machine. By the start of the twenty-first century, the ownership of fridges, washing machines, televisions and phones was virtually 100 per cent, ownership of personal computers about 60 per cent and car ownership among households including a person in employment was 83 per cent. Between 1951 and 1998, total household expenditure had more than tripled in real terms and over the same years expenditure on televisions, and video and audio equipment had quadrupled (Higgs 2006). More recently the ownership of personal electronic appliances has increased hugely – mobile phones, laptops, tablets etc. are now almost ubiquitous, especially among the young.

Although housing conditions have improved significantly since the end of the war and the ownership of so-called labour-saving devices has become widespread, the hours spent by women doing unwaged housework have not fallen at the same rate.

TABLE 4 *Households with selected domestic appliances, 1988 (%)*

Households with:

	Deep freezers (incl. fridge freezers)	Washing machine	Tumble drier	Microwave oven	Dishwasher
Professional	88	93	60	51	32
Employers and managers	91	95	62	60	27
Other non-manual	84	89	45	50	19
Skilled and semi-skilled manual	85	91	50	48	6
Unskilled manual	75	83	36	32	1
Economically inactive	61	72	25	21	4
All	77	84	42	39	10

Source: Adapted from Beynon et al. (2003) data from Social Trends and Family Expenditure, Survey, ONS.

TABLE 5 *Patterns of change affecting the market for consumer durables*

	Average HH size	No. hholds	Women working	Stock of dwellings
		(m)	(000s)	
1970	2.91	18.3	8,962	16.1
1975	2.78	18.8	9,719	16.9
1980	2.70	19.5	10,347	17.5
1985	2.56	21.1	10,173	18.5
1990	2.48	22.4	11,604	19.4
1995	2.40	23.5	11,599	20.3
2000	2.29	24.5	12,647	21.1

Source: Adapted from Beynon et al. (2003) data from Social Trends and Family Expenditure, Survey, ONS.

While there is no doubt that the labour involved in keeping a house clean and a family clean and fed is now much easier, the association between femininity, domesticity and care remains strong. For many women, looking after their family and doing housework is a measure of their care and perhaps their own sense of self-worth and so hours spent on domestic tasks have not fallen as fast as was once predicted (Cowan 1983; Oakley 1974).

Patterns of transport and journeys to work have changed enormously over the post-war period. The most significant change has been in the pattern of car ownership. By 1971 there were 29 million cars in the UK, an increase from 13 million in 1951. These figures include cars for lease and off the road. Since 1951 the rise in the number of households with at least one car has been rapid – from 14 per cent in 1951 to 69 per cent in 2001 (Leibling 2008). While men are still more likely to have a driving licence than women, among younger age groups the gender difference is insignificant and it is older women who are less likely to be able to drive.

Appendix 2

Interviewees in Alphabetical Order

All names are pseudonyms.

Name	Country of birth	Date of birth	Year arrived in the UK
Adele	New Zealand	1948	1970
Aileen	Ireland	1930	1949
Amalie	France	1971	1997
Amrita	India	1957	1977
Ani	Romania	1968	1993
Anya	Estonia	1947	2004
Bashira	Pakistan	1961	1979
Beatta	Poland	1982	2006
Bina	Tanzania	1959	1978
Brie	Trinidad	1948	1967
Brigita	Latvia	1930	1947
Catherine	Kenya	1978	1999
Caro	Canada	1952	1978
Dagnija	Latvia	1919	1947
Diana	Latvia	1920	1947
Dominika	Poland	1974	1999
Eidothea	Greece	1981	2006
Ellen	Hong Kong	1962	1975 (?)*
Elvira	Latvia	1920	1947

Name	Country of birth	Date of birth	Year arrived in the UK
Erica	Latvia	1921	1947
Eva	Latvia	1928	1947
Farah	Kuwait	1966	1991
Fida	Uganda	1950	1989
Fitore	Yugoslavia (Kosovo)	1970	2002
Flora	Colombia	1952	1974
Georgina	Trinidad	1941	1957
Grieta	Latvia	1918	1947
Hana	Ethiopia	1970+	2005
Harshini	India	1948	1962
Illona	Latvia	1926	1947
Isobel	New Zealand	1957	1982
Jaba	India	1933	1968
Jane	Brazil	1952	2005
Janice	New Zealand	1951	1970
Jasbir	Kenya	1953	1977
Jelena	Latvia	1931	1948
Jenny	Latvia	1980	2002
Karina	Latvia	1982	2003
Kate	New Zealand	1960	1982
Li Jing	Hong Kong	1973	1999
Lina	Latvia	1931	1947
Mari	Brazil	1970	2002
Maria	East Timor	1983	2007
Marianna	Yugoslavia (Kosovo)	1973	1999
Marta	Latvia	1930	1948
Martine	South Africa	1974	2000
Mary	Ireland	1943	1961
May	Thailand	check Jane's	2009
Meg	USA	1978	2006
Milda	Latvia	1930	1947
Moira	Ireland	1937	1954

Nadia	Poland	1981	2005
Natalija	Latvia	1930	1947
Natasha	USSR	1965	1990
Papla	Kenya	1946	1971
Parnal	India	1974	2002
Parvani	Kenya	1941	1966
Phyllida	Ireland	1934	1958
Posha	Indian	1979	2006
Raksha	India	1950	1968
Ruta	Latvia	1929	1947
Sahdev	India	1952 (?)**	1977
Sai	India	1936	1968
Saran	India	1955	1971
Shami	India	1951	1988
Simone	France	1982	2008
Surjit	India	1948	1995
Taslima	Bangladesh	1978	1997
Tracey	South Africa	1945	1966
Valda	Latvia	1919	1947
Velta	Latvia	1926	1947
Vieda	Latvia	1930	1948
Victoria	Singapore	1975	2004
Vijaya	Kenya	1943	1968

Notes:

+Hana did not know exactly when she was born but was given 1970 as her date of birth by Dutch immigration officials.

*Ellen was unsure exactly when the family moved to the UK but remembered it was sometime in the mid-1970s.

**Sahdev's passport recorded her date of birth as five years earlier than she thought it was and so she said this 'official' date was incorrect.

Appendix 3

Post-War Immigration Legislation

The list that follows includes the major legislative changes regulating in-migration between 1945 and 2015.

1948 British Nationality Act: introduced a new status Citizen of the United Kingdom and Colonies (CUKC) consisting of all those British subjects who had a close relationship, either through birth or descent with the United Kingdom and its remaining colonies, and guaranteed right of free entry to British subjects and Commonwealth citizens.

1962 Commonwealth Immigrants Act: beginning of restrictions. Before this Act all Commonwealth citizens could enter and remain in the UK without restrictions. Through this Act, citizens of the United Kingdom and Colonies (CUKCs) whose passports were not directly issued by the UK government (passports issued by a Governor of a Colony or by the Commander of a British Protectorate) now became subject to immigration control, with the exception of those who held passports issued at a British High Commission in an independent Commonwealth country or by a British Consul. The Act also increased the residence period for Commonwealth citizens, British subjects and Irish citizens applying for registration as Citizens of the UK and Colonies from one year to five years. Employment vouchers were also required to gain entry into the UK.

1968 Commonwealth Immigrants Act: this Act widened controls to include people who were citizens of the UK and Colonies either by birth in a colony or by registration in a Commonwealth country before it became independent. It sharpened the distinction between citizens of the UK and Colonies (CUKC) who had close ties with the UK and who were free to enter and those citizens who had no such ties and were therefore subject to immigration control. It had the effect, especially in the newly independent East African countries, of abolishing the right to residence in the UK.

1971 Immigration Act: control of immigration into the UK or people of all nationalities, new provisions for deportation orders; altered rights of appeal against immigration decisions and excluded certain categories of its nationals from the right of abode. This is the Act that created the concept of partiality or right of abode only for those CUKCs and other Commonwealth citizens who if they, their husband (if female), their parents or grandparents were connected to the United Kingdom and Islands. It meant that some of the UK's nationals were now forbidden entry into the country of their nationality.

1987 Immigration (Carriers' Liability) Act: provided for a charge of £1,000 to be levied on the owners or agents of a ship or aircraft where a passenger requiring leave to enter the UK arrives without valid travel documentation or visa. This Act seriously undermined the substantive rights of refugees to claim asylum.

1988 Immigration Act: the main effect of this Act was to end the exemption of certain Commonwealth citizens from the need to meet the marriage tests and the maintenance and accommodation requirements when bringing their families into the UK for settlement.

1993 Asylum and Immigration Appeals Act: provides new rights of appeal for asylum applicants refused asylum; introduced strict time limits of all stages of processing appeals and a swifter procedure for dealing with 'manifestly unfounded' cases. The Act also abolished the right of appeal for people from other countries wishing to visit the UK as a tourist, to visit a relative, as a prospective student, or those seeking to extend their duration of stay beyond the maximum period permitted should their application be refused.

1996 Asylum and Immigration Act: this Act widens the scope of the accelerated appeals procedure in asylum cases, outlines various punitive measures targeted at immigration offenders and those abetting them and restricts accommodation and welfare provisions for asylum applicants and introduces provisions to remove them from the UK. The Act makes it a criminal offence for an employer to employ anyone subject to immigration control, punishable with fines of up to £5,000. Employers must ask new employees taken on or re-employed for evidence of residential status, such as national insurance documents and EU passports; this request must be made in a manner that does not breach racial discrimination legislation. The Act also makes provisions for returning asylum seekers to other 'third' countries even if they have recently transited though this country on the way to their destination and effectively removes the right of appeal against decision to return asylum seekers to these 'safe third countries'.

1999 Immigration and Asylum Act: this Act replaces mainstream welfare benefits entitlement for asylum seekers. It created the National Asylum

Support Service (NASS) to provide basic support – vouchers worth £35 a week for an adult – and accommodation on the basis of a forced dispersal policy.

2002 Nationality, Immigration and Asylum Act: this Act created a 'white' list of 'safe countries' whose citizens cannot remain in the UK while they mount an appeal once their asylum applications are rejected. It denies asylum seekers' support unless they make their claim 'as soon as reasonably practicable' after their arrival in the UK – at a port or airport – and they can explain how they reached the UK. This Act provides for the creation of a network of induction centres to house destitute asylum seekers.

2004 Asylum and Immigration (Treatment of Claimants) Act: this Act introduced a new single tier appeals process (Asylum and Immigration tribunal) to consider all appeals against immigration and asylum decisions. Further appeals to the High Court can only be made on the grounds that a tribunal made an error of law. It also abolishes back dated support payments, creates new offences for undocumented migrants and for non-cooperation with removal.

2006 Immigration, Asylum and Nationality Act: this Act restricts the right of appeal for refusal of entry clearance, leaving open only grounds for appeal based on human rights and race discrimination reasons. The Act introduces civil (not criminal) penalties for employers who take on people subject to immigration control and provisions empowering the Home Secretary to deprive a person of British citizenship or right of abode if it is considered such deprivation is 'conducive to the public good'.

2008 Criminal Justice and Immigration Act: among other things this introduces a special immigration status for those believed to have been involved in terrorism and other serious crimes and for their spouses. Recipients have no formal leave to enter or remain in the UK and the Home Secretary can impose conditions on their residence and require them to wear an electronic tag.

2009 The Borders, Citizenship and Immigration Act introduced some changes to the British Nationality Act 1981, increased age at which a spouse might be admitted and altered rules for Tier 1 (highly-skilled) and Tier 5 (unskilled) economic migrants. A Condition of Acceptance letter for students at higher educational institutions from 2010 and restrictions on dependents were also introduced. Asylum seekers waiting for a decision for more than a year permitted to seek work. Introduced changes to regulations for domestic servants in diplomatic households. Introduced higher income thresholds for sponsoring dependents and strict rules on admission of elderly parents requiring care. New immigration appeals (family visitor) regulations came into effect from July 2012. New doctorate extensions scheme introduced in April 2013, giving eligible applicants twelve months after completing a PhD to find skilled work or set up as an entrepreneur.

2014 Immigration Act introduced changes to the Immigration and Asylum Act 1999 about removal of persons unlawfully in the UK. Changed the removals and appeals system, ends the abuse of Article 8 of the European Convention on Human Rights – the right to respect for family and private life, and prevents illegal immigrants accessing public services.

Appendix 4

Questions Raised by the Narratives

Some questions to think about while reading

How do women tell stories about migration? Why do women leave home?

How has the transformation of the UK economy over time been reflected in women's working lives?

What elements of continuity are there in the jobs women do, the conditions under which they work and the pay they receive?

How has the growth in the numbers and the diversity of migrants living and working in the UK been reflected in women's working lives?

Is there still gender segregation in the labour market? Do migrant women work in the main in women-only jobs and why?

Do women work not only with other women but women from their own class and ethnic backgrounds and, if so, why?

Are women discriminated against and exploited; how and why?

Are women who were not born in the UK particularly disadvantaged; are they more likely to work across their lifetime than British born women?

Do women need mentors to succeed, especially in professional occupations? Are they more likely to be another woman or a man?

Why do women often work in casual jobs or part-time?

Why are women paid so poorly in many sectors?

How do women combine waged work and other responsibilities, especially caring for their families? How has this changed over time?

Are migrant women likely to join trade unions? In what sorts of jobs? Do unions protect women's interests on the whole?

How has women's waged work changed over time and why; has it improved?

How have patterns of migration changed and why?

Have attitudes to non-British women changed and how might this affect opportunities in the labour market?

What do women emphasize in their stories about work and home, and why?

How reliable are the stories? Does it matter when they were told and about which time period? How often do stories change or do they become sedimented in a particular version?

Is it possible to read these narratives 'against the grain' thinking about what might have been left out and why?

NOTES

Chapter 1

1 11 September 2001 when the Twin Towers in New York City were attacked, 7 July 2005 when bombs were detonated on the London Underground and a London bus and 7 January 2015 when the offices of weekly magazine *Charlie Hebdo* and a Jewish supermarket in Paris were attacked: all in the name of radical Islam.

Chapter 2

1 Fifteen thousand Latvians were deported to Siberia – intellectuals, high ranking officials, business owners, and members of the armed forces and the police service, including over 5,000 women and just over 3,000 children.

2 Many of the women leaving the Baltic States were recruited into the German war effort, often working with, but regarded as superior to, the forced labourers who were a significant component of the labour force in Nazi Germany.

3 Serbian attacks on Kosovans who were forced to flee in 1999.

4 Under the agreement signed by Churchill, Roosevelt and Stalin at the Yalta Conference in 1945, refugees from the territories that became part of the USSR, including the Baltic States, were to be handed back. However, many displaced people from the Baltic States escaped this fate through various routes, including recruitment as EVWs.

5 Powell, a Conservative Member of Parliament, had been Minister of Health between 1960 and 1963 but in 1966 was Shadow Secretary of Defence in Heath's Shadow Cabinet. Labour politician Harold Wilson was Prime Minister from 1964 to 1970.

6 Kenya became independent in 1963 and Jomo Kenyatta was the first president of the republic from 1964. Asians had been significant in the commercial life of the country before independence and were discriminated against and so many families decided to leave. Those who held British passports left in greater numbers in 1968 as the UK government passed a restrictive act (1968 Commonwealth Immigrants Act) that sharpened the distinction between Commonwealth citizens with close ties to the UK and those without. People with the new Kenyan citizenship, for example, were excluded.

7 Another Indian woman rather than a blood relative.

8   Communal violence based on religious and language differences.

9   Eritrea became independent in 1991 after a war with Ethiopia between 1961 and 1991.

10 11 September 2001 when the twin towers of the World Trade Center in New York City were destroyed.

Chapter 3

1   A Victorian mill in Stockport, Cheshire, now converted to light industrial use and office space.

2   Typically mills shut for a week or a fortnight in June or July.

3   Taking off the rough parts from the inner surface of a skin by short oblique cuts with a currier's knife.

4   EVWs had to gain permission to move between jobs in the initial years in the UK.

5   Then an artificial fibre (viscose and rayon) producer in Coventry in the Midlands.

6   Lina rented a room from an English couple she called Pop and Ma.

7   A two generational family. Bashira lived with her in-laws.

8   The Transport and General Workers Union (also known as TGWU and T&G) that merged with Amicus in 2007 to become Unite.

9   Her monthly union subscription.

Chapter 4

1   The equivalent of £68 in 2014.

2   EVWs were permitted to change their job but had to remain in the same type of employment to which they were allocated initially. Most women had to work for three years before being released from their contract and able to seek employment in the open market.

3   This was the second scheme introduced after the Baltic Cygnet scheme and for men as well as women 'volunteers'.

4   In 2006 when Karina moved, the national minimum wage was £5.35 for workers aged 22 and over.

Chapter 5

1   Polio or poliomyelitis was a major public health issue in Victorian times. It has now been eradicated in the UK but in the late 1940 and early 1950s there was a worldwide epidemic in which half a million people died, including over a thousand in the UK. Others were left with degrees of paralysis. About 120,000 affected are currently still living in the UK.

2   As nurses from the Caribbean were to find, there were two training routes in the 1950s and 1960s – three years to become an SRN (State Registered Nurse) and two to become an SEN (State Enrolled Nurse). Only the former, as Aileen remarked, was the 'proper' route, leading to seniority and promotion.

3   There were several strikes by dock workers in the 1960s when many men were still employed on a casual basis.

4   The SRN was a three-year professional route leading to promotion; the SEN lasted only two years and so was a less prestigious qualification. The SRN-trainee was termed a student nurse, the SEN-trainee a pupil nurse. The distinction was abolished in the mid-1990s when all courses became three years.

5   Brie is referring to the concept of institutionalized racism in organizations, a concept introduced by the Macpherson Report (1999) about attitudes in the Metropolitan Police revealed during the inquiry into the death of Stephen Lawrence, a black teenager, in London.

6   The replacement of the State Registered Nurse qualification was the Registered General Nurse training.

7   General Certificate of Secondary Education, then the qualifications taken at age 16.

8   Registered General Nurse: the new name for the SRN.

9   Ear, nose and throat.

10 Royal College of Nursing.

11 Parnal was recruited by a Singapore hospital through an agency operating in Kerala.

12 National Insurance Number.

13 Parnal worked on the cardiology ward whereas the CCU (coronary care unit) provides more specialist care for more seriously ill patients, and the nurses there are on a higher pay grade.

14 Farah worked as a shop assistant at Matalan, a clothes retailer, for two years and then five years at Tesco, a large grocery store, but left as she found working as a cashier on the till exacerbated her epilepsy.

Chapter 6

1   A bear market is when investors anticipate losses and as selling continues, pessimism grows. Its opposite, a bull market, is when prices are rising or expected to, often leading to over-optimism.

2   Caro was referring the events of Black Wednesday in September 1992 when sterling left the European Exchange Rate Mechanism (ERM) and George Soros, a currency market investor, made over £1 billion by short selling sterling.

3   The interview was in July 2009, not long after the financial crisis of late 2007–8.

4   A gas leak at the Union Carbide pesticide plant in northern India in 1984 in which over 500,000 people were exposed to noxious chemicals. The immediate

death toll was 2,259 and several thousand people have since died from gas-related symptoms.

5   Singapore declared independence in August 1965.

Chapter 7

1   United Nations Relief and Rehabilitation Administration.

2   The steel tube manufacturer in Corby, owned by Stewart and Lloyds until 1967, when it was nationalized, relied heavily on male migrant workers, including Scots in the inter-war years and afterwards, and EVWs in the late 1940s.

3   The equivalent of approximately £150 in 2010.

4   In 1975 seven Irish men were sentenced to life imprisonment for bombing a public house in Birmingham. The convictions were declared unsafe and quashed in 1991.

5   Lord Mountbatten, uncle of Prince Philip, a statesman and naval officer, was killed by an IRA (Irish Republican Army) bomb in 1979.

6   It is the responsibility of individuals to obtain a national insurance number before accepting employment.

7   Jenny had done the first two years of an economics degree in Latvia.

8   Jenny was interviewed in 2009 not long after the banking crisis.

9   Nadia has a BA in history and philology from a Polish university.

Chapter 8

1   The Clean Air Acts of 1956 and 1968 were introduced to combat the smogs of the 1950s and 1960s which were the consequence of burning coal by both households and industry. As well as health benefits, homes became easier, as well as less onerous, to keep clean.

2   Idi Amin Dada was the third president of Uganda between 1971 and 1979. The expulsion of South Asian heritage people from Uganda in 1972 increased the number of South Asians in the UK. He was a brutal despot and was involved in ethnic persecutions, including Fida's family. During the Ugandan–Tanzanian War between 1978 and 1979, Amin was deposed and fled to Libya.

3   Acholi is the language of the Luo people from the north of Uganda.

SELECT BIBLIOGRAPHY

References cited in the text

Amin, A 2012 *Land of Strangers*, Polity Press, Cambridge.

Anderson, B 1991 *Imagined Communities*, revised edition, Verso, London

Arthur, M 2004 *Forgotten Voices of the Second World War*, Ebury Press, London.

Ashcroft, L 2013 *Small Island: public opinion and the politics of immigration*, available at http://lordashcroftpolls.com (accessed 28 June 2015).

Augé, M 1995 *Non-places: an introduction to an anthropology of supermodernity*, Verso, London.

Bartram, D, Poros, M and Monforte, P 2014 *Key Concepts in Migration*, Sage, London.

Benhahib, S and Resnik, J (eds) 2009 *Migrations and Mobilities: citizenship, borders and gender*, New York University Press, London.

Betts, A 2011 *Global Migration Governance*, Oxford University Press, Oxford.

Beveridge, W 1942 *Social Insurance and Allied Services*, HMSO, London.

Beynon, H, Cam, S, Fairbrother, P and Nichols, T 2003 *The rise and transformation of the UK domestic appliances industry*, Working Paper Series, Paper 42, School of Social Sciences, Cardiff University.

Brush, L 1999 'Gender, work, who cares? Production, reproduction, deindustrialisation and business as usual', pp. 161–189 in M M Ferree, J Lorber and B Hess (eds), *Revisioning Gender*, Sage, London.

Centre on Dynamics of Ethnicity 2012 *How has ethnic diversity grown, 1991–2001–2011?* ESRC Centre, University of Manchester.

Chambers, I 1989 'Narratives of nationalism: being "British"', *New Formations* 7, 88–103.

Connerton, P 1989 *How Societies Remember*, Cambridge University Press, Cambridge.

Connolly, S and Gregory, M 2007 'Women and work since 1970', pp. 142–77 in N Crafts, I Gazeley and A Newell (eds) *Work and pay in 20th century Britain*, Oxford University Press, Oxford.

Cowan, R S 1983 *More Work for Mother: the ironies of domestic technology from the open hearth to the microwave*, Basic Books, New York.

Duffy, B and Frere-Smith, T 2014 *Perceptions and Reality: public attitudes to immigration*, Ipsos-MORI, London.

Dustmann, C, Fabbri, F, Preston, I and Wadsworth, J 2003 *Labour market performance of immigrants in the UK labour market*, Home Office Online Report 05/03, available at discovery.ucl.ac.uk (accessed 10 June 2015).

Dyer, R 1997 *White*, Routledge, London.

Eatwell, R and Goodwin, M (eds) 2010 *The New Extremism in 21st Century Britain*, Routledge, London.

Eksteins, M 1999 *Walking Since Daybreak: a story of Eastern Europe, World War II and the heart of the twentieth century*, Houghton Mifflin, New York.

Eliot, T S 1973 *Notes towards the Definition of Culture*, Faber and Faber, London.

Fawcett Society 2010 *Sexism and the City: the manifesto – what's rotten in the City and what we can do about it*, Fawcett Society, London.

Gabriel, Y 2000 *Story Telling in Organizations*, Oxford University Press, Oxford.

Garfield, S 2004 *Our Hidden Lives: the everyday diaries of a forgotten Britain 1945–1948*, Ebury Press, London.

Gilroy, P 2002 *There ain't no Black in the Union Jack: the cultural politics of race and nation*, Routledge, London (re-issued with a new introduction, originally published by Hutchinson in 1987).

Goodwin, M 2011 *New British Fascism: the rise of the British National Party*, Routledge, London.

Hall, S 1990 'Cultural identity and diaspora', pp. 222–37 in J Rutherford (ed.) *Identity: Community, Culture, Difference*, Lawrence & Wishart, London.

Haque, R 2002 *Migrants in the UK: a descriptive analysis of their characteristics and labour market performance*, RDS Occasional Paper No. 82, Department of Work and Pensions.

Harrison, B 2009 *Seeking a Role: the United Kingdom 1951–1970*, Oxford University Press, Oxford.

Hicks, J and Allen, G 1999 *A Century of Change: trends in UK statistics since 1990*. Research Paper 99/111, House of Commons Library, London.

Higgs, P 2006 *From passive to active consumers*, Cultures of Consumption Working Paper Series, Paper no. 28, Centre for Behavioural and Social Sciences in Medicine, UCL, www.consume.bbk.ac.uk (accessed 14 November 2014).

Hobsbawm, R and Ranger, T (eds) 2012 *The Invention of Tradition*, Cambridge University Press, Cambridge.

Holmes, R 2007 *The World at War: the landmark oral history*, Ebury Press, London.

Kingsnorth, P 2015 'Rescuing the English', *The Guardian Review* 14 March, 2–4.

Leibling, D 2008 *Car Ownership in Britain*, RAC Foundation, London.

Madood, T 2007 *Multiculturalism*, Polity Press, Cambridge.

Mandela, N 1994 *Long Walk to Freedom*, Little, Brown, London.

Marshall, H E 2005 *Our Island Story: a child's history of Britain*, Galore Park Civitas, London (originally published in 1905).

McCrindle, J and Rowbotham, S (1977) *Dutiful Daughters: women talk about their lives*, Allen Lane, London.

McDowell, L 2005 *Hard Labour: the forgotten voices of Latvian migrant volunteer workers*, UCL Press, London.

McDowell, L 2013 *Working Lives: gender, migration and employment in Britain, 1945–2007*, Wiley-Blackwell, Oxford.

McDowell, L, Anitha, S and Pearson, R 2014 'Striking narratives: representing the "Great Grunwick Strike"', *Women's History Review* 23, 595–619.

Oakley, A 1974 *Housewife*, Allen Lane, London.

Patterson, S 1963 *Dark Strangers: a study of West Indians in London*, Tavistock, London.

Paul, K 1997 *Whitewashing Britain: race and citizenship in the postwar era*, Cornell University Press, Ithaca NY.

Powell, E 1976 Speech at the Hampshire Monday Club, Southampton, 9 April.

Purvis, T and Hunt, A 1993 'Discourse, ideology, discourse, ideology, discourse, ideology', *The British Journal of Sociology* 44, 473–99.

Rawicz, S 1999 *The Long Walk: the true story of a trek to freedom*, Constable and Robinson, London.

Roediger, D 1991 *The Wages of Whiteness: race and the making of the American working class*, Verso, London.

Roediger, D and Esch, E 2012 *The Production of Difference: race and the management of labor in US history*, Oxford University Press, Oxford.

Samuel, R 1999 *Island Stories: unravelling Britain – theatres of memory*, Verso, London.

Standing, G 2011 *The Precariat: the new dangerous class*, Bloomsbury, London.

Terkel, S 1977 *Working: people talk about what they do all day and how they feel about what they do*, Penguin, Harmondsworth (first published in 1974 in the USA).

Thompson, E P 1963 *The Making of the English Working Class*, Victor Gollancz, London.

Todd, S 2014 *The People: the rise and fall of the working class 1910–2010*, John Murray, London.

Toynbee, P 2003 *Hard Work: life in low pay Britain*, Bloomsbury, London.

Women's Sport and Fitness Foundation 2013 *Trends in women's participation in sport*, Sport England's Active People Survey, London.

United Nations 2013 *World migration in figures*, joint report by UN Department of Economic and Social Affairs, Population Division and OECD, New York, available at www.oecd.org.els/mig (accessed 10 June 2015).

Winder, R 2004 *Bloody Foreigners: the story of immigration to Britain*, Abacus, London.

YouGov 2012 *The perilous politics of immigration*, available at yougov.co.uk (accessed 28 June 2015).

Other interesting books about migration, gender and work

Migration into the UK

Fryer, P 1984 *Staying Power: the history of Black people in Britain*, Pluto Press, London.

Phillips, M and Phillips, T 1998 *Windrush: the irresistible rise of multi-cultural Britain*, Harper Collins, London.

Visram, R 2002 *Asians in Britain: 400 years of history*, Pluto Press, London.

General texts about global migration and its implications

Boswell, C and Geddes, A 2011 *Migration and Mobility in the European Union*, Palgrave Macmillan, Basingstoke, Hampshire.

Brettell, C B and Hollifield, J 2008 *Migration Theory: talking across disciplines*, Routledge, London.

Castles, S and Davidson, A 2000 *Citizenship and Migration: globalisation and the politics of belonging*, Routledge, London.

Castles, S, De Haas, H and Miller, M 2009 *The Age of Migration: international population movements in the modern world*, Palgrave Macmillan, Basingstoke, Hampshire.

Collier, P 2013 *Exodus: immigration and multi-culturalism in the twenty first century*, Allen Lane, London.

Cohen, R 2006 *Migration and its Enemies: global capital, migrant labour and the nation state*, Ashgate, Aldershot, Hampshire.

Cohen, R 2008 *Global Diasporas: an introduction* (second edition), Routledge, London.

Dabydeen, D, Gilmore, J and Jones, C 2007 *The Oxford Companion to Black British History*, Oxford University Press, Oxford.

Glick-Shiller, N and Faist, T (eds) 2010 *Migration, Development and Transnationalisation: a critical stance*, Berghahn, New York.

Gilroy, P 1993 *The Black Atlantic: modernity and double consciousness*, Harvard University Press, MA.

Gilroy, P 2007 *Black Britain: a photographic history*, Saqi, London.

Goldin, I, Cameron, G and Balarajan, M 2011 *Exceptional People: how migration shaped our world and will define our future*, Princeton University Press, Princeton, NJ.

Khory, K 2012 *Global Migration: challenges in the twenty-first century*, Palgrave Macmillan, Basingstoke, Hampshire.

Koser, K 2007 *International Migration: a very short introduction*, Oxford University Press, Oxford.

Marfleet, P 2006 *Refugees in a Global Era*, Palgrave Macmillan, Basingstoke, Hampshire.

Madood, T 2007 *Multiculturalism*, Polity, Cambridge.

Palmary, I, Burman, E, Chantier, K and Kiguwa, P (eds) 2010 *Gender and Migration: feminist interventions*, Zed Books, London.

Panayi, P and Virdee, P (eds) 2011 *Refugees and the End of Empire: imperial collapse and forced migration in the twentieth century*, Palgrave Macmillan, Basingstoke, Hampshire.

Portes, A and De Wind, J (eds) 2007 *Rethinking Migration: new theoretical and empirical perspectives*, Berghahn, Oxford.

Ruhs, M 2013 *The Price of Rights: regulating international labour migration*, Princeton University Press, Princeton, NJ.

Shelley, T 2007 *Exploited: migrant labour in the new global economy*, Zed, London.

Thomson, A, Cave, P, Good, G, Pickett, J and Wright, D 2011 *Moving Stories: an intimate history of four women across two countries*, Manchester University Press, Manchester.

Vertovec, S 2009 *Transnationalism*, Routledge, London.

Book-length case studies/personal stories

Delap, L 2011 *Knowing their Place: domestic service in twentieth century Britain*, Oxford University Press, Oxford.

McGowan, B 2009 *Taking the Boat: the Irish in Leeds, 1931–81*, self publication.

Nguyen, N 2009 *Memory is Another Country: women of the Vietnamese diaspora*, Praeger, Santa Barbara.

Searle, K 2010 *From Farms to Foundries: an Arab community in industrial Britain*, Bern, Peter Lang AG International Academic Publishers.

Thomson, A, Cave, P, Good, G, Pickett, J and Wright, D 2011 *Moving Stories: an intimate history of four women across two countries*, Manchester University Press, Manchester.

Ugolini, W 2011 *Experiencing war as the 'enemy other': Italian Scottish experience in World War II*, Manchester University Press, Manchester.

Valk, A and Brown, L (eds) 2010 *Living with Jim Crow: African American women and memories of living in the segregated south*, Palgrave Macmillan, New York.

Yu-ling, K, Khoo, A, Naifei, D and Parry, A E 2011 *Our Stories: migration and labour in Taiwan*, Strategic Information and Research Development Center, Selangor, Malaysia.

Studies of post-war change

Beckett, A 2009 *When the Lights Went Out: Britain in the seventies*, Faber and Faber, London.

Harrison, B 2010 *Finding a Role: The United Kingdom, 1970–1990*, Oxford University Press, Oxford.

Hennessy, P 2006 *Having it so Good: Britain in the fifties*, Allen Lane, London.

Kynaston, D 2007 *Austerity Britain 1945–51*, Bloomsbury, London.

Kynaston, D 2009 *Family Britain 1951–57*, Bloomsbury, London.

Kynaston D 2013 *Modernity Britain 1957–59*, Bloomsbury, London.

Sandbrook, D 2005 *Never Had it so Good: a history of Britain from Suez to the Beatles*, Little, Brown, New York.

Sandbrook, D 2006 *White Heat: a history of Britain in the swinging sixties*, Little, Brown, New York.

Sandbrook, D 2010 *State of Emergency – the Way we Were: Britain 1970–1974*, Allen Lane, London.

Sandbrook, D 2012 *Seasons in the Sun: the battle for Britain, 1974–1979*, Allen Lane, London.

Books on the changing meaning of waged work in UK

Kirk, J and Wall, C 2011 *Work and Identity: historical and cultural contexts*, Palgrave Macmillan, Basingstoke, Hampshire (based on 110 oral interviews, and change since 1970s).

McDowell, L 2013 *Working Lives: gender, migration and employment in Britain, 1945–2007*, Wiley Blackwell, Oxford.
McIvor, A 2013 *Working Lives: work in Britain since 1945*, Palgrave Macmillan, Basingstoke, Hampshire.

Migration stories using interviews and narratives

Baldassar, L 2001 *Visits Home: migration experiences between Italy and Australia*, Melbourne University Press, Melbourne.
Block, D 2005 *Multilingual Identities in a Global City: London stories*, Palgrave Macmillan, London.
Eastmond, M 2007 'Stories as lived experience: narratives in forced migration research', *Journal of Refugee Studies* 20, 248–64.
Gardner, K 2002 *Age, Narrative and Migration: the life course and life histories of Bengali elders in London*, Berg, London.
Hopkins, P and Hill, M 2008 'Pre-flight experiences and migration stories: the accounts of un-accompanied asylum-seeking children', *Children's Geographies* 6, 257–68.
Lawson, V 2000 'Arguments within geographies of movement: the theoretical potential of migrants' stories', *Progress in Human Geography* 24, 173–89.
Ryan, L 2002 '"I'm going to England": Irish women's stories of migration in the 1930s', *Oral History* 30, 42–53.
Sorhaindo, C and Pattullo, P 2009 *Home Again: stories of migration and return*, Papillote Press and the Dominica UK Association, London.
Tannenbaum, M 2007 'Back and forth: immigrants' stories of migration and return', *International Migration* 45, 147–75.
Thomson, A 1999 'Moving stories: oral history and migration stories', *Oral History* 27, 24–37.

On writing personally: two examples

Light, A 2014 *Common People: the history of an English family*, Fig Tree, London.
McDowell, L 2014 'Border crossings: reflections on women's lives in 20th century Britain', *Gender, Place and Culture* 21, 152–73.

About memory, narrative and biography

Connerton, P 1989 *How Societies Remember*, Cambridge University Press, Cambridge.
Crownshaw, R, Kilby, J and Rowland, A (eds) (2010) *The Future of Memory*, Berghahn, Oxford.
Cubitt, G 2007 *History and Memory*, Manchester University Press, Manchester.

Eakin, P J 2008 *Living Autobiographically: how we create identity in narrative*, Cornell University Press, Ithaca, NY.

Fentress, J and Wickham, C 1992 *Social Memory*, Blackwell, Oxford.

King, N 2000 *Memory, Narrative, Identity: remembering the self*, Edinburgh University Press, Edinburgh.

Radstone, S and Schwartz, B (eds) 2010 *Memory: histories, theories, debates*, Fordham University Press, New York.

Ricouer, P 2004 *Memory, History, Forgetting*, University of Chicago Press, Chicago (first published in French in 2000; translated by K Blamey and D Pellauer).

Wood, H H and Byatt, A S (eds) 2008 *Memory: an anthology*, Chatto and Windus, London.

Useful guides to doing oral history

Abrams, L 2010 *Oral History Theory*, Routledge, London.

Bornat, J and Tetley, J (eds) 2010 *Oral History and Ageing*, Centre for Policy on Ageing, London.

Perks, R and Thomson, A (eds) 2006 *The Oral History Reader* (second edition), Routledge, London.

Plummer, K. 1983 *Documents of Life: An introduction to the problem and literature of a humanistic method*, George Allen and Unwin, London.

Ritchie, D A 2003 *Doing Oral History: a practical guide*, Oxford University Press, Oxford.

Ritchie, D A 2011 *The Oxford Handbook of Oral History*, Oxford University Press, Oxford.

Sommer, B W and Quinlan, M K 2009 *The Oral History Manual*, Plymouth, Altamira Press.

Key journals

History Workshop
Oral History
Oral History Review
Women's History Review

Useful sources

International Forced Labourers Documentation project (IFLDP) research project carried out between 2004 and 2007 by the Institute for History and Biography, University of Hagen, by 33 interview teams – interviews in original language when French, German or English or translated. 600 interviews in 24 European States, Israel, South Africa and the USA, funded by the German Foundation – Remembrance, Responsibility and Future (Stiftung, Reinnerung, Verantwortang und Zukunft).

Novels about migration and multicultural Britain

Aboulela, Leila 2005 *Minaret*, Bloomsbury, London.
Ali, Monica 2003 *Brick Lane*, Doubleday, London.
Craig, Amanda 2009 *Hearts and Minds*, Little, Brown, London.
Emecheta, Buchi 1994 *Second Class Citizen* (second edition), Heinemann, London.
Evaristo, Bernadine 1999 *Lara*, Bloodaxe Books, London.
Gee, Maggie 2002 *The White Family*, Saqi Books, London.
Kureishi, Hanif 1990 *The Buddha of Suburbia*, Faber and Faber, London.
Levy, Andrea 1994 *Every Light in the House Burnin'*, Headline, London.
Levy, Andrea 2004 *Small Island*, Review, London.
MacInnes, Colin 1959 *Absolute Beginners*, Allison and Busby, London.
Okri, Ben 1991 *The Famished Road*, Jonathan Cape, London.
Phillips, Caryl 1985 *The Final Passage*, Faber and Faber, London.
Riley, Joan 1985 The *Unbelonging*, The Women's Press, London.
Rhys, Jean 1966 *The Wide Sargasso Sea*, Andre Deutsch, London.
Rushdie, Salman 1981 *Midnight's Children*, Random House, London.
Selvon, Samuel 1956 *Lonely Londoners*, Penguin, London.
Smith, Zadie 2000 *White Teeth*, Penguin, London.
Tremain, Rose 2007 *The Road Home*, Chatto and Windus, London.
Valmorbida, Elise 2009 *The Winding Stick*, Two Ravens Press, London.

Index

abuse, abusive comments 51, 108, 190
academia, academic 2, 6, 16, 139, 146,
        157, 158, 160, 163, 165–168, 202
academic dress 167
accent 15, 22, 23, 134, 151, 152, 156,
        165, 177, 183, 190, 217
Adele 122, 124, 237
agency work 100, 119, 122, 123, 237
Aileen 111, 112, 114, 137, 237
airline meals 69, 237
Albania 50–52
Amalie 146, 237
Amin, Idi 4, 36, 209, 224, 250
Amrita 56, 77, 78, 178, 237
Ani 157, 163, 202, 204, 237
antenatal appointments 200
Anya 86, 104, 105, 237
appearance 184
Athens 144
au pair 86, 98, 99, 195

back office jobs 184
bakery 74, 75, 76, 90
Baltic 4, 11, 18, 22–24, 28, 42, 45, 86,
        98, 122, 173, 185, 197, 233,
        247, 248
Baltic Cygnet 22, 24, 28, 86, 173, 185,
        197, 233, 248
Baltic States 4, 11, 18, 23, 42, 45, 86,
        98, 185, 247
Bangalore 125, 149
Bangladesh 57, 107, 137, 193, 200,
        215, 230, 231, 233, 239
bank 8, 11, 102, 140, 142, 147–149,
        172, 202, 219
    investment 8, 140, 141, 149, 202
    private 149, 152
banking 6, 18, 40, 139–141, 143,
        147–149, 152, 153, 202, 250

Bashira 56, 62–65, 200, 237, 248
Beatta 100–102, 219, 237
belonging 4, 60, 195, 196, 213, 215,
        217, 219, 220, 222, 223, 226
    and unbelonging 223
Berlin 26
Beveridge Report 12
Bhopal 149, 150
Bina 23, 38, 54, 109, 118, 120, 237
Birmingham bombing 178
BMW 80, 82–84, 200
body shopping 153, 155
bonds 140, 141, 196
Bradford 26, 58–60, 94, 95, 133, 134
brain work 139
Bray 30
Brazil 104, 105, 182, 238
breadwinner wage 12
Brie 23, 33, 40, 53, 109, 114, 115, 237,
        249
Brigita 56, 58, 60, 199, 237
British Airways 69, 71
British Social Attitudes Survey 226
Britishness 220, 221
British identity 217, 218, 220,
        226
bus driver 18, 44, 187–189, 216
butler 92

camps 22, 24, 29, 50, 57, 87, 88,
        91–94, 222
    displaced persons 22, 24, 27, 28,
        57, 88, 91, 94, 222
Cape Town 40
car industry 56, 57, 80, 84
car seats 5, 18
care 6, 8, 11, 18, 30, 33, 45, 79, 84,
        85, 104, 106–109, 112, 114, 120,
        121, 123, 124, 126–128, 130–134,

136, 137, 194, 196–200, 202–204,
219, 236, 243, 249
care assistant 30, 132, 134
care home 6, 79, 109, 132, 133, 136,
137, 219
care work/er 11, 79, 108, 130, 132,
133, 135, 136, 137
Caribbean 3, 4, 7, 9, 11, 22, 23, 30,
32–34, 53, 109, 114, 117, 119,
122, 192, 193, 197, 212, 217,
221, 231, 233, 249
caring 6–8, 11, 18, 19, 30, 55, 69, 85,
86, 104, 105, 108, 109, 114,
135, 170, 196, 218, 226, 232,
246,
Caro 140–142, 202, 237, 249
Castle, Barbara 56
Catherine 42, 45, 78, 79, 132, 133,
199, 237
Catholic Church 208
childcare 3, 8, 65, 85, 104, 106–108,
194, 196–200, 202–204
childminder 107, 108, 203–205
chip shop 113, 182
City of London 8, 40, 149, 171
class 4, 6, 9, 13, 16, 17, 23, 36, 40, 54,
96, 129, 219, 222, 226, 231,
234, 245
middle class 4, 6, 9, 17, 23, 36, 40,
234
working class 9, 16, 17, 222, 226,
234
class position 17, 54, 219
cleaners 11, 53, 100
clinic, gynaecological 186
clocking in 77
cohesion 220, 224
Colberg 25
Colombia 98, 238
Commonwealth 4, 7, 33, 42, 139, 241,
242, 247
Commonwealth, New 4, 7
Commonwealth, Old 139
community work/er 191, 193, 194, 210
Compstall 58
Corby 173, 250
cosmopolitan, cosmopolitanism
186, 216, 217, 224, 226
Courtaulds 61, 92, 198

Cowley 80, 82
culture, national 222

Dagenham 12, 55, 56, 66, 199
Dagnija 9, 172, 237
Danzig 25
Dar es Salaam 38
deference 8
deindustrialization 5
Delhi University 165, 168
democracy 220
deportation 24, 28, 242
Diana 10, 23, 27, 28, 30, 60, 197, 202,
207, 237
diaspora 221, 224
difference, politics and production of
7, 220, 221
discrimination 7, 19, 117, 118, 120,
139, 146, 170, 190, 220, 242,
243, 271
dislocation 19
displaced people/persons 11, 22, 24,
27, 28, 57, 87, 88, 91, 93, 97,
172, 212, 222, 247
disruption 19
divorce 44, 136, 160, 166, 167, 208
doctorate, PhD 150, 158, 159,
161–165, 167, 168, 214, 244
doctors 7, 9, 11, 40, 54, 87, 115–117,
127, 139, 163, 200,
domestic service 6, 86, 87, 92
Dominika 42, 43, 45, 53, 237
dot-com 153, 154
dry cleaners 186
dual roles 8, 9, 12

East Africa 3, 11, 23, 36, 37, 39,
54–56, 70, 217
Eidothea 144, 237
Eire 11, 23, 30, 111 see also Ireland
Ellen 180, 181, 194, 237, 239
Elvira 7, 21–27, 60, 61, 199, 201, 237
emotions, emotional, emotional labour
7, 84, 104, 108, 117, 124, 132,
143, 189, 196, 212, 215
Empire 10, 11, 22, 33, 222
employment 1, 3–8, 11–13, 15, 18,
19, 23, 38, 43, 54, 56, 57, 62,
69, 72, 78, 80, 85, 86, 98, 100,

104, 134, 138, 143, 153, 163,
    172, 173, 185, 194, 195, 203,
    213, 215, 218, 219, 226, 227,
    231–234, 241, 248, 250
  manufacturing 1, 18, 56, 62, 78
  pink collar 5
  service sector 18
engines, engine plant 12, 55, 56, 66
Equal Pay Act 56
Erica 201, 238
Eritrea 46–49, 50, 248
Estonia 9, 59, 87, 94, 102, 104–107,
    172–173, 237
EU expansion 42, 45, 230
European Union 2, 3, 44, 100, 102,
    105, 169
Eva 22, 95, 97, 238
EVWs (European Volunteer Workers)
    22, 36, 54, 57, 59, 60, 62, 109,
    211, 212, 222, 234, 247, 248,
    250

family business 39, 180, 192
family reunification 197
Farah 133, 134, 238, 249
fashion 41, 42, 186, 191–193
femininity 6, 8, 12, 236
feminist 7, 12, 16, 21, 85
Fida 209, 210, 238, 250
finance, financial services 143, 144,
    146, 149
Fitore 42, 51–54, 238
floor supervisor 102, 103
Ford 5, 18, 54, 55, 65–69, 80, 196,
    199, 233,
foreign exchange dealer 140

Gate Gourmet 196, 233
gender equality 220
Georgina 32, 33, 40, 53, 109, 207,
    212, 238
Germany 9, 11, 22, 25–29, 54, 57, 59,
    87, 91, 93–95, 172, 197, 205,
    230, 247
Gilroy, Paul 220, 223
government 3, 4, 9, 13, 15, 16, 22, 29,
    33, 38, 40, 41, 42, 46, 48, 53,
    56, 92, 107, 136, 154, 176, 191,
    209, 215, 224, 234, 241, 247

Labour 15, 56
Grieta 9, 211, 238
Grunwick 69, 196, 225, 233

hairdresser 136, 137
Hall, Stuart 221, 223
Hana 42, 46, 47, 49, 54, 238, 239
harassment 16, 54, 131, 139, 171
Harbhanan 11
Harshini 65, 66, 238
Harwell 176–178
Heathrow (airport) 41, 51, 71, 73,
    178
Holland 46, 49, 50, 105, 163
Home Office 46, 104, 126
home 1, 3–9, 11–14, 18–22, 28–30, 32,
    33, 37, 38, 41, 42, 44, 51, 53–59,
    62–65, 69, 70, 71, 73, 74, 76,
    77, 84–86, 91, 96, 98–101, 103,
    105, 107, 108, 110–113, 117,
    120–123, 125, 128–132, 134,
    144, 150, 157, 161, 163, 166,
    170, 171, 174–178, 180, 186,
    192, 194–197, 201, 202,
    204–210, 212, 213, 215, 218,
    221, 227, 234, 245, 246, 250
homeland 4, 19, 176, 197, 211, 212,
    218, 221, 224
Hong Kong 41, 42, 180, 182, 191,
    193, 230, 237, 238
hospital 6, 8, 11, 22, 26, 27, 30, 32, 33,
    35, 41, 60, 75, 88, 91, 93–98,
    105, 108–117, 119–126, 129,
    130, 132, 137, 139, 170, 172,
    181, 198, 201, 207, 219, 249
  isolation 97, 112
  mental 22, 93, 95, 96
hostility 217
hotels 18, 100, 103, 108, 171, 172,
    182, 183
housework 8, 45, 85, 86, 99, 165, 174,
    195, 197, 199, 204, 205, 234,
    236
HSBC 151–153
hybrid, hybridity 23, 220, 221, 223,
    224

identity, national 4, 221, 224
Illona 94, 95, 198, 238

India 3, 4, 9, 23, 36–39, 62, 66, 69, 70,
    72, 74–76, 78, 117, 119,
    124–126, 149, 150, 152, 165,
    166, 168, 178, 204–206, 214,
    215, 230, 231, 237–239, 249
institutionalised racism 249
interactive work, interactive exchanges
    18, 172
IRA (Irish Republican Army) 250
Ireland 4, 9, 23, 30, 32, 105, 122, 163,
    174, 175, 178, 205, 208, 212,
    222, 229, 230, 237–239 see also
    Eire
Islamophobia 220
Isobel 202, 238

Jaba 23, 37, 38, 40, 69, 85, 86, 238
Jamaica 9, 116, 230
Jane 104, 105, 238
Janice 213, 238
Jasbir 73, 74, 75, 78, 178, 238
Jelena 57, 58, 238
Jenny 185, 187, 194, 238, 250

Karina 9, 100–102, 104, 238, 248
Kate 142, 238
Kenya 9, 36, 37, 45, 66, 78, 117, 132,
    199, 209, 214, 230, 237–239,
    247
Kenyatta, Jomo 36, 37, 247
Kikuyu 45
knitting 56, 61, 209, 210, 211
knowledge work 6, 171
Kosovo 9, 27, 50, 51, 238
KPMG 149
Kuwait 133, 134, 238

labour 1–13, 15, 17, 19, 20, 23, 27, 30,
    53–57, 61, 65, 84–88, 92, 93,
    97, 104, 108, 109, 120, 137,
    169, 171, 173, 196, 202, 206,
    215, 218, 219, 224–227, 229,
    231–234, 236,
    245–247
    affective 7, 196
    directed 30, 88
    domestic 7, 8, 9, 11, 88, 93, 108
    emotional 84, 104
labour exchange 61, 86, 88, 92, 97

language 15, 18, 38, 49, 63, 67, 68, 79,
    94, 97, 99, 120, 128, 129, 132,
    134, 135, 151–153, 161, 165,
    172, 189, 200, 201, 204–206,
    208–211, 215, 219, 220, 222,
    223, 248, 250
Latvia 7, 9, 10, 15, 21, 23, 25–28, 45,
    57, 87–94, 100–102, 110, 172,
    185, 186, 201, 211–213,
    237–239, 250
law firms 147–148
lawyers 7, 54, 139
Leipaj 25
Li Jing 41, 42, 191, 192, 194, 238
Lina 62, 86, 87, 238, 248
Lister's Mill 59
long hours 41, 139, 142, 143, 145,
    146, 148, 149
low pay 84, 137, 185, 219

machining 66
    seat covers 54, 55, 65, 66
    shirts 5, 37, 54, 55, 58, 65, 66, 85,
        86
machinist 65, 67–69
Marianna 42, 50, 54, 238
maid 28, 47, 88–90, 93, 103, 110, 174,
    219
Mari 182–184, 238
Maria 11, 80, 83, 84, 200, 203, 238
Market Harborough 88
Marks and Spencer 5, 54, 65
Marple 57, 58
marriage 15, 17, 23, 36, 38, 51, 52, 70,
    118, 125, 133, 136, 138, 160,
    165, 166, 175, 176, 200, 205,
    207, 208, 242
Marta 61, 86, 173, 198, 238
Martine 40, 41, 238
Mary 30, 32, 238
masculinity 11
    heroic 11
maternity leave 8, 124, 159, 202, 203
May 136, 238
meat 69, 70, 90, 181
medicine 18, 40, 113, 139
Meg 128, 129, 132, 238
memory 16, 26
Middlesex Hospital 32

Milda 206, 207, 238
milking 45, 89, 90
mill hands 18, 53, 54
Mini plant 82 *see also* BMW
minimum wage 85, 103, 219, 248
Moira 174, 176, 177, 208, 238
Moscow 160–162, 170
multicultural, multiculturalism 4, 36,
    145, 146, 217, 220, 224

Nadia 43–45, 53, 187, 194, 239, 250
nanny 8, 27, 93, 98, 105–107, 174,
    195, 202
Natalija 86, 88, 100, 239,
Natasha 160, 161, 163, 170, 239
national identity 4, 221, 224
National Insurance number 185, 249,
    250
New Zealand 3, 9, 122, 123, 128, 202,
    213, 214, 229, 230, 237, 238
NHS (National Health Service) 5, 22,
    40, 53, 84, 105, 109, 110, 121,
    122, 212
nostalgia 11, 16
nurse, matron 33, 93–97, 110, 112,
    113, 125
nurse, sister 33, 98, 110, 113, 115,
    117, 119, 124, 201,
nurse, staff 110, 123, 124
nursery 29, 57, 81, 93, 107, 124, 185,
    200–205, 219
nursing 17, 18, 32, 33, 35, 40, 93,
    95–97, 108–114, 118–126, 128,
    132, 134, 136, 249

occupational therapy 109, 128
on the line 5, 18, 61, 66, 72, 78
oral histories 17, 233
oral narratives 2, 17
Other, otherness 2, 4,16, 54, 216, 217,
    219, 224, 225, 227
Oxbridge (Oxford, Cambridge) 44, 51,
    63, 80, 82, 134, 157, 158, 162,
    164, 165, 167, 173, 175, 200

packing 18, 55, 69, 70, 71, 73, 76, 78,
    79, 199
Pakistan 3, 4, 9, 59, 62, 68, 73, 133,
    134, 200, 230, 231, 237

Papla 214, 215, 239
Paris 13, 146, 147, 159, 186, 247
Parnal 124, 125, 128, 129, 239, 249
Parvani 36–38, 40, 56, 66, 68–70, 84,
    199, 239
Patterson, Sheila 217
pension fund 140, 141
Phyllida 205, 239
physiotherapist, physio 40, 109, 129,
    130
piece work 59, 60
Plessey 62
Poland 4, 9, 18, 29, 42–45, 53, 100,
    101, 137, 230, 231, 237, 239
polio 3, 112, 137, 248
poor work 219
Posha 149–151, 170, 204, 239
post-war refugees 4, 10
Powell, Enoch 34, 222, 223, 247
Precariat 219
precariousness, precarity 11, 219
Preston 57, 58
production of difference 7
public 5, 101, 171–194, 219, 224, 225,
    243
public transport 22, 172
Punjab 65, 70–73

race riots 225
racism 7, 167, 168, 169, 223, 249
Raksha 69, 239
rape 16, 50, 54
ration books, rations 59, 90, 93
RCN (Royal College of Nursing) 249
receptionist 11, 18, 80, 182, 183, 185,
    186
refugees 4, 10, 14, 22, 23, 26, 27, 36,
    42, 53, 54, 95, 122, 210, 242,
    247
research 139, 144, 145, 152, 157, 158,
    160–162, 164, 165, 167, 168,
    171, 176, 221, 229
respect 10, 33, 71, 74, 78, 81, 95, 103,
    115, 116, 150, 184, 193, 244
retail assistant 134
retirement 1, 9, 19, 69, 71, 194, 195,
    208, 211, 212,
return 9, 10, 12, 19, 42, 133, 210, 212,
    213, 215, 226, 242,

RGN (Registered General Nurse) 118, 121, 249
Riga 28, 88, 95, 101, 102, 172, 185
Romania 157, 158, 202, 237
Rostock 25
Royal Mail 73, 178
rude 71, 74, 103, 134, 140, 183, 184, 189
rural backgrounds 9, 17
Russia 9, 29, 161, 162, 163
Russian occupation of Latvia 24
Ruta 93, 95, 100, 211, 213, 239

Sai 196, 205, 206, 239
Saran 69, 70, 72, 73, 178, 239
secretary 56, 91, 172, 185, 186, 243, 247
Second World War 2, 3, 10, 12, 13, 16, 111, 197, 227
sector/zone 1, 5, 6, 18, 19, 22, 26, 27, 29, 30, 40, 55, 57, 72, 80, 84, 88, 104, 107, 132, 134, 139, 140, 143, 146, 149, 171, 172, 218, 226, 232
  American 26, 27
  British 30, 88, 172
  Russian 26, 29
SEN (State Enrolled Nurse) 114, 115, 118, 119, 121, 249
sexism 140, 143
Shami 165–170, 239
shoes, shoe factory 60, 90, 92, 101, 180, 197
shops 126, 144, 171, 172, 181, 197
Simone 163–165, 239
Singapore 124–126, 153–155, 157, 239, 249, 250
skill 55, 164, 166, 232, 233
skiving 60
social life 170, 201, 207, 220
software 153
soldering 61, 62
Somalia 46, 48, 49
South Asia 23, 217
spinning 57, 58, 61
SRN (State Registered Nurse) 112, 114, 115, 249
Standing, Guy 219
stereotypes, stereotypical assumptions 7, 109, 70, 165, 172, 194, 205

Stettin 26
strangers 2, 4, 19, 71, 216, 217, 220, 224
strikes 3, 55, 56, 67, 71, 98, 196, 225, 233, 249
Sudan 46, 47, 48, 49, 50, 168, 209
Surjit 69, 70, 71, 239
Switzerland 106

takeaway 180, 181, 216
talent 55
Tanzania 9, 23, 37–39, 69, 85, 118, 205, 209, 237
Taslima 107, 108, 200, 201, 215, 239
TB (tuberculosis) 3, 97, 98, 110–112, 137, 174
teachers 7, 9, 11, 23, 25, 45, 47, 54, 139, 153, 171, 226
teaching 2, 17, 18, 32, 45, 60, 79, 80, 112, 123, 132, 139, 157, 158, 160, 164, 165, 166, 168, 191, 192, 211
textile industry 7, 11, 18, 56, 57, 68, 199
Thailand 136, 238
The Lady 6
third space 223
Thompson, E. P. 16
Toynbee, Polly 219
Tracey 212, 239
trade unions 12, 67–70, 76, 77, 80, 83, 85, 92, 233, 248
trading room 141
tradition 30
Trinidad 23, 32–36, 114, 115, 207, 237, 238
Trinidad and Tobago 32, 33, 35
tropes 15

Uganda 9, 13, 36, 117, 209, 210, 230, 238, 250
unemployment 1, 105, 168, 219, 232
uniform 80, 96, 100, 101, 103, 110, 129, 130, 175
United Biscuits 72
university teaching 18
UNRRA (United Nations Relief and Rehabilitation Administration) 172

Valda 22, 97, 239
vegetarian 69
Victoria 153, 239
Victoria and Albert Museum 192, 193
Vieda 10, 26, 93, 100, 105, 110, 211,
    212, 213, 215, 239
Vijaya 117, 118, 239

waitress 174, 175, 192
ward orderly 97
Warsaw 45
weaver/weaving 26, 57–60
web designer 154
white swan 57
white, whiteness 71, 74, 75, 109, 115,
    116, 118, 120, 132, 139, 179,
    193, 217, 218, 221, 223–225,
    227, 231, 233
Wilson, Harold 56, 247
women of colour 10, 42, 137
Woolf, Virginia 14
woollen industry 8, 58, 60

work 1, 15, 16–18, 20, 22, 23–30,
    32–34, 37, 38, 40, 42–45, 47,
    50, 52–80, 81, 83–97, 99–110,
    112–115, 119–124, 126–140,
    142–156, 158–168, 169–181,
    183–188, 191–200, 203, 204,
    206, 207, 209–215, 218, 219,
    226, 227, 231, 236, 243, 245,
    246, 248
  agency 100, 119, 122, 123
  body 6, 18, 109, 171
  dirty 6, 76, 104
  home 55, 62, 63, 65, 70, 85
  knowledge 6, 171
  waged 1, 2, 5, 7–9, 11, 12, 18, 20,
    54, 84, 85, 100, 108, 170, 172,
    195, 196, 200, 212, 218, 219,
    246
work culture 142
work permit 42, 102, 126, 128, 158,
    168, 191, 192
WVS (Women's Voluntary Service) 173